global

beginner teacher's book

Kate Pickering, Rob Metcalf & Frances Watkins

MACMILLAN

Macmillan Education
Between Towns Road, Oxford OX4 3PP
A division of Macmillan Publishers Limited
Companies and representatives throughout the world

ISBN: 978-0-230-03287-3

Designed by eMC Design Limited
Cover design by Barbara Mercer

These materials may contain links to third party websites. We have no
control over, and are not responsible for, the contents of such third party
websites. Please use care when accessing them.

Teacher's Resource CD

Ilustrated by Stephen Dew, Celia Hart and eMC Design.

The authors and publishers would like to thank the following for
permission to reproduce their photographic material:

iStock/Luis Portugal; iStock/Kkgas; iStock/gibson ff; iStock/fpm;
iStock/Pertunisas; iStock/idrutu; iStock/Cloki; iStcok/tacojim.

Printed in Thailand

2014 2013 2012 2011
10 9 8 7 6 5 4 3 2

Contents

Coursebook contents map

EV – Extend your vocabulary   (P) – Pronunciation   (W) – writing   (FL) – functional language

Course overview

Components for the learner

Coursebook
see pages viii–xiii

eWorkbook
see pages xiv–xv

Components for the teacher

**Teacher's book &
Teacher's Resource disc**
see page xvi

Class Audio CDs
see page xvii

Global Website
see page xvii

Global Digital
See pages xviii–xix

Coursebook: lessons 1 and 2 of a unit

Unit structure

Each unit is divided in six two-page lessons. The first four lessons are the core part of the unit. The last two lessons include additional material (e.g. Games, Review). In this unit, the first two lessons are about numbers, the next two spreads are about prices and shops.

Headings

Clear headings throughout the book show what you are teaching at each stage of the lesson.

UNIT 4 Big & Small

Part 1

Vocabulary
Numbers 20-100

Vocabulary & Reading
Shopping in numbers

Grammar
There is / there are

Pronunciation & Speaking
schwa /ə/

Writing
Describing a hotel

Vocabulary

1 Write the words in the box with the numbers.

sixty	forty	ninety	seventy
eighty	thirty	twenty	fifty	hundred

20	_twenty_	70	_____
30	_____	80	_____
40	_____	90	_____
50	_____	100	_____
60	_____		

2 1.63 Listen, check and repeat.

3 Write the words for the numbers.

50	_fifty_	7	_seven_	→	57	_fifty-seven_
30	_____	9	_____	→	39	_____
60	_____	1	_____	→	61	_____
24	_____
82	_____
33	_____

4 Match the numbers with the words.

23 — forty-six
46 — ninety-eight
89 — sixty-four
32 — eighty-nine
64 — thirty-two
98 — twenty-three

5 1.64 Listen and write the numbers you hear as words.

1 _forty-two_   3 _____
2 _____   4 _____

Vocabulary and Reading

1 1.65 Look at the pictures of places in a town. Listen and repeat the words.

2 Is there a big shopping mall in your town?

3 Read about a shopping mall on page 25. Complete the text with the numbers.

Language note:

one	two	many
★	★★	★★★

4 1.66 Listen and check.

a supermarket

b restaurant   c car park   d shopping mall   e cinema   f shop

BURKE

Grammar

> *There's a big supermarket.*
> *There are 48 restaurants.*
> *Is there a cinema?*
> *Are there any banks?*
>
> *Yes, there are.*
> *No, there aren't.*
>
> • Use *There's (There is)* with singular nouns
> • Use *There are* with plural nouns
> • Start questions with *Is there...?* or *Are there...?*
> • Use *any* after *Are there...?*

1 Read the sentences about a shopping mall. Decide which four sentences are incorrect. Then correct them.

There's four restaurants. ✗
There are four restaurants. ✔
1 There's two floors.
2 There are one cinema.
3 There's six floors for shopping.
4 There is a big car park for eighty cars.
5 There are two supermarkets.
6 There's many people.

2 Underline the correct words.

1 *Is there / Are there* any restaurants?
2 *Is there / Are there* a bank?
3 *Is there / Are there* a supermarket?
4 *Is there / Are there* a car park?
5 *Is there / Are there* any cinemas?

ⓖ **Grammar focus** ~ explanation & more practice of *there is* and *there are* on page 108

Pronunciation and Speaking

1 1.67 Listen to how the underlined sound is pronounced. Repeat the sentences.

1 There's a cinema.
2 Is there a bank?
3 It's busy on Saturday.

2 Work in pairs. A: turn to page 96. B: turn to page 100. Talk about two other shopping malls.

Shopping in Numbers

There are shopping malls everywhere from **A**lgeria to **Z**ambia but they're not just for shopping.

48 restaurants
cinemas   4   shops

"In this mall there are _____ floors for shopping and a big car park with _____ floors for cars. There are many interesting shops and there's a big supermarket. But it's not just for shopping: there are _____ restaurants and a cinema with _____ screens."

floors   6   screens
supermarkets   11

Cevahir shopping mall, Istanbul, Turkey

Writing

1 Look at this information about the Allstar Hotel. Write some sentences. Use the text about the shopping mall to help you.
• 20 floors
• 4 restaurants
• 2 cafés
• 25 shops
• one bank
• one big car park for 60 cars
In the Allstar Hotel there are twenty floors ...

Big Little 4 25

Contents sidebar

Content is summarised on every spread so you can see at a glance what the lesson is about.

Grammar practice

Grammar practice is highly contextualised and meaningful, often in texts that provide additional information about the topic of the lesson. Many grammar practice exercises are designed in a similar way to the reading texts.

Short writing tasks

Some lessons end with a short writing task to give students the opportunity to develop fluency in writing as well as speaking.

Functional language

Some units include a *Functional language* section. This contains frequent functional and situational language that is immediately useful outside the classroom.

Texts

Texts draw on real places, people and events. Background information is provided to give the students extra cultural knowledge about these. Many of the texts are also on the class audio, so learners can read and listen to them.

Big & Small

Part 2

Vocabulary & Speaking
Prices

Functional language
In a shop

Reading & Vocabulary
A small shop near my house; adjectives

Writing & Speaking
A shop near your house

Vocabulary and Speaking

1 1.68 Listen and repeat the prices.
$4.50 £39 €10.99 £75.42 $25

Language note: $ = dollar, £ = pound, € = euro

2 1.69 Listen to the conversations and Circle the price you hear.
1 a £24 b £42 c £25
2 a £19 b $90 c $99
3 a £13.30 b €3.30 c €1.30
4 a £7.49 b £6.49 c £6.90

3 Write four prices. Work in pairs. Say the prices to your partner. Your partner writes the prices. Then swap roles and repeat.

4 Work in pairs. Look at the pictures and prices. Ask and answer with a partner.
A: How much is the cola?
B: It's $1.

5 Compare the prices with your country. Are they cheap, expensive or the same?
A: The magazine is $3.00. In my country that's about 39 pesos. That's expensive!
B: Oh, for me it's cheap.

Functional language

1 Complete the conversation with the words in the box.

| Thank you | Bye | How much is | Hello |

Shop Assistant: _____
Customer: Hi, _____ the magazine?
Shop Assistant: $3.00, please.
Customer: Here you are. Thanks.
Shop Assistant: _____ Goodbye.
Customer:

2 1.70 Listen and check.

3 Work in pairs. Practise the conversation.

4 Work in pairs. Look at the pictures and prices again. Make a similar conversation.

Useful phrases
• How much is ... ?
• Here you are.
• Thank you.

Reading and Vocabulary

1 1.71–1.74 Read and listen to four people talking about a shop near their house. Match 1–4 to the pictures a–d.

2 Look at the pairs of opposite adjectives. Complete the words with the adjectives in **bold** from the text.

★★★★★ ★★★★★
g _ _ d   bad

f _ _ _ _ _ y   unfriendly

big   s _ _ _ _
o _ _ n   closed

interesting   b _ _ _ _ g

o _ d   new
c _ _ _ p   e _ _ _ _ _ _ _ e

3 1.75 Listen, check and repeat.

4 Underline the adjectives you can use to describe the nouns.
city: big closed old
1 student: good friendly expensive
2 café: open small unfriendly
3 book: boring closed new
4 holiday: boring cheap closed
5 grandfather: old expensive interesting

Writing and Speaking

1 Think about a small shop near your house. Make some notes.
name of the shop: _____
adjectives to describe the shop: _____

2 Write a short description about the shop. Use the descriptions about the four shops to help you.

3 Work in small groups. Tell the other students about your shop.

A small shop near my house

1
'There's a bakery near my house. The bread is very **good** and the people are **friendly.**'

2
'The shop near my house is very **small** but there are lots of things to buy. It's **open** 17 hours a day from 6.00am to 11.00pm.'

3
'*Bob's News* is a **small** shop in my street. There are lots of newspapers and magazines. There are other things too – Coke®, milk and chocolate.'

4
'There's a **small** bookshop near my house. There are many **interesting**, **old** books in the shop. It isn't an **expensive** shop, the books are **cheap.**'

cola $1   milk $1.38   bread $1.97
newspaper $1.25   magazine $3.00

Unit 4 Small   Small Unit 4

Balance of skills

Each lesson has a balance of skills work and language work.

Vocabulary

Vocabulary is presented in a meaningful context with clear visual support and opportunities for students to begin using the language right away.

Coursebook: extra material at the end of a unit

Global games, Global voices and Global readings

Every unit has either a Global game, Global voices or Global reading page. Global games revise language from the unit in a motivating and fun way.

Global review

Revision is crucial for language learning. Each unit contains review activities that cover the main grammar and vocabulary points.

Global game

1 Work in pairs. Look at the picture and say what you can see. How many sentences can you say?

There is a cinema.
The camera is £89.

2 1.76 Work in pairs. Listen and answer the questions.

Unit 4 Global game

Global review

c i n e m a   b_____   r_____   h_____

Vocabulary

1 Write the name of the places under the pictures.

2 Write eight more numbers in the table. Work in pairs and read the numbers to your partner.

| 63 | | | | | | | |

3 Listen and write your partner's numbers here.

| 63 | | | | | | | |

4 Work in pairs. Say a number from 11 to 99. Your partner says the opposite.
A: 23   B: 32
A: 45   B: 54

5 Put the tiles in the correct order to make adjectives.

| L | AL | SM |
| SM | AL | L |

| OS | FD | CL |

| EA | P | CH |

| PE | IV | NS | E | EX |

| IE | LY | FR | ND |

| TE | I | NG | IN | RE | ST |

Grammar

Tick (✔) the correct sentence or question.

a There's a shopping mall. ✔
b There a shopping mall.
1 a There are 85 shops in the mall.
  b There's 85 shops in the mall.
2 a There's many people shopping on Saturdays.
  b There are many people shopping on Saturdays.
3 a Is there two or three bookshops?
  b Are there two or three bookshops?
4 a Is there a car park?
  b Are there a car park?

Listen again

1 1.77–1.80 Listen to the speakers from page 27. Complete the sentences with the adjectives in the box.

| expensive | friendly | good | interesting | open | small |

1 There's a bakery near my house. The bread is very _____ and the people are _____.
2 The shop near my house is very small but there are lots of things to buy. It's _____ 17 hours a day from 6.00am to 11.00pm.
3 Bob's News is a _____ shop in my street. There are lots of newspapers and magazines. There are other things too ~ Coke®, milk and chocolate.
4 There's a small bookshop near my house. There are many _____, old books in the shop. It isn't an _____ shop, the books are cheap.

2 Listen again and check.

3 Look at A small shop near my house again on page 27. Choose one of the speakers and practise reading what they say.

Global review Unit 4

Extra vocabulary practice

Vocabulary tasks provide an extra opportunity to revise and consolidate vocabulary from the unit.

Listen again

The review page includes extra listening tasks for one of the recordings from the unit and allows students to practise the phrases and dialogues.

Coursebook: lesson 1 of a unit

Reading tasks

Each text is accompanied by a different kind of reading activity, which focuses on comprehension.

Putting it into practice

The listening task is followed by a choice of speaking activity so that students can put the new language to use immediately.

Topics and texts

Topics and texts are chosen to appeal to the learners' intellectual curiosity. Stylish design makes the text attractive and motivating to read.

Listening

Every lesson has a reading and / or listening text. Listening texts are supported by different tasks for gist and specific listening. The listening texts in *Global* include a variety of genres, including interviews and dialogues.

Real world people

Reading and listening texts in *Global* are about real people and the real world.

---

5 Work & Play

Part 1

Reading
VSO

Grammar
There isn't / There aren't

Listening
Describing jobs

Vocabulary & Speaking
Jobs

Reading

1 Read the introduction to the text about VSO in the information box on page 31. Then look at the pictures of VSO volunteers and complete the sentences with the words in the box.

school   farm   hospital

2 2.01 Listen and read more about VSO. Choose the best title for the text.
- VSO – an International Organisation
- Working for VSO
- The History of VSO

3 Are the following sentences true (T) or false (F)?
1 VSO is an American organisation. ____
2 Many volunteers work in Africa and Asia. ____
3 There are volunteers in North Africa. ____
4 Guyana is a South Asian country. ____
5 There isn't a lot of time for fun. ____

4 Do you think working for VSO is interesting? Why?
Yes, because …
No, because …

Useful language
- boring
- busy
- difficult
- easy
- friendly
- fun

Grammar

*There **isn't** a lot of money for volunteers.*
*There **aren't** any volunteers in North Africa.*

- use *there isn't* with singular nouns
- use *there aren't* with plural nouns
- use *any* after *there aren't*

---

1 Underline the correct words.
1 There *isn't / aren't* any volunteers in Brazil.
2 There *isn't / aren't* a VSO office in Egypt.
3 There *isn't / aren't* any volunteers who are seventeen years old.
4 There *isn't / aren't* any volunteers on farms.

2 Complete the sentences with *There isn't* or *There aren't*.
1 _____ any volunteers in my country.
2 _____ a teacher in the classroom.
3 _____ any friendly students here.
4 _____ a school café for the students.

3 Are the sentences in exercise 2 true or false for you?

G **Grammar focus** – *exploration & more practice of there isn't and there aren't* on page 110

Listening

1 2.02–2.07 Listen to six people talking about their jobs. How many people work for VSO?

2 Listen again and match the names to the sentences.
Jim — I work outdoors, it's *easy / difficult*.
David — I work in a hospital, it's *quiet / busy*.
Ingrid — I work in a shop, it's *boring / interesting*.
Maria — I work in an office, the people are *friendly / unfriendly*.
Richard — I work in a restaurant, it's *quiet / busy*.
Julie — I work in a school, it's *boring / interesting*.

3 Listen again and underline the correct words.

Language note: use *I work…* to talk about your job.
*I **work** in a restaurant / outdoors.*

Vocabulary and Speaking

1 Turn to page 104 and match the jobs to the pictures.

2 Look at the table. Choose **one** of the tasks below.

A Tick (✔) the sentence which is true for you.

B Choose a job from page 104. This is your job. Tick (✔) the true sentence.

		you
I work …	in a school	
	in an office	
	in a shop	
	in a restaurant	
	outdoors	
	at home	
	…	
I'm a student		
I'm unemployed		
I'm retired		

Language note: someone who is **unemployed** does not have a job. Someone who is **retired** does not have a job because they are over 60 or 65 years old.

3 Speak to five other people in the class and make a note of their answers.
A: *I work in a shop. And you?*
B: *I'm a student.*

4 Are these sentences true (T) or false (F)?
In my group …
- three people work in an office. ____
- two people are unemployed. ____
- one person is a student. ____
- nobody is retired. ____

VSO is a British organisation; it works with people in many countries. VSO workers are called *volunteers*.

Sharing skills Changing lives

There are 1,500 VSO volunteers and they work in over 40 countries. There are many volunteers in Asian countries including China, India and Indonesia. There are also many volunteers in African countries but there aren't any volunteers in North Africa. Volunteers also work in South America in Guyana, Bolivia and Peru.

Volunteers are from 18 to 75 years old; the average age of a volunteer is 42. Most volunteers work for two years. They work in many different places including schools, hospitals, offices and outdoors on farms.

There isn't a lot of money for volunteers – only for food and a house. There's a lot of work but there's time for fun too.

A volunteer in a _____ in Malawi.

A VSO volunteer in a _____ in Guyana.

A volunteer on a _____ in Kenya.

Unit 5 Work

Coursebook: lesson 2 of a unit

Listening

Students hear conversations in various situations which help contextualise the language and provide a model.

Grammar explanations

Short grammar explanations are provided on the page, with a cross reference to further explanation and practice at the back of the book.

UNIT 5 Work & Play

Part 2

Vocabulary & Speaking
Sports

Listening
Talking about sports

Grammar & Pronunciation
Like

Reading & Speaking
The Human Race

Vocabulary and Speaking

1 Write the missing vowels (*a, e, i, o, u*) to complete the names of the sports.

2 2.08 Listen and repeat the sports.

3 Work in pairs. Look at the bar chart of countries and their national sports. Guess the sports. Choose from the sports in exercise 1.
A: I think number one is swimming. What do you think?
B: I think it's basketball.

4 2.09 Listen and check.

5 Work in pairs. Ask and answer the questions.
• Which sports are popular in your country?
• Which sports are *not* popular?
• Is there a national sport?

National sports of the world

sw__mm__ng   r__nn__ng   t__bl__ t__nn__s

cr__ck__t   b__sk__tb__ll   m__r__t__ t__ll   f__ __tb__ll

Listening

1 Do you like the sports in Vocabulary and Speaking exercise 1? Write +++ (I love it), ++ (I like it), + (it's OK) or x (I don't like it) in the boxes.

2 2.10 Listen to two people talking about some sports. Tick (✔) the table.

		+++ I love it	++ I like it	+ It's OK	x I don't like it
football	Man				
	Woman			✔	
swimming	Man				
	Woman				

3 Listen again and put the conversation in the correct order.
No, I don't. ___
Really? I love it. ___
Do you like football? _1_
Well, it's OK. ___
What about swimming, Steve? Do you like swimming? ___
Yes, I do. And you? ___

4 2.11 Read and listen to these sentences from the Listening on page 32. Notice how the words connect.
Do you like football?
Yes, I do.
Do you like swimming?
No, I don't.

5 Listen again and repeat.

6 Work in pairs. Ask and answer questions 1–4 from exercise 2. Remember to connect the words. Use short answers.
A: Do you like tennis?
B: Yes, I do.

G Grammar focus – explanation & more practice of *like* on page 110

Grammar and Pronunciation

Do you like football?
Yes, I do. / No, I don't.

• start questions with the auxiliary verb *do*
• use *do* for short answers, **not** the main verb (*Yes, I like*)

1 Underline the correct words.
A: Do you *like / likes* basketball?
B: Yes, I *do / don't*. It's a very popular sport in my country. In Argentina we love all ball sports – football, tennis, basketball. *Like you / Do you like* basketball?
A: No, I *don't / I don't like*. It's boring. I *do like / I like* running.

2 Write words to complete the questions.
Do you like *tennis* (a sport)?
1 Do you like _____ (a sport)?
2 Do you like _____ (a sportsman or sportswoman)?
3 Do you like _____ (a nationality) restaurants?
4 Do you like _____ (an actor)?

3 Write your answers to the questions.
Do you like tennis?   No, I don't

Reading and Speaking

1 Work in pairs. Do you like running? Ask your partner.

2 Look at the picture of a race and read the information. Then answer the questions.
1 What's the name of the race?
2 Where is it?
3 How many kilometres is the race?
4 What's special about this race?

3 Work in pairs. A: turn to page 97. B: turn to page 101. Tell your partner about another race.

4 Work in pairs. Are there any important races in your town or country? Tell your partner.

• The Human Race
• 10 kilometres
• 1 million runners worldwide
• Races in many cities (including London, Istanbul, Lima, Taipei, Warsaw ...) or run where you live

---

Pronunciation

A focus on sounds, stress and intonation are included at regular intervals in *Global*. Pronunciation is integrated into the language points of the lesson. The aim is for students to achieve international intelligibility.

Further practice

There are grammar explanations and exercises as well as communication activities at the back of the book for further practice of new language.

Coursebook: extra material at the end of a unit

Global voices

Every other third unit contains a listening section featuring authentic and unscripted recordings of a wide range of native and non-native speakers of English, which expose learners to real English as it is being used around the world today.

Global reading

Every other third unit contains an extra reading lesson, called *Global English* featuring a text by David Crystal, which provides interesting information about the English language.

Global voices

 capoeira
 ski-jumping
 dancing
 judo
 motorbike racing

Warm up

1 🔊 2.12 Listen and repeat the names of the sports in the pictures.

2 Look at the sports in the box.

basketball	capoeira	dancing	football	golf
judo	motorbike racing	running	ski-jumping	
swimming	tennis			

Find sports you ...
* play with a ball.
* normally do indoors.
* normally do with one other person.
* do alone.

Listening

1 🔊 2.13–2.17 Listen to five people answer the questions *Do you like sport?* and *What's your favourite sport?* Write the speaker's number next to the phrases.
* Not football. ____
* Well, I mean, yes, quite a bit, not too much, but yes. ____
* I do like sport, but not too much. ____
* Yes, I do. ____
* I love sports. *1*

2 Listen again and write the speakers' favourite sports from the list in Warm up exercise 2.
1 Mireille, US ____
2 Christina, Germany ____
3 Francesco, Italy ____
4 Jolanta, Poland ____
5 Eva, Switzerland ____

Language focus: questions

Language note: for questions starting with *do* we normally give *yes / no* answers. For *Wh* questions (*Where, What* etc) we give information in the answer.
Do you like sport?   Yes, I do.
What's your favourite sport?   My favourite sport is golf.

Underline the correct answer for each question.
1 A: Do you like sport?
  B: *My favourite? Cricket. / Yes, it's OK.*
2 A: What's your favourite type of music?
  B: *I love it. / Opera – I love opera.*
3 A: Do you like the cinema?
  B: *Well, yes, but not too much. / I like Titanic.*
4 A: What's your favourite food?
  B: *No, I don't. / Chinese food.*
5 A: Do you like Italian restaurants?
  B: *Yes, I do, they're great. / My favourite is pizza.*

Speaking

Work in pairs. Ask and answer the questions from the Language focus section.

Unit 5 Global voices

Global review

Vocabulary

1 Write six places where people work in the crossword puzzle. Use the pictures to help you.

r e s t a u r a n t
c
h
o
o
l

2 Complete the words.
A person over 65 who doesn't work is *r* ____
A person who doesn't have a job is *u* ____

3 Put the letters in the correct order to spell six sports.
1 lachsbktal
2 snetin
3 folatobl
4 tckrcie
5 nsimgiwm
6 nungirn

Grammar

1 Read a teacher's description of her school. Complete the sentences with *there's, there are, there isn't* or *there aren't*.

'I work in a school, it's a small school. ____ one head teacher and ____ 5 teachers. It's a school for girls. ____ 80 girls in the school. The girls are from 5 to 11 years old. ____ any boys. I like my job, ____ a boring day – every day is busy and interesting!'

2 Look at the table. Write five more sentences.

		+++ I love it	++ I like it	+ It's OK	x I don't like it
tennis	I	✓			
	You		✓		
swimming	I			✓	
	You			✓	
cricket	I				✓
	You	✓			
football	I		✓		
	You				✓

1 I love tennis.
2 I think swimming is OK.
3 ____ cricket.
4 ____
5 You like tennis.
6 You ____
7 ____
8 ____

3 Underline the correct answer.
1 Do you like tennis? Yes, I *like / do.*
2 Do you like cricket? Yes, I *love it / I do like.*
3 Do you like swimming? *Is OK / It's OK.*
4 Do you like football? No, I *don't / not like.*

Writing

1 Complete the sentences with information about yourself.
Hello, my name's ____, I'm from ____
I work ____. I'm ____
In my country the national sport is ____
I like ____ but I don't like ____

Listen again

1 🔊 2.18 Read and listen to these sentences from the Listening on page 30. Notice how the words link together.
I work in a shop, it's a small shop.
It's open every day.
It's OK, but it's a bit boring.

2 Repeat the sentences. Remember to link the words.

3 Read these phrases from the listening and decide which words link together.
I work outdoors on a farm.
It's a good job, but it's a difficult job too.

4 🔊 2.19 Listen and check. Repeat the sentences.

Global review Unit 5

Extra speaking and writing practice

Speaking and writing tasks based on the unit topic provide an extra opportunity to revise and consolidate the language from the unit in a freer and more open-ended format.

eWorkbook

Comprehensive component for self-study

The *Global* eWorkbook represents an evolution in self-study materials for learners. Within a rich multimedia environment it provides a wealth of resources for the learner, enabling them to continue their studies at their own pace, and in their own time.

Language Work

The eWorkbook contains a wide range of activities which allow for extra practice and review of the language presented in the Coursebook. These activities cover all aspects of language learning. Grammar, Vocabulary, Listening and Pronunciation practice activities are available both as fully interactive activities and in a printable pen-and-paper format. There are also worksheets to practise reading and writing skills.

global

BEGINNER

eWorkbook

 LANGUAGE PRACTICE

 PRINT AND WORK

 LISTEN

 WATCH

 ON THE MOVE

 DICTIONARY

 WORD LISTS

 GRAMMAR HELP

 WRITING TIPS

 TESTS

 PORTFOLIO

 CONTENTS MAP

Software Update   v1.0

Tools for reference and support

The eWorkbook offers all the support the learner may need. For instance, links to the Macmillan Dictionary Online, word lists per unit and grammar help organized by topic. The Writing tips section includes information on general aspects of writing, such as spelling, punctuation, paragraphing, etc.

Learning on the Move

The Global eWorkbook provides a wide variety of authentic extra listening and video materials supplied in commonly used file formats, so learners can load them onto their portable music and video players and study and review 'on-the-go'.

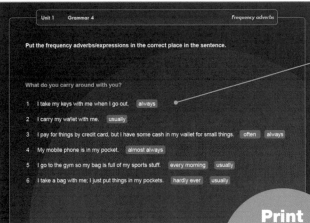

Unit 1   Grammar 4   Frequency adverbs

Put the frequency adverbs/expressions in the correct place in the sentence.

What do you carry around with you?

1 I take my keys with me when I go out. always
2 I carry my wallet with me. usually
3 I pay for things by credit card, but I have some cash in my wallet for small things. often always
4 My mobile phone is in my pocket. almost always
5 I go to the gym so my bag is full of my sports stuff. every morning usually
6 I take a bag with me; I just put things in my pockets. hardly ever usually

Interactive activities

Meaningful practice.

Video

Extracts from BBC programmes as well as original videos that can be downloaded and used on the move.

Big & Small

Vocabulary 3A
Adjectives (1)

Complete the puzzle.

Across
2 The opposite of *new*.
4 The opposite of *interesting*.
5 The opposite of *expensive*.
6 The opposite of *big*.

Down
1 The opposite of *good*.
2 The opposite of *closed*.
3 The opposite of *unfriendly*.

Vocabulary 3B
Adjectives

Complete the sentences with the correct adjective.

1 The coffee is very g_____
2 The shopping mall is very b_____There are 100 shops.
3 He's very un_____
4 The shop is c_____
5 This camera is very ex_____
6 Is this n_____?
7 The film is in_____

Functional language
In a shop

Put the conversation in the correct order.

a Goodbye.   ____
b Hello.   ____
c Here you are. Thanks. ____
d Hi. How much is this bag? ____
e It's £90.   ____
f Thank you. Goodbye. ____

Pronunciation
Schwa /ə/

Listen and complete the sentences.

1 There's ____ restaurant.
2 Is there ____ car park?
3 There isn't ____ bank.
4 There is ____ cinema.
5 Is there ____ bookshop?

Global Beginner eWorkbook   © Macmillan Publishers Limited 2010

Print and Work

For those who prefer to work offline.

50 Questions   15.25

Choose how or what to complete the question.

● What   ○ How

_____ kind of car do you drive?

Previous Question   Next Question   Submit Test

Listening

Comprehensive listening section, with tracks that can be downloaded and used on the move.

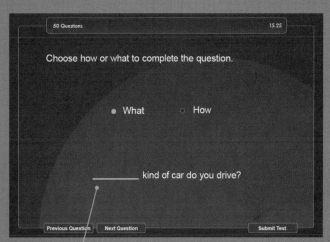

global
BEGINNER   eWorkbook

Word List   Grammar Help   Writing Tips

acceptable
accepted   Click the correct answer.
bring
basketball   1. When do you not use commas?
dynamo
pootle   a. to join sentences
practical
twistor   b. to separate prepositional phrases
dynamo
pootle   c. to separate items in a list   ✓
practical
twistor   previous   next
words
speaker

LANGUAGE PRACTICE   DICTIONARY

WORD LISTS   CONTENTS MAP

global
BEGINNER   eWorkbook

Useful Phrases   ● Describing people
                      ● The human body
In Conversation   ● Feelings
                      ● Describing people and things
Vocabulary Builder   ● Work
                      ● Technology
                      ● Time and money
                      ● House and home
                      ● Sports and activities
LISTEN ON THE MOVE   ● New words

Self assessment

Test generator and Common European Framework checklists for self assessment.

Tools

Comprehensive tools for self study.

Teacher's Book

David Crystal: The future of Englishes: going local

When people talk about 'global English' they are usually referring to the common features which identify the variety we call standard English. Increasingly, however, attention has been drawn to the regional features which differentiate one part of the English-speaking world from another. So today we happily talk about British, American, Australian, South African, Indian, and other 'Englishes', and studies are accumulating of the way these varieties make distinctive use of pronunciation, orthography, grammar, vocabulary, and discourse. Much of the distinctiveness resides in the area of lexicology, the linguistic domain which most closely reflects cultural identity, and dictionaries have been compiled of the distinctive lexicons encountered in these regions.

It does not take long before these lexicons reach many thousands of words. When a country adopts a language as a local alternative means of communication, it immediately starts adapting it, to meet the communicative needs of the region. Words for local plants and animals, food and drink, customs and practices, politics and religion, sports and games, and many other facets of everyday life soon accumulate a local wordstock which is unknown outside the country and its environs. When someone in South Africa says 'The bakkie had to stop at a red robot', we need to know that a bakkie is a truck and a robot is a traffic-light. There are thousands of such words in a dictionary of South African English. And other parts of the English-speaking world display the same kind of creativity.

This seems to be the pattern, as English becomes a local alternative language. When a group of people in a country switch into English, for whatever reason, the subject-matter of their conversation inevitably incorporates aspects of their local environment. They talk about the shops, streets, suburbs, bus-routes, institutions, businesses, television programmes, newspapers, political parties, minority groups, and a great deal more. They make jokes, quote proverbs, bring up childhood linguistic memories (such as nursery rhymes), and recall lyrics of popular songs. All this local knowledge is taken for granted, and used in sentences without gloss. Visitors who hear such sentences, or read them in local newspapers, need to have them explained. Conventional dictionaries will not help, for they do not include such localisms, especially if the expressions are encyclopedic in character (referring to local people, places, institutions, and suchlike).

Every English-speaking location in the world has usages which make the English used there distinctive, expressive of local identity, and a means of creating solidarity. From this point of view, notions such as 'Swedish English' take on a fresh relevance — going well beyond traditional conceptions of English spoken with a Swedish accent, or English displaying interference from Swedish grammar. Swedish English, for me, I define as the kind of English I need to know about when I go to Sweden, or I will be unable to converse efficiently with Swedish speakers in English. It would be amazingly useful to have a glossary of the English equivalents of Swedish cultural references, but I know of none. This seems to be a neglected area for any language.

We need regional cultural dictionaries or glossaries. It is something everyone could do, and something to which everyone who learns English can contribute. It would take only an hour or so to accumulate a list of dozens of culturally specific items. And once these are written down, in the style of a glossary, it has an interesting effect on the participants. They feel they have somehow made the English language their own. I don't suspect such projects add greatly to their linguistic confidence and self-esteem, that no-one else in the world knows their home-grown variety of English as well as they do. And they can take pride in the fact that they have added their own small piece to the global jigsaw puzzle that comprises the English language.

UNIT 5 Work & Play

Part 2

Vocabulary and Speaking (SB page ...)

1 Ask students to look at the pictures and write the missing vowels to complete the names of the sports. They then compare answers with a partner. Ask if they have the same answers before you check them with the class.

| swimming |
| running |
| table tennis |
| cricket |
| basketball |
| American football |
| football |

2 🔊 2.08 Students listen and repeat the sports. Write these on the board and mark the stress, which is usually on the first syllable of each word. Also note that *table* in *table tennis* is stressed more than *tennis*, and that in *American football*, the second syllable of *American* is stressed, and both words are given equal emphasis. Point out, too, that the final *e* of *table* is silent.

3 Focus students on the bar chart of national sports. Working in pairs, students guess the sports 1–4 from ... in exercise 1. Tell them to use the countries ... decide, and draw attention to the example ... Write *I think ...* and *What do you think?* on ... they talk and explain that they are used ... put an opinion. Drill the pronunciation ... don't give a grammatical explanation ... formed at this point. When ... invite some pairs to tell the class ... others agree. Don't confirm ...

... and check their answers.

... rica, Africa & Europe, **football** is ... Australia, **cricket** is the most ... the national sport is football – ... **tennis** is very popular.

... airs, students ask and answer the ... students time to read through the ... and deal with any queries they have before they ... ting. When pairs finish, discuss the questions with ... lass so that students can share their knowledge if ... hey come from different countries, or try to agree if they ... all come from the same country.

The Teacher's Book includes comprehensive teaching notes with answer keys and audioscripts, and to bu... about (something ...). Point to the sports pictures and ask *Do you like (sport)?* Use gestures, eg thumbs up and down, or happy and sad faces, to clarify the meaning of *like*. Find out whether a majority of class members like or don't like each sport.

1 Go through the meaning of each symbol. Start by explaining what *like* means, either through gesture or by saying *It's good*. Then explain that *love* means 'like a lot', and that *I don't like it* is the negative form of *I like it*. Also tell them that *it* is a pronoun and refers to the sport (basketball, etc.). Students write the symbols in the box for each picture. When they've finished, call out the name of a sport and invite different students to tell you what they think of it. Work on pronunciation as they do this, and drill any problem phrases as necessary.

2 🔊 2.10 Tell students they are going to listen to two students talking about football and swimming. Ask them to look at the table and explain that they need to tick the man and the woman's opinions of the two sports.

The woman likes football and she loves swimming.
The man thinks football is OK and he doesn't like swimming.

3 Students listen and write the conversation in the correct order. Check answers and tell students that they will study the language in this conversation in the grammar section.

🔊 2.10
A: Do you like football?
B: Yes, I do. And you?
A: Well, it's OK.
B: What about swimming, Steve? Do you like swimming?
A: No, I don't.
B: Really? I love it.

Grammar and Pronunciation (SB page 33)

Here the focus is on questions with *like* and short answers.

Focus students on the example question and tell students it comes from the conversation in *Listening* on page 32. Read through the rules with them and check that they ...

Callouts

Teach Global Think Local

The Teacher's Book includes comprehensive teaching notes with answer keys and audioscripts, and detailed background and language notes.

It also provides 'Teach Global Think Local' ideas: extra activities that can be adapted to individual teaching situations.

Specialist essays

The Teacher's Book features a number of specialist essays, each focusing on a different aspect of language teaching. These have been written by a range of well-known and award-winning guest ELT authors and teacher trainers, and will be of interest to teachers of all levels of experience.

Teacher's Resource CD

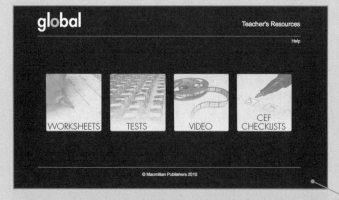

global   Teacher's Resources
                                                        Help

WORKSHEETS   TESTS   VIDEO   CEF CHECKLISTS

© Macmillan Publishers 2010

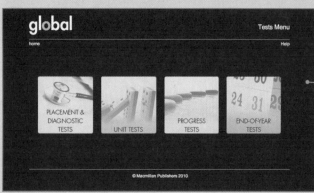

global   Tests Menu
home   Help

PLACEMENT & DIAGNOSTIC TESTS   UNIT TESTS   PROGRESS TESTS   END-OF-YEAR TESTS

© Macmillan Publishers 2010

global   Video
home   right click and 'save target as' to save the file | Help

Video			
Unit 1	Iris recognition	Watch	Print worksheet
Unit 2	Tea break	Watch	Print worksheet
Unit 3	Art fraud	Watch	Print worksheet
Unit 4	The sun (contd.)	Watch	Print worksheet
Unit 5	Computer games (contd.)	Watch	Print worksheet
Unit 6	Birth of Horror: Frankenstein (contd.)	Watch	Print worksheet
Unit 7	The history of money (contd.)		
Unit 8	Thomas Cook (contd.)		
Unit 9	A history of sum...		
Unit 10	New Zeal...		

Communication activities, tests, videos

The Teacher's Resource CD includes printable communication activity worksheets that practise areas of language from the Coursebook units and printable communication activity worksheets to do at different stages of the course. In addition, it provides a wide range of tests (diagnostic, progress tests, end-of-year test etc) and additional video clips and video worksheets for the teacher.

Audio CDs

global BEGINNER
Class CD 1

Units 1–4
(Tracks 1–80)

© Macmillan Publishers Limited 2010

This recording is copyright and unauthorized copying is illegal.

ISBN 978-0-230-03286-6

Class CD 2

Units 5–10
(Tracks 1–78)

ISBN 978-0-230-03286-6

Class CD 3

Units 11–15
(Tracks 1–72)

ISBN 978-0-230-03286-6

The *Global* Beginner class audio is contained on three CDs. They include the listening material from the Coursebook.

Website

The Global website consists of author blog, teaching tips, extra resources and much more.

www.macmillanenglish.com/global

Global Digital

Enhancing the teaching experience in the classroom

Global Digital is a digital component designed for classroom use. It can be used with an interactive whiteboard or with a computer and projector.

The Digital Book

The Digital Book allows the teacher to access and display an interactive version of any page from the Coursebook in front of the class. All of the relevant audio, video and reference materials are instantly accessible right on the page.

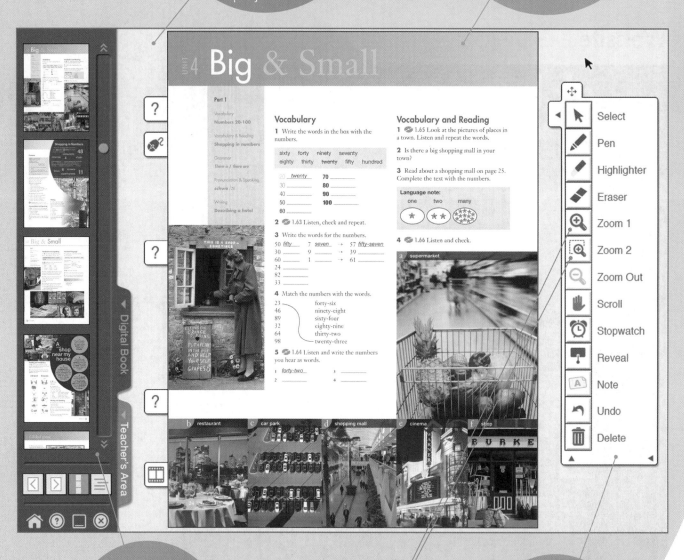

Navigation pane

The navigation pane allows you to select a page from anywhere in the book.

Zooming in and out

The Zoom tools allow you to zoom in either on pre-defined areas or any part of the page that you choose.

Toolbox

The toolbox provides a number of tools which enable you to interact with the Digital book page.

Navigation pane

The navigation pane displays thumbnails of the pages you have created in the Teacher's area.

The Teacher's Area

The Teacher's Area can be used to create your own material either before or during the class. You can insert and edit text and images, add links to pages from the digital book and insert audio and website links.

Open Game

Create Game

Teacher's Area

Select

Pen

Highlighter

Eraser

Text

Shape

Image

Audio

Hyperlink

Stopwatch

Reveal

Copy

Paste

Background

Undo

Delete

Games section

The games section provides interactive game templates to which you can add your own content.

Toolbox

A toolbox which includes some different tools from the ones for the digital book enables you to make annotations and create and edit materials.

Introduction

Ideas about language teaching, like languages themselves, are subject to change. For much of the twentieth century different 'methods' were presented as the best way to learn or acquire a new language. Some argue that we are now 'beyond methods', or in a 'post-method' condition in the twenty-first century. However, suggestions and approaches, useful tips, techniques and advice for good teaching practice are still as important as they ever were.

We know that language teachers often like to be informed of the newest developments in our field. With current technology we know more about the English language than ever before. Additionally, we as teachers are harnessing technology and the internet in new and exciting ways that help us help our students in ways we could not have imagined twenty years ago. And yet, there are some things that remain the same in the classroom.

What follows are a series of short essays, each written by experts in the field. The aim of these essays is to provide you, the language teacher, with up-to-date information about your subject matter. Like the material in *Global* itself, they are thought-provoking pieces. We also believe that learning more about what we do is extremely useful for our ongoing professional development. We hope you find them useful.

Lindsay Clandfield

Contents

Lindsay Clandfield: Why *Global*?

Every book is a product of its times. Nowhere is this truer than in educational materials. Notions of how people learn, of what they learn and of what is important are shaped by the world around us and the period we live through. What then, are the times that have shaped *Global*?

We live in an era of fast communication. More and more people are gaining access to internet and quicker communications technology. This means that we are writing and reading more than before, be it emails, text messages, blogs or web pages. Language learners need to work on quick and unplanned writing (writing for fluency) just as they do for speaking.

We live in an era of information. New technologies enable us to communicate more and with more people, but they have also made more and more information available than ever before – and it is available faster. Much of this information is still in English. Students need to be able to access information and assimilate it quickly.

We live in an era of uncertainty. Precisely because so much information is out there, we are often unsure what is accurate and what is opinion or even misleading. To succeed in an information-rich world one has to learn how to discern, analyse and evaluate what one sees or hears. Fostering critical thinking skills has long been an important goal of educaton.

We live in an era of global English. One of the most important realisations in the field of English Language Teaching of the past decade or so is that English is an international language, spoken all over the world, by people with different accents and different 'Englishes'. A learner is just as likely, if not more likely, to use his or her English with another non-native speaker as with a native speaker.

Given all this, the goals of *Global* are threefold:

1   For your students to **learn English**. This, as for any language course, is the primary goal of *Global*, which reflects modern developments in language teaching and learning. There is a strong lexical focus as well as a complete grammar syllabus, language presentation and practice is highly contextualised with many opportunities for personalisation, and there is plenty of meaningful communicative practice which in *Global* extends to mean writing as well as speaking fluency. *Global* includes a wide variety of reading and listening genres and practises a range of reading and listening skills. With the addition of sections to develop functional language, writing and study skills and review language, we are confident this course provides your students with the tools to become competent users of the language.

2   For your students to **learn through English**. The texts and topics of *Global* are selected so that in every lesson you and your students will be learning something new. We have chosen material that is thought-provoking, interesting, intelligent and above all, real. We have also included tasks that encourage students to examine the information they receive critically, and to find out more about a topic if they are interested. Unlike many other courses, texts and topics steer away from the light human interest or celebrity-related story. We use real world information from a wide variety of domains and the power of literature to unlock students' self-expression.

3   For your students to **learn about English**. This course also includes a focus, through extra reading and listening activities, on the English language as a subject itself. What is it? How is it changing? What kinds of English are appearing around the world? What are the implications of this? We believe these are important questions, worthy of being touched on in the language class. It is why we asked the foremost world expert author on these matters, David Crystal, to contribute to this new and innovative thread of *Global*.

David Crystal: The future of Englishes: going local

When people talk about 'global English' they are usually referring to the common features which identify the variety we call standard English. Increasingly, however, attention has been drawn to the regional features which differentiate one part of the English-speaking world from another. So today we happily talk about British, American, Australian, South African, Indian, and other 'Englishes', and studies are accumulating of the way these varieties make distinctive use of pronunciation, orthography, grammar, vocabulary, and discourse. Much of the distinctiveness resides in the area of lexicology, the linguistic domain which most closely reflects cultural identity, and dictionaries have been compiled of the distinctive lexicons encountered in these regions.

It does not take long before these lexicons reach many thousands of words. When a country adopts a language as a local alternative means of communication, it immediately starts adapting it, to meet the communicative needs of the region. Words for local plants and animals, food and drink, customs and practices, politics and religion, sports and games, and many other facets of everyday life soon accumulate a local wordstock which is unknown outside the country and its environs. When someone in South Africa says 'The bakkie had to stop at a red robot', we need to know that a bakkie is a truck and a robot is a traffic-light. There are thousands of such words in a dictionary of South African English. And other parts of the English-speaking world display the same kind of creativity.

This seems to be the pattern, as English becomes a local alternative language. When a group of people in a country switch into English, for whatever reason, the subject-matter of their conversation inevitably incorporates aspects of their local environment. They talk about the shops, streets, suburbs, bus-routes, institutions, businesses, television programmes, newspapers, political parties, minority groups, and a great deal more. They make jokes, quote proverbs, bring up childhood linguistic memories (such as nursery rhymes), and recall lyrics of popular songs. All this local knowledge is taken for granted, and used in sentences without gloss. Visitors who hear such sentences, or read them in local newspapers, need to have them explained. Conventional dictionaries will not help, for they do not include such localisms, especially if the expressions are encyclopedic in character (referring to local people, places, institutions, and suchlike).

Every English-speaking location in the world has usages which make the English used there distinctive, expressive of local identity, and a means of creating solidarity. From this point of view, notions such as 'Swedish English' take on a fresh relevance, going well beyond traditional conceptions of English spoken with a Swedish accent, or English displaying interference from Swedish grammar. Swedish English, for example, I define as the kind of English I need to know about when I go to Sweden, otherwise I will be unable to converse efficiently with Swedish speakers in English. It would be amazingly useful to have a glossary of the English equivalents of Swedish cultural references, but I know of none. This seems to be a neglected area for any language.

We need regional cultural dictionaries or glossaries. It is something every region can do, and something to which everyone who learns English can contribute. It takes only an hour or so to accumulate a list of dozens of culturally specific items. And when these are written down, in the style of a glossary, it has an interesting effect upon the participants. They feel they have somehow made the English language their own. I suspect such projects also add greatly to their linguistic confidence and self-esteem, for no-one else in the world knows their home-grown variety of English as well as they do. And they can take pride in the fact that they have added their own small piece to the global jigsaw puzzle that comprises the English language.

David Crystal is honorary professor of linguistics at the University of Bangor, and works from his home in Holyhead, North Wales, as a writer, editor, lecturer, and broadcaster. He read English at University College London, specialized in English language studies, then joined academic life as a lecturer in linguistics, first at Bangor, then at Reading, where he became professor of linguistics. He received an OBE for services to the English language in 1995. His books include *The Cambridge Encyclopedia of the English Language* and *The Stories of English. Just a Phrase I'm Going Through: my Life in Language* was published in 2009.

Amanda Jeffries: Developing study skills and encouraging learner autonomy

Learner autonomy can be defined as the ability of a learner to take charge of their own learning, not only by learning specific strategies or study skills but also by developing an entirely new attitude to learning. A truly independent learner of English is aware of their learning needs and goals, can reflect on how they learn, has a positive and proactive attitude to language-learning, and can make the most of learning opportunities both in and out of class.

Study skills are strategies and approaches that can lead to more effective learning. The *Global* series follows a comprehensive study skills syllabus covering metacognitive strategies (thinking about, planning, and evaluating learning) and affective and social strategies (monitoring your attitude to learning and working with others) as well as dictionary and reference skills. It also develops specific strategies for learning and practising listening, speaking, reading, writing, vocabulary, and grammar more effectively. All learners are different and research suggests that effective learning depends on choosing the right strategy, or combination of strategies, for the task, the learning context, or the particular individual.

Why deal with learner autonomy in class?

Most teachers recognise the importance of learning effectively, but many have reservations about doing learner training or learning awareness activities in class: 'It wouldn't work with my group'; 'There's already too much to do in class'; or 'I wouldn't know where to start'. It is important to remember, however, that a focused and independent learner is not only more efficient but also more motivated. Moreover, learner autonomy activities provide a valuable extra practice opportunity.

How can I help my learners to develop these skills?

You may find some of the following suggestions useful in your teaching situation.

- Include short regular learner training slots in your timetable, so that your learners get used to the idea of study skills as a key part of their learning.

- Offer students a 'menu' of possible strategies for, say, planning an essay, or memorising vocabulary to help them choose the strategy that works best for them. Comparing ideas in pairs or groups can also suggest new and useful ideas. Suggest they try out a new strategy for a week and report back on how effective they found it.

- When doing class activities, share your aims with your students and suggest useful strategies; for example, explain that you are asking them to read primarily to understand the gist of a passage and offer good gist reading tips.

- Ask students regularly to note down or discuss how well they have learned and what they have enjoyed or found puzzling, and make resolutions for how to improve.

- Find out how your students learn. You could ask them to write you a short letter about their progress and write back with suggestions!

- Make students aware of the range of practice opportunities and materials available – in a library or study centre, online, or in the media. Students can also keep a record of work outside class that they can discuss with you.

- More advanced groups might find writing learner diaries a good way to reflect on their learning styles and preferences.

- Above all, show you are convinced that developing good learning habits is a valuable learning focus – that way, your own attitude is more likely to rub off on your students.

Amanda Jeffries teaches university students and works on teacher development programmes in Oxford. She has contributed to the Macmillan *Straightforward* and *New Inside Out* series. She has written the writing, study skills and review pages for the *Global* series, and is the co-author of *Global Advanced*.

Pete Sharma: Blended learning

The term 'blended learning' is a 'buzz' term, yet one that means different things to different people. The 'classic' definition of blended learning is a course consisting of traditional 'face-to-face' language lessons, combined with 'distance learning' i.e. the opportunity to study 'beyond the classroom'. Such a course can provide many benefits for language learners.

In our book *Blended Learning*, we suggest a broader definition, taking blended learning to mean a combination of classroom teaching and the *appropriate* use of technology. Technology such as an interactive whiteboard can be used inside the classroom to enrich the learning experience. In addition, the students could have 24/7 access to their interactive learning materials, allowing them to study at anytime, anywhere.

Principles

Whichever definition is used, new technology has had a major impact on language teaching and learning. We describe four key principles for successfully integrating technology into language teaching:

- Differentiate the role you play as a teacher, and the role the technology is playing. For example, the teacher can clarify 'fuzzy' areas of grammar. The interactive exercises on a CD-ROM could then offer extra practice in 'crisp' areas of language, with students receiving feedback from the computer.
- Teaching should be principled. In other words, there should be a sound pedagogical reason for using the technology.
- The technology should complement and enhance what the teacher does. It is not a replacement for the teacher.
- 'It's not what it is, but what you do with it'. The interactive whiteboard in itself is just a 'tool'. It is how teachers actually use it, to help provide engaging language lessons, which can lead to better learning outcomes.

Integrating technology into language courses

There are many ways to integrate technology into a language course. A teacher can:

- support their face-to-face teaching with a Virtual Learning Environment, a web based platform which learners can access at any time. The VLE can be used, for example, to post language feedback for students to study after a class discussion.
- run 'learner training' sessions to show students how to benefit from the digital material in the eWorkbook at the back of their course book. For instance, you can download the audio files to their mp3 players to allow learning 'on the go'; use the 'QuickFind' feature on their electronic dictionary, and download the free interactive version of the phonemic chart from the web.
- use technology before a class. Before a fluency lesson, email students a pre-discussion reading task to get them thinking about the topic.
- use technology during a class. If you use an interactive whiteboard, you can save the electronic flip-charts you create. This allows you to build up a bank of personalised digital materials including photographs and sound files to support each of the course book units.
- use technology after a class. Students focusing on writing can collaborate together to produce an essay using a wiki, a website which contains editable web pages.

If teachers continue to provide pedagogically sound and interesting lessons, and allow the technology to support learning both inside and outside the classroom, then a blended learning approach can certainly enrich the language learning experience of students.

References

Barrett, B and Sharma, P *Blended Learning* – using technology inside and beyond the language classroom (Macmillan, 2007); Jones, C (1986) 'It's not so much the program, more what you do with it: the importance of methodology in CALL' System 14 / 2, 171-178

Pete Sharma is an associate Lecturer at Oxford Brookes University, UK. He has written books on technology in language teaching, and is co-author of *Blended Learning: using technology in and beyond the language classroom* (Macmillan 2007). Pete is a Director of Pete Sharma Associates, which runs training in educational technology: www.psa.eu.com. He has edited the CALL Review, the newsletter of the Learning Technologies SIG of IATEFL, and blogs on technology at: www.te4be.com

Duncan Foord: How we can develop as teachers

Development means change and change is inevitable. You are not the same teacher (or person) you were a year ago. Working with a new coursebook, new students and colleagues, taking part in in-service training, preparing classes – all of these challenging elements of your day-to-day routine have changed you. You are always developing, you just have to decide how.

Our choices are framed by the culture we live in, the school we work in, government policy, students' expectations and so on. Some schools may encourage and support teacher development, others less so, but you will always have choices to make about how you teach and how you deal with challenges inside and outside the classroom. Focus on what you can do rather than what you can't.

Guiding principles

Just like a lesson, your working life needs some aims to guide your choice of development activities, your development plan, if you like. Here are six which I like.

- Take an interest in my students.
- Enjoy teaching.
- Take on challenges.
- Manage stress.
- Balance work and home life.
- Share my enthusiasm with others.

Give your teaching a 'developmental twist'

Here are some ideas for practical activities which are easy to integrate into your teaching routine and not time consuming.

- **Get feedback** from your students. Five minutes before the end of the lesson ask the students to write on a piece of paper three things they liked about the class and one thing they didn't like, or a 'suggestion' if they prefer. Thank your students and collect the papers in. In the next class (or via email) respond to the comments.

- **Make a short video** of your class. For this you need a small hand-held camera or mobile phone with video. Get a colleague or student to video your class for about 5–10 minutes. Watch the video afterwards more than once. The first few times you will be cringing at your appearance and mannerisms! After that you will notice more interesting things about your choice of language, gestures and facial expressions and get a good idea how your students see you.

- **Try activities out first**. Before you use a speaking activity, try it out with a colleague. Afterwards assess how much time you needed, whether the instructions were clear, if you needed preparation time, what language you used, whether your students would find it easy or difficult and what help they might need. Adjust your lesson plan accordingly.

- **Break your routine**. This can be a very good way to help you understand your teaching better and add an element of surprise and fun to your classes. For example, let one of your students become the teacher for ten minutes and you become a student, move the seating arrangement, supplement the coursebook text with one you find which will particularly interest your students…

- **Create a staff 'sharing board'**. This is a place where you can share materials and teaching ideas with your colleagues. Once it catches on, the board will help build staff rapport as well as provide a source of interesting lessons and save you preparation time.

Duncan Foord is the Director of the teacher training institution OxfordTEFL. He is responsible for teacher training and development in the company and teaches on Trinity Certificate and Diploma courses in the Barcelona centre. He is co-author (with Lindsay Clandfield) of *The Language Teacher's Survival Handbook* (It's Magazines, 2008) and *The Developing Teacher* (Delta Publishing, 2009) winner of the Duke of Edinburgh ESU English Language Award 2009 for Best Entry for Teachers.

Jim Scrivener: Different kinds of beginner learner

When I started teaching, I found low level classes quite puzzling. I met 'beginners' who seemed to know quite a lot of the grammar already or who could say a large number of unusual chunks of language with perfect pronunciation (but do little else) – or learners who could read some complex technical texts in their field of work but not understand anything I said. At the same time, I was meeting 'elementary' students who seemed to be struggling with some absolute basics of the language. What was going on?

Zero beginners and false beginners

A zero beginner or true beginner may arrive in your class with only a few internationally known words, product names, catch phrases, and song lyrics. In fact zero beginners are quite rare nowadays in some countries and many teachers will never meet one. As more learners study English at school, there are nowadays very few adult true beginners.

A false beginner, in contrast, is someone who has learnt English at some time previously, though they may have forgotten most of it (or think that they have). In class they may be reactivating things they already half-knew rather than learning them from scratch.

However, even these terms include quite a range of different types of beginner and elementary learners. Let's unpack a few variations of the low-level learner.

Professionally-skilled learners

Some beginners have learnt to cope professionally in a narrow area of English. For example, a telecom engineer may have become very skilled at reading technical telecom manuals but be weak in other skills and knowledge – even in other kinds of reading. This can be confusing for a teacher who sees the learner cope with their own work-related texts and wrongly assumes a higher level of competence than exists.

Acquisition-rich learners

Some students have never formally studied the language but have been exposed to lots of English speech (e.g. in film soundtracks or TV programmes) learning chunks of colloquial English. I think of this as the 'Cartoon Network effect'. Learners may have little idea what phrases actually mean nor any idea of the underlying grammar.

Special needs learners

Not all students are necessarily very strong at reading and writing in their own language. If a learner seems to be having problems with some classroom work, it's possible that this doesn't reflect difficulty with English alone. They may be dyslexic. They may have a range of other problems. Clearly, it's important for a teacher to recognise and find ways of working with these needs as early as possible.

False false beginners

These are students who believe themselves to be beginners and book into a beginner's course, but aren't really. Their teacher may only realise over time that they are rather better at English than they appeared to be at first. So where do these students come from? Some adult students feel strongly that they want to study in a beginners class, maybe because they don't feel confident or want a less challenging course that covers more familiar ground. The presence of a 'false false beginner' in a beginner's class can demotivate other students who may wonder why their own progress seems so much slower. I once had a student in a beginner's class who eventually turned out to be upper intermediate; it took me a few days to realise exactly what the problem was!

Jim Scrivener is Head of Teacher Development for Bell International based at Bedgebury School in Kent, UK, where he developed and runs the Online Delta course. He is the author of *Learning Teaching* (Macmillan), Basics: *Teaching Grammar* (OUP) as well as the Teacher's Books and Portfolios for the *Straightforward* coursebook series (Macmillan).

Rose Senior: Teaching beginner learners in class-centred ways

What is class-centred teaching?

Class-centred teaching is a framework for understanding the behaviour of effective classroom teachers that can help all language teachers to teach more successfully. As its name suggests, class-centred teaching puts emphasis on the class group and makes the learning and social wellbeing of the class the focal point of the teacher's attention. The holistic notion of class-centred teaching is based on the premise that cohesive classes (characterised by overall feelings of openness, trust, and mutual respect and trust) provide optimum environments for language learning.

Balancing teacher talking time with student talking time

Teachers of low-level classes should be prepared to be the focal point of the class for a significant part of each lesson. During this time they will be setting up activities, giving instructions, asking questions, eliciting responses, correcting errors, explaining things, providing general feedback – and of course modelling new language – for the benefit of the whole class.

At the same time, it's important to keep in mind the class-centred principle of balance: alternating between teacher talking time and student talking time in such a way that your students sense that they are progressing both individually and collectively towards the achievement of worthwhile learning goals.

Teaching tips

When teaching low-level classes it's important to remember that your goal is to maintain a sense that your class is moving ahead in unison – with no-one feeling lost or left out. To achieve this goal you could do the following:

- Always speak clearly and at a speed that enables your class to follow what you are saying. Don't worry if you feel that your speech is somewhat unnatural: all effective speakers adjust their speech patterns to the people with whom they are talking.

- Model linguistic forms in a deliberate way, providing your class with a range of opportunities to mimic and repeat them (through chorus work, hand and body movements, structured question and answer sequences with a partner and so on). Don't give up too soon: continue until students can reproduce words and phrases intelligibly and with a degree of confidence.

- Focus on the linguistic items presented in the book in such a way that your students can clearly identify recurring language patterns. Adult learners welcome the opportunity to understand the structure of English; applying their cognitive as well as their imitative abilities provides them with a welcome additional learning tool. This is particularly important when their exposure to English is limited to the classroom.

- Remember the role that humour can play in language classrooms. Spontaneous whole-class laughter (provided it is not derisory in tone) can affirm the feeling that the class functions as a unified classroom community.

Developing a feeling of mutual support in low-level classes

The level of supportiveness of the overall class group is particularly important for adult beginners and elementary students, who naturally feel nervous and vulnerable as they embark on learning English and practising their interactive skills in class. If students feel that the class is behind them as they struggle to overcome difficulties with pronunciation, memorization or formulating responses they are more likely to make steady linguistic progress and to develop the confidence to speak in front of others.

Rose Senior is a language teacher, teacher educator and classroom researcher. Author of *The Experience of Language Teaching* (CUP, 2006), Rose presents at conferences, runs professional development workshops and writes on a range of aspects of classroom language teaching in both academic and teacher-oriented journals. She has a regular column in *English Teaching Professional*.

Hanna Kryszewska: Teaching new words versus teaching lexical chunks

For many years English language teaching focused on teaching grammar and vocabulary had a subservient role. Teaching vocabulary tended to be about single words and an occasional collocation, and a successful learner mastered vocabulary lists. More recent trends have changed the focus, and put lexis in the central position. The works of Nattinger and DeCarico, of Michael Lewis and Dave Willis emphasise the role of lexis, with lexical chunks as the building blocks of the language.

What is a lexical chunk?

Imagine a pile of multicoloured building blocks of various sizes. This is a 'picture' of the brain of a native speaker when it comes to language. Each building block is a lexical chunk stored in the native speaker's brain, waiting to be used. When a native speaker wants to produce an utterance, they retrieve a ready-made chunk or chunks, usually stringing them together by means of grammar. A chunk is a unit of meaning which can be a single word, a phrase or even a sentence, but no longer than eight words as that is the most the brain can successfully store or retrieve. A given word can appear in many different chunks, e.g. *Catch!*, *It caught fire*, *catch the bus to town*, etc.

Language corpora and frequency lists

We have been able to learn more about language chunks thanks to language corpora. A corpus is a body of language created from spoken and written texts, produced by native speakers. Such a body may contain 400 million words, and computer analysis of these corpora helps lexicographers and grammarians to determine frequencies, to detect certain language patterns, to discover the environment of a word or chunk and helps to write new generation dictionaries as well as re-write the English grammar.

Computer analysis of the corpus reveals not only facts but also figures about the language. One interesting finding is that the first 1000 most common words in English constitute 74.1% of text, the next 1000 add only 7.2%, and 12,500 word families constitute 95% of text. Learners must be aware that some words are more useful (the *Macmillan Essential Dictionary* codes the most frequent words with stars) and that a word learnt at lower levels, may be used in more idiomatic contexts to create a more advanced chunk, such as in *He thinks he is the **cat**'s whiskers* where the meaning of the word 'cat' is not transparent.

Tips

Language teachers need to encourage the storage of whole chunks as part of learner training and design activities to promote the right storage and retrieval of chunks. For example a teacher can:

- supervise the way learners record new language in their notebooks and how they go about learning new lexical items. Encourage them to record new lexis as chunks.

- collect chunks around a common word from a corpus – ie record chunks that begin with, contain, and end with a given word e.g. *home*. You can also ask students to go through the coursebook and collect chunks that contain a given word e.g. *take* or collect chunks around a theme, e.g. travel.

- get students to make chunks or sentences using the top 100 words in English; design activities around the top 20 adjectives or the top 100 phrases in English, etc.

Focus on lexical chunking can easily supplement the coursebook and enrich our classroom practice. By adding a new dimension to language learning, it ensures faster progress. After all if native speakers learn language successfully through chunking, why shouldn't we incorporate it in our language teaching?

Hanna Kryszewska is a senior lecturer at the University of Gdańsk, Poland and teacher trainer with Pilgrims Language Courses, UK. She is the co-author of a number of resource books, including *Learner Based-teaching* (OUP), *Language Activities for Teenagers* (CUP) and the series of coursebooks *ForMat* (Macmillan Polska). Her latest book (with Paul Davis) on lexical chunking will soon be published by Delta Publishing. She is the editor of *Humanising Language Teaching* website magazine.

Jamie Keddie: Words and pictures: flashcards and flash images

When we incorporate an element of image into the activities that we plan for our language learners, the result may be a classroom experience which is more engaging and memorable for everyone involved. One example of a well-established visual aid is the picture flashcard.

Traditional picture flashcards

Imagine, for example, we have a set of action pictures to represent the following words: *climbing, running, skiing, shopping, fishing, dancing, sightseeing, surfing, camping* and *windsurfing.* After using the flashcards to elicit and drill the verb forms, a teacher could do any of the following:

- Place the flashcards at different points around the room and ask learners to point to the correct picture in response to the instructions: *Let's go camping, Let's go dancing,* etc.

- Place the flashcards on a table and remove one of them while students have their eyes closed. When they open their eyes, the first student to identify the missing flashcard gets a point and the procedure is repeated.

- Play 'Back to the Board': A student comes to the front of the class and faces the others. The teacher sticks a picture on the board. The student can't see the picture and has to guess what it is from the other students' descriptions.

- Play Bingo: Students choose and write down three of the activities. The teacher calls out items, pieces of equipment or places that are necessary for them (*credit card*, *rope*, *gloves*, *the beach*, etc). When one of these corresponds to an activity that a student has chosen, he or she can cross it off, but only one activity at a time. The winner is the first to cross off all three activities. Fun arguments usually follow.

- Use the flashcards to practise a wide range of substitution drills such as: *Have you ever been _____ in _____?* or *Tomorrow we're going _____ in _____ .* (NB for this drill, students have to think of a place that begins with the same letter as the verb – *camping in Cameroon*, *fishing in Finland*, *shopping in Shanghai*, etc.)

Other kinds of images

Picture flashcards are usually obtained from ELT resource books or online libraries and understandably teachers will be limited to what is on offer. They are usually small and categorized into topics such as food and drink, weather, professions, animals, etc. We are about to look at two possible ways of expanding our choices.

The internet: The internet offers an inexhaustible supply of images to flash at learners. Visit an image search engine, type in any of the example words we considered above (*skiing, shopping, surfing,* etc) and see what you get. Resulting images can be engaging and thought-provoking. A search for *climbing*, for example, could result in a photograph of a rock climber negotiating a death-defying overhang. As well as bringing the target language into the classroom, such an image could also introduce discussion on dangerous sports, vertigo, human endeavour and more.

Teachers can download images and create slideshows to show in class or print the pictures out to use when a computer screen or projector is not an option.

Students: Another way for teachers to get around the problem of limited flashcard resources is to turn to students themselves as a creative resource. Write a set of linguistic items on the board (*sightseeing, running, surfing,* etc). Give out pieces of scrap paper and ask students to decide among themselves who draws what. Some students will need to do more than one drawing - a job for the enthusiastic artists - while others will be more reluctant to get involved. This isn't a problem.

When students draw the target language, they 'experience' it and the results can be fun. Student-generated flashcards can be laminated or scanned, stored and displayed digitally. Happy flashing!

Jamie Keddie is a teacher, teacher trainer and writer. In 2008, he founded TEFLclips.com, a site dedicated to the possibilities for online video-sharing in the classroom. He is the author of Images in the *Resource Books for Teachers* series published by Oxford University Press. He is also a teacher trainer at Norwich Institute for Language Education.

Nick Bilbrough: Building confidence through dialogues

My first teaching experiences were with classes of teenagers and adults in Japan and Brazil. As a newly-qualified teacher, being suddenly faced with fairly large groups of low-level learners and trying to help them develop their abilities to speak in English was a real challenge; one that I met with only limited success. In retrospect I think that there was a fundamental problem with my approach.

The need for noticing

Principally I was underestimating the need for models of the kind of language that learners could use to perform the speaking activities I was trying to set up. It's all very well finding relevant and motivating speaking tasks, but without enough language support, beginners and elementary learners are pushed into either relying on the limited English that they already have, or worse, speaking entirely in the mother tongue. The language they needed to perform the tasks could not simply materialize out of thin air. I quickly realized the need for what Earl Stevick (in *Memory, Meaning and Method*, Heinle & Heinle) refers to as 'span' activities – those which provide a link between input and output, and which encourage learners to think deeply about language use. One way of incorporating a healthy amount of 'span' activities is through the use of dialogues. By encouraging learners to read, to practise, to perform and even to memorize dialogues, we are effectively 'slowing down' spoken language and providing more opportunities to notice aspects of linguistic form. Consequently these forms are more likely to move towards being owned by the learners.

Some example activities

- Ask learners to write dialogues themselves. This allows space for them to plan their own speech far more, and, through consultation with their peers, the teacher, or dictionaries, hopefully also to improve it. A really nice way of doing this is for learners to pass written notes between themselves, having a sort of conversation in writing. And because there is a written record of it, mistakes can also more easily be identified and improvements made.

- Provide models through interacting with the learners as much as possible. Teachers are often concerned about talking too much and so reducing the time that is available for the learners to talk to each other. But many low level learners really appreciate the simultaneous challenge and support that interacting with a more advanced speaker can give. In some contexts we may be the only people who can provide this.

- When using a roleplay with a low level class, model the activity yourself with a confident learner so that the class clearly understand what they have to do and can observe the areas of language that may be used.

- Follow up a student-to-student roleplay with a student-to-teacher roleplay in front of the class to increase the level of challenge. With small groups it can also be really useful sometimes for the teacher to take an active role throughout the whole of the roleplay, to provide constant scaffolding and linguistic support.

One of my favourite activities, using all of these principles, is dialogue building. To set the context the teacher displays a photo or does a simple drawing on the board showing two people interacting. The learners, speaking in either L1 or L2, suggest what a character might be saying. With each line supplied by the learners, the teacher reformulates it if necessary and then drills it around the class. When a dialogue of 6 or 7 lines has been constructed in this way, the learners practise it in pairs and go on to memorise it completely, before personalizing it by making their own versions, e.g.

A: *Did you have a nice holiday?*
B: *Great, thanks*
A: *Where did you go?*
B: *I went camping in Wales.*
A: *What was the weather like?*
B: *Lovely!*

Nick Bilbrough has been involved in language teaching for more than 20 years and has taught and trained teachers in many varied contexts in Europe, Asia and South America. He is the author of *Dialogue Activities* (2007) in the Cambridge Handbooks for Language Teachers series, and is currently working on his second book *Memory Activities for Language Learning* to be published in Spring 2011 in the same series. He now teaches on a freelance basis and runs short teacher development courses at Horizon Language Training in Totnes, UK.

Teaching notes

Name & Address

Coursebook

Unit 1	Language	Texts	Communicative skills
Part 1 SB page 6	Vocabulary and Listening Common English words Pronunciation Word stress Grammar Regular plural nouns	Listening and Speaking Introducing yourself Listening and Speaking The alphabet	Speaking Spelling words Functional language Meeting people
Part 2 SB page 8	Vocabulary and Listening Numbers 1–10 Grammar *What's*	Reading and Listening Postcodes	Functional language *How are you?* Writing and Speaking Filling in a form
Global game SB page 10	Board game: *You know lots of English!*		
Global review SB page 11	Ordering words in a conversation Number dictation		

Additional resources

eWorkbook	Interactive and printable grammar, vocabulary, listening and pronunciation practice Extra reading and writing practice Additional downloadable listening and audio material
TB resource CD	Communication activity worksheets to print and photocopy
Go global Ideas for further research	**Name** Look for 'international English' words in the street, eg *hotel, bar, taxi*. Find three more words and tell your teacher. **Address** Ask students to find the postcodes for these famous buildings: the White House; 10 Downing Street (British Prime Minister); the European Parliament; the International Red Cross and Red Crescent, Geneva.

Part 1

Lead-in

You may wish to do some basic introductions before starting the book. Make eye contact with the class, smile, wave and say *Hello, I'm ...* Greet different students, alternating *Hello* and *Hi*. Then choose a student and ask *And you?* Ask a few more students in this way, then gesture for the students to stand up and mingle, introducing themselves to other students. If space is limited, they can remain seated, introducing themselves to students sitting nearby.

Listening and Speaking (SB page 6)

1 💿 **1.01** The first listening requires students to distinguish the use of *Hello* and *Hi*. Write *page 6* on the board, then hold up your book so students can check as they open their books to the correct page. Point to the photos and read aloud the names. Write *Hi / Hello* on the board. Then play the example part of the listening and demonstrate underlining the answer.

Gesture and demonstration are essential in the early stages of teaching beginners, when students lack the language to understand verbal instructions.

Students continue and complete the exercise. At this stage they ignore the part about *I'm from*. Ask (and gesture) students to check their answers in pairs before doing whole class feedback. This is an important way to boost student confidence and avoid them feeling exposed in front of the class.

> 💿 **1.01**
> 1 **Hello**. I'm Tom.
> 2 **Hi**. I'm Liz.
> 3 **Hello**. I'm Atul.
> 4 **Hi**. I'm Steve.
> 5 **Hi**. I'm Sasha.
> 6 **Hello**. I'm Pam.

2 💿 **1.02** Point to exercise 2, read the cities and ask students to repeat them. On the board write *Hello, I'm Tom. I'm from _____* . Then play the recording, stopping after the first sentence, elicit the answer (London) and complete the sentence. Gesture for students to continue, working in pairs, and play the rest of the recording. Then go through the answers with students.

> 💿 **1.02**
> 1 Hello, I'm Tom. I'm from **London**.
> 2 Hi. I'm Liz. I'm from **Sydney**.
> 3 Hello. I'm Atul. I'm from **Mumbai**.
> 4 Hi. I'm Steve. I'm from **Cape Town**.
> 5 Hi. I'm Sasha. I'm from **New York**.
> 6 Hello. I'm Pam. I'm from **Toronto**.

Extra activity

To check that students know where all these places are, you could download photos of these places from the internet and ask students to identify them. You could also use the opportunity to teach *I don't know*, eg:

T: *Where's this? London?*

S: *I don't know.*

T: *Yes, it's London. / No, it's Toronto.*

Language note

In English, names of people, places, countries, etc have an initial capital letter, eg *Tom*, *London*, *Australia*.

Extra activity

If you have students who use a different script or have different conventions for capitalisation, point out the use of capital letters in names. For additional practice, you could choose some international words you think the students will know and write them on the board, mixing in some names, but writing all the words in lower case (eg *pizza*, *san francisco*, *photo*, *steve*) and ask students to capitalise where appropriate.

3 Copy the sentences on the board and complete them for yourself. Ask students to do the same, monitoring carefully as they work.

4 Gesture to students to work in pairs. Ask them to read and compare.

Listening and Speaking (SB page 6)

1 💿 **1.03** Either use the recording, or say the letters yourself, giving students time to repeat.

Pronunciation extra

Before continuing, you may want to do some more alphabet practice. One idea is to say two or three letters in sequence, then pause to elicit the next letter. After demonstrating, students can do the same activity in pairs or small groups. Alternatively, prepare individual cards for each letter and hold them up at random to elicit the pronunciation.

2 💿 **1.04** The conversation focuses on a name with two potential spellings and two place names which could be confused due to similarities in pronunciation. Draw two faces on the board. Under one write *Pedro – Madrid*; under the other write *Leslie / Lesley – Torquay / Tokyo*.

Pedro – Madrid   Leslie / Lesley – Torquay / Tokyo

Play the conversation; students listen for the correct spelling. Let them check in pairs before doing class feedback.

UNIT 1 Name & Address

1.04

A: Hi. I'm Lesley.
B: Lesley? Can you spell that?
A: L – E – S – L – E – Y
B: L – E – S – L – E – Y
A: That's right. I'm from Torquay.
B: Can you spell that?
A: T – O – R – Q – U – A – Y
B: T – O – R – Q – U – A – Y
A: That's right.
B: I'm Pedro.

3 Draw a speech bubble, with a question mark coming from Pedro's mouth. Play the first part of the conversation again, stopping after *Can you spell that?* and elicit the question. Play again and ask students to repeat.

Now ask two students to read the dialogue on page 6. Then demonstrate the activity with students asking you. Put students into groups and ask them to do the same, writing their partners' names and cities.

Vocabulary and Listening (SB page 7)

1 **1.05** Point at the pictures. Play the recording and ask students to say the words. Note: students are not expected to know this vocabulary, though the words are all international words which have close equivalents in many languages. If your students are unlikely to know the words, move straight to exercise 2. Check that students understand that *café* and *hotel* are places (not *coffee* and *key*).

2 **1.06** Play the recording and ask students to read the conversation while they listen. After that, ask them to read it in pairs. Then ask them to close their books and see if they can remember the dialogue.

3 Put students into pairs and ask them to choose three of the words illustrated by the pictures to spell to each other, using the conversation in exercise 2 as a model. You could practise this with a student yourself first as an example.

Language note

When spelling, we tend to say *double* for repeated letters, eg:
coffee = C – O – double F – double E

4 Demonstrate the activity with a stronger student. Say *I am Student A and (Olga) is Student B. (Olga), write the words. 1 Passport* etc. Remind students they can ask *Can you spell that?* and put this question on the board to remind / help them.

Divide students into As and Bs. On the board write *A – page 96* and *B – page 100*. Ask students to find the page and check they all have the right one. As students work in pairs, monitor to check and help.

5 **1.07** Tell students they will hear four conversations where someone is spelling his or her name. Write the word *Brawn* on the board. Play the first dialogue as an example, ask students what is different and underline the incorrect letter *o*. Then play the whole recording.

```
1  a
2  u
3  e
4  P
5  m
```

1.07

1 A: Name?
  B: Brown. B – R – O – W – N.
2 A: Name?
  B: Ball. B – A – L – L.
3 A: Can you spell spell that?
  B: C – L – A – R – K.
4 A: Can you spell your name?
  B: Barker. B – A – R – K – E – R.
5 A: Can you spell that, please?
  B: J – A – N – E – S. Janes.

Pronunciation (SB page 7)

The activity helps students become sensitive to the number of syllables and to identify the main stress. It's a good idea to copy the table on the board and number the three columns.

1 **1.08** Do the example together. Then you can either ask students to listen and tick directly, or give them a chance to guess the answers before listening to check.

	●	●•	•●
hi	✔		
hello			✔
coffee		✔	
phone	✔		
camera		✔	
café		✔	
hotel			✔
bus	✔		
passport		✔	

BEWARE diff. in Sr book

2 Check answers, then listen and repeat.

Grammar (SB page 7)

Here the focus is on regular plural forms.

Language note

Most nouns form the plural with -s. Nouns ending -ch, -s, -sh or -x add es.

Nouns ending in consonant + y change to -ies.

Note that the same rules apply to the formation of the 3rd person singular of regular verbs.

Read the rules with students, then ask them to complete the exercise individually. Give time for students to check their answers in pairs before doing class feedback.

1	coffees
2	phones
3	taxis
4	cameras

G Grammar focus

Show students the icon. Write *page 106* on the board and ask them to find it. Show students the language summary on nouns.

You can use exercise 1 on page 107 for:

a) extra practice now

b) homework

c) review a couple of lessons from now.

The answers are on page 116 of the Teacher's Book.

Functional language (SB page 7)

This section focuses on introducing yourself.

1 Here students listen and order two separate greeting conversations. Give students time to read the conversations before listening to number them in the correct order.

Correct order
Conversation 1: 2, 3, 1
Conversation 2: 3, 1, 2

🔊 **1.09**		
1	Tom:	Hi. I'm Tom.
	Liz:	Hello Tom. I'm Liz.
	Tom:	Nice to meet you, Liz.
2	Sasha:	Hello. I'm Sasha.
	Atul:	Hi Sasha. I'm Atul.
	Sasha:	Nice to meet you, Atul.

2 Draw students' attention to the *Useful phrases* on page 7. Ask students to stand up and mingle, introducing themselves and greeting other students.

Part 2

Functional language (SB page 8)

This section focuses on asking *How are you?*

1 🔘 **1.10** Focus students on the illustrations. Then listen and read. Point at the first picture and ask *Conversation 1 or Conversation 2?* Then do the same with the second picture.

1	a
2	b

2 Listen to the recording again, pausing after each line for students to repeat. Ask students to read the conversations in pairs.

3 Read through the *Useful phrases* with students. Students then stand up and mingle or speak to students sitting near them and ask *How are you?*

Vocabulary and Listening (SB page 8)

1 🔘 **1.11** Students listen and repeat the numbers.

> **TEACH GLOBAL THINK LOCAL** **Alternative procedure**
>
> If you prefer, you can present the numbers with books closed. Options include counting round the class, using Cuisenaire rods or counters, or using flashcards of individual numbers to elicit the word. It's important initially to work with numbers in sequence, before asking students to say numbers at random.

2 Ask students to match the numbers with the words. For feedback, write a number (or show the flashcard) and ask students to spell the word. This reviews alphabet and spelling while checking.

3 🔘 **1.12** Students listen to four *incorrect* sequences and have to write the missing number. Listen and follow the example with the class. Remind them to write the missing number in full (to practise spelling). Then ask students to listen and work individually, pausing the recording to give them time to write. Let students check in pairs before class feedback.

a	1, 2, 3, 5	four
b	4, 5, 6, 8	seven
c	2, 3, 4, 6	five
d	6, 7, 9, 10	eight
e	9, 8, 7, 5	six
f	5, 3, 2, 1	four

Language note

We pronounce '0' as *zero*. In the US people use this for phone numbers, but most British people say *oh*, eg '405601' as *four oh five six oh one*.

We write '2441' and can say digits individually or use the word *double*, eg *two double four one*.

4 Demonstrate the activity. Write five random numbers in your notebook and then dictate to the students who write the number in words. After checking, show the class the numbers in your notebook. Ask them to work in pairs and do the same. Monitor to check, help and correct spelling.

5 🔘 **1.13** The extracts focus on five real-world situations when we use numbers. The first listening simply requires students to listen and identify the situation by matching the conversations they hear with pictures a–e. Reassure students that they are not expected to understand everything in the dialogue.

1	b
2	d
3	a
4	c
5	e

> 🔘 **1.13**
> 1 Manchester United 3, Liverpool 2
> 2 Yeah! Six! One, two, three, four, five, six.
> 3 A: Good morning.
>   B: 2 –1 – 3 please.
>   A: 213. Here you are.
> 4 8 – 3 – 4 – 1 – 9. That's it … Oh no!
> 5 4 – 5 – 2 – 6 – 9 – 8 – 8

6 Students now listen again for the numbers in each extract.

1	Manchester United 3, Liverpool 2 (picture b)
2	Game: 6! 1, 2, 3, 4, 5, 6! (picture d)
3	Room 213 (picture a)
4	Safe combination: 83419 (picture c)
5	Phone number: 452 6988 (picture e)

Name & Address

Reading and Listening (SB page 9)

The text is about postcodes in different countries.

Background note

Postcodes (also called 'postal codes' and 'zip codes') were first introduced in the Ukraine in 1932 and in Germany in 1941. In a 2005 study, 117 countries had a postal code system. Most countries only use numbers which indicate an area or region, but some use alphanumeric codes (mixing letters and numbers) to identify a more precise location. In the UK the postcode identifies a group of two or three houses in some areas.

1 Show students the illustration of different envelopes. Copy the first onto the board, elicit the name and address and then elicit and circle the postcode. Ask students to continue doing the same. Check their answers.

1	520651
2	B3 1XQ
3	L5R 3F8
4	GA 30302
5	119123

2 💿 **1.14** Students listen and correct the postcodes on the envelopes.

1	520**7**51
2	**C**3 1XQ
3	L**5**R 3F**6**
4	GA 31302
5	11**5**123

3 Read the text once to students, while they follow it. Then ask students to read again silently to answer the questions. Give them time to check in pairs before class feedback.

1	F (*zip code* is the US term.)
2	T
3	F (An Australian postcode is a number.)
4	F (A Manchester postcode starts with *M*, the first letter of 'Manchester'.)

This important *Language note* focuses on the use of the indefinite article. After reading the note, give extra practice by writing some words from the unit on the board and asking them to sort into two columns *a* and *an*.

Language note

Note that the key issue is whether the first *sound* (not letter) is a vowel. For example, we say *an umbrella* because it starts with the vowel sound /ʌ/, but we say *a university* because the first sound is /j/.

Extra activity

If your students come from different countries, ask them if they have postcodes and whether postcodes in their countries use letters and numbers or only numbers.

4 Drill the question *What's your postcode?*, then put students into pairs to ask each other and write down their partner's postcode. If all your students are likely to share the same postcode, omit this activity.

5 If postcodes are used in your country, write a local postcode on the board. In front of it write a question mark. Elicit and drill the question *What's the postcode?* Divide students into pairs and tell them to decide who is A and who is B. Write *Student A – page 96* and *Student B – page 100* on the board. Monitor as students work.

Grammar (SB page 9)

Read the grammar note with students or write the two questions on the board, omitting the question word and eliciting *What*.

1 The exercise brings together various personal information questions. Read the four options with students, then read the first question and elicit the answer. Students continue working individually.

2 💿 **1.15** Students listen and check.

1	name
2	phone number
3	address
4	postcode

Ⓖ Grammar focus

Show students the icon. Write *page 106* on the board and ask them to find it. Show students the language summary on *What's*.

You can use exercise 2 on page 107 for:

a) extra practice now

b) homework

c) review a couple of lessons from now.

The answers are on page 116 of the Teacher's Book.

Writing and Speaking (SB page 9)

Pairwork. Students consolidate the questions and ways to check and clarify through personalisation. Draw students' attention to the *Useful phrases* on page 9. Write *name, address, postcode* and *phone number* on the board; elicit and drill the question forms (*What's your name?* etc) . Then write *spell* and *repeat* and elicit and drill the questions (*Can you spell that?* etc).

Put the students in pairs to ask and answer questions, check spelling and note answers.

Option A: If appropriate, students can use their own personal details.

Option B: Otherwise, refer students to the invented information at the back of the book. Write *Student A – page 96; Student B – page 100* on the board.

Monitor while students work.

Global game

Global game (SB page 10)

The game is designed to boost students' confidence by making them aware of the amount of English they know already, both from the unit and through international English.

Put the students into groups of between three and five, ideally sitting in a circle. Each group needs one copy of the book, open at page 10. You also need one dice per group.

Demonstrate the game: throw the dice, tell students the number you threw and elicit the question (for example *Number 4 – Say a country*). Elicit some possible answers from students, eg *France, Italy …*

Give students counters, or tell them to each take a different coin and place it on 'Start'. On the board write the phrases *You start* and *It's your turn*. If you speak the students' language, translate the phrases. If not, point out the phrases at appropriate moments.

Students play the game. Monitor to help and correct.

TEACH GLOBAL THINK LOCAL **Mixed ability**

If some groups finish before others, ask them to list all the words they can think of for the different categories in the game.

Global review

These activities can be used at home but are designed to be used in class with students working together in pairs.

Aim: to review the language of the unit.

Tips:

- Encourage students to work together.
- Allow them to look back through the unit or consult their notes.
- In feedback, elicit more examples or the reason why an answer is correct.

Vocabulary (SB page 11)

1

Across

2 six
3 seven
7 two
8 three
9 one

Down

1 nine
4 eight
5 four
6 five
8 ten

2

C	A	M	E	R	A	W	L
O	H	O	T	E	L	P	B
F	G	U	T	A	X	I	O
F	O	U	R	C	Y	F	O
E	P	H	O	N	E	V	K
E	K	C	A	F	E	A	S
P	A	S	S	P	O	R	T

Pronunciation (SB page 11)

	●	● ·
taxi		✔
phone	✔	
café		✔
bank	✔	
camera		✔

Grammar (SB page 11)

1

1 c
2 a
3 d
4 e
5 b

2 Students' own answers.

Listen again (SB page 11)

The first *Listen again* exercise in this unit comes from the *Functional language* section on page 7. Here, students listen again to order the conversation.

1, 2 💿 **1.16**

Tom: Hi. I'm Tom.

Liz: Hello Tom. I'm Liz.

Tom: Nice to meet you, Liz.

Exercise 3 in this *Listen again* reviews *Vocabulary* on page 8.

3 💿 **1.17**

a 1, 2, 3, 5
b 4, 5, 6, 8
c 2, 3, 4, 6
d 6, 7, 9, 10
e 9, 8, 7, 5
f 5, 3, 2, 1

UNIT 2 Me & You

Coursebook

Unit 2	Language	Texts	Communicative skills
Part 1 SB page 12	Vocabulary and Listening Countries and nationalities Grammar Subject pronouns; *be* Grammar *Yes / No* questions Pronunciation Intonation of *Yes / No questions*	Reading and Listening *Four students at the International School of English, London*	Functional language Introductions
Part 2 SB page 14	Grammar Possessive adjectives (1) Vocabulary Numbers 11–20	Reading *Interview with Luis Ruiz* Listening Asking questions	Writing and Speaking Personal details
Global voices SB page 16	Listen to people from round the world giving personal information. *What* and *where*		
Global review SB page 17	A conversation with an immigration officer Identifying additional words		

Additional resources

eWorkbook	Interactive and printable grammar, vocabulary, listening and pronunciation practice Extra reading and writing practice Additional downloadable listening and audio material
TB resource CD	Communication activity worksheets to print and photocopy
Go global **Ideas for further research**	**Me** Ask students to write the names of six countries near their own, then check on the internet how we say the names of the countries in English, and find the nationality. **You** The following organisations are all connected with the police in the USA. Use the internet to find what the letters mean: CIA, LAPD, FBI, NYPD.

Part 1

Lead-in

It's often a good idea to start the lesson with books closed, doing a short, fun activity to review input and relax the students by starting the class with familiar language.

Review the alphabet and spelling from Unit 1, by dictating the following words: *coffee, camera, taxi, address, postcode, English*. Use gesture to indicate that students have to listen and write, but accompany this with verbal instructions so students gradually become familiar with classroom language. After checking spelling, ask each student to write two more words and dictate them to their partner.

Vocabulary and Listening (SB page 12)

1 The map uses a colour code to show the principal world languages (which aside from Arabic and Hindi are also nationality words). Point to the orange shading on the map and say *number 1?* Drill the pronunciation of *Chinese* and continue with the other languages. Then point to the other three languages in exercise 1. On the board write:

A: Number 1?

B: English?

A: No, Chinese.

Ask students to work in pairs, using this simple dialogue to do the activity in English.

1	Chinese
2	English
3	Spanish
4	Russian

2 🔊 **1.18** Listen to check answers. Pause after each language to repeat.

Language note

Some words are the same for both language and nationality. Arabic and Hindi are the only two shown on the map that refer to language only. If your students come from a country that uses one of these languages, or another language that has a different word for the nationality, make sure they understand the words for the nationality and the language.

3 This activity encourages students to spot and follow patterns. This is a very important strategy in encouraging students to make educated guesses about English and thus to make them more independent learners.

Students work in pairs to complete the table. Quickly copy the table to aid feedback; then monitor as they work.

Country	Nationality
Italy	Italian
Russia	Russian
Germany	German
Brazil	Brazilian
Egypt	Egyptian
China	Chinese
Japan	Japanese
Portugal	Portuguese
Britain	British
Spain	Spanish
Poland	Polish
France	French

4 🔊 **1.19** Listen to check answers. Pause after each nationality to repeat.

Extra activity

If your students have some prior knowledge of English you could ask them to add some more countries and nationalities to the table. On the board write *How do you say 'Deutsch' in English?* and *Can you spell that?* so that they can do the activity in English.

Alternatively, take in photos of famous people or things from the countries in the table, and hold them up to elicit the nationality.

5 🔊 **1.20** Read the words and ask students to repeat. Ask them which words are countries and which are nationalities. Explain that they will hear three conversations. They have to listen and underline the words they hear.

1
A: Hello. I'm Lucian.
B: Are you from France?
A: No, I'm not. I'm **English**.
2
A: Hi. My name's Maria.
B: Are you **Italian**?
A: No, I'm not. I'm **Spanish**.
3
A: We're Olga and Tatiana.
B: Are you **German**?
A: No, we're not. We're **Russian**.

If you like, your students can listen again, following the audioscript on page 120.

6 Here, students see how we use *be from* + country or *be* + nationality adjective. Look at the example with students and then ask them to work individually to complete the sentences.

1	He's English.
2	She's Spanish.
3	They're Russian.

7 Now students personalise the language. Write two sentences on the board about yourself and elicit the country and nationality. Ask students to do the same. If you have a multinational class, ask students to read their sentences to each other when they finish.

Grammar (SB page 12)

The grammar box focuses on the use of personal pronouns and the verb *be*. Read the examples.

TEACH GLOBAL THINK LOCAL **Lead-in**

For more consolidation of the pronouns before written practice, play a quick drill game with books closed. Elicit the personal pronouns in order on the board. Point to yourself and elicit *I*; point to a male student and elicit *he* and so on. After a few minutes, put students in small groups to continue doing the same.

Language note

Some languages (eg Russian) do not have a verb *be* in the present. For speakers of these languages you may need to stress the importance of this verb in English. By contrast other languages (eg French) have different verb forms for each person, so the English system, with only three different forms *am / is / are*, is relatively simple. Speakers of languages such as Spanish will need to realise that pronoun use is essential and cannot be omitted in English.

1 Read the example. Ask students to work individually to complete the sentences. Check that students know that Fatima is a woman's name.

1	She
2	We
3	They
4	I

2 Go back to the grammar box and read the first example (*I am / I'm Polish*). Show on the board how we write the apostrophe where we omit a letter.

TEACH GLOBAL THINK LOCAL **Extra activity**

Do a quick drill to practise the pronunciation of contractions. Hold up the first finger of your right hand and say *I*. Then hold up the first finger of your left hand and say *am*. Ask students to repeat the words as you raise first one finger, then the other. Then bring the two fingers together (to indicate the contraction) and say *I'm* and have students repeat. Continue with other forms.

Students complete the exercise, writing the contracted form.

1	We're
2	He's
3	You're
4	She's

3 Ask students to make the sentences in exercise 2 negative. Do the example together (I'm not Russian.)

1	We aren't French.
2	He isn't Spanish.
3	You aren't German.
4	She isn't from Egypt.

Language note

Note that for all pronouns except *I* there are two negative forms for the verb *be*: in addition to the form shown in the grammar box, we can use *you're not, he's not, she's not, we're not, they're not*. It doesn't matter which form you use and it is important to expose students gradually to both forms, but you may choose to keep to one form initially to avoid overload.

Ⓖ Grammar focus

Show students the icon. Write *page 106* on the board and ask them to find it. Show students the first part of the language summary on *be*: the table of pronouns and the positive and negative of the verb *be*.

You can use exercise 3 on page 107 for:

a) extra practice now

b) homework

c) review a couple of lessons from now.

The answers are on page 116 of the Teacher's Book.

Extra activity

For more practice write the following words (or similar) on the board: *the USA, England, Portuguese, Japan, my teacher, the students in this class, spaghetti, Audi and BMW, burgers, Coca Cola, my phone*.

Write a couple of sentences using the words and ask students if the sentences are true or false, eg *The students in this class are from England. My phone is Japanese*.

Ask students to write their own *True / False* sentences, monitoring as they work. Then they form groups and read their examples to their group.

Reading and Listening (SB page 13)

The text is about four female students in a London language school. Note that the text describes them as students because they are studying in London, but they are not all students in their own country.

1 Ask students to look at the photos and read the texts.

2 **1.21–1.23** Now students listen to interviews with three of the women. As they listen, they complete the box with *Y* or *N*.

3 Comparing the answers with the original texts, students now decide the name of each woman. Do the first one together as an example. Ask students which woman is not in the table.

	1 Carola	2 Adriana	3 Chun Hei
Europe?	N	Y	N
Married?	Y	Y	N
Student?	N	N	Y

Missing speaker: Elisaveta

🔘 **1.21–1.23**

Speaker 1
A: Are you from Europe?
B: No, I'm not.
A: Are you married?
B: Yes, I am.
A: Are you a student?
B: No, I'm not.

Speaker 2
A: Are you from Europe?
B: Yes, I am.
A: Are you married?
B: Yes, I am.
A: Are you a student?
B: No, I'm not.

Speaker 3
A: Are you from Europe?
B: No, I'm not.
A: Are you married?
B: No, I'm not.
A: Are you a student?
B: Yes, I am.

Grammar (SB page 13)

On the board write *married?*

Elicit the question *Are you married?* and appropriate short answers. Read the grammar note.

1 Explain that this is the interview with the fourth woman. Students complete the text.

2 🔘 **1.24** Listen and check.

Interviewer:	Are **you** from Europe?
Elisaveta:	Yes, **I** am.
Interviewer:	**Are you** married?
Elisaveta:	No, **I'm not**.
Interviewer:	**Are you** a student?
Elisaveta:	**Yes, I** am.

G **Grammar focus**

Show students the icon. Write *page 106* on the board and ask them to find it. Show students the second part of the language summary on *be*: question forms and short answers.

You can use exercise 4 on page 107 for:

a) extra practice now

b) homework

c) review a couple of lessons from now.

The answers are on page 116 of the Teacher's Book.

Pronunciation and Speaking (SB page 13)

1 **1.25** Students listen and repeat, copying the intonation of each sentence.

> ### Pronunciation note
>
> Although there are exceptions, the general rule is that intonation rises on *Yes / No* questions and falls on *Wh-*questions.

2 Put students into AB pairs. Write *A – page 96* and *B – page 100* on the board and make sure they find the correct page. Students use the prompts to write *Yes / No* questions (eg *Are you from Italy?*). Monitor as students work. When they finish, they can use the questions to interview a partner. Note: if students do not wish to give their own personal information, tell them they can invent things.

Functional language (SB page 13)

This section focuses on introducing yourself.

1 Students read the conversation and write numbers beside each sentence to put it in order.

2 **1.26** Students listen and check.

> A: Hi. I'm Cem.
> B: Hi Cem, I'm Andrea.
> A: Nice to meet you, Andrea.
> B: You too. Where are you from, Cem?
> A: I'm Turkish. I'm from Istanbul. And you?
> B: I'm French. I'm from Paris.

Highlight the use of *where* to ask about places.

3 Pairwork. Using the conversation as a model, students write their own version.

4 Students practise the conversation with books closed. To end the class, ask students to stand and mingle or work with others sitting near them and introduce themselves.

Part 2

TEACH GLOBAL THINK LOCAL **Lead-in**

Play 'Beat the box', which is a variation on 'Hangman'. It's a good way to review vocabulary and spelling. Think of a word and write a dash for each letter, eg _ _ _ _ _ (*Italy*).

Students guess letters from the word. If they are correct, write the letter into the word, eg _ *I* _ _ _ . If not, draw the first line of a 6-line box. Continue, seeing if students can complete the word before you finish the box.

–	

Use this to review recent vocabuary. Lead in to the lesson by finishing with the word *POLICE*.

Reading (SB page 14)

The pictures are of law enforcement officers in different situations. Look at the pictures with students and ask them to tell you any words they know (eg *car*, *police*, *passport*).

1 Ask students to look at the photo of Luis. Ask students questions, eg *Is he English? Is he Chinese? Is he a teacher? What's this?* (pointing at the dog). Students read the text to match the questions and answers.

2 **1.27** Students listen and check their answers.

> **1.27**
> A: Are you English, Luis?
> B: **No, I'm not. I'm American.**
> A: Where are you from?
> B: **I'm from Miami**.
> A: Are you a police officer?
> B: **Yes, I am.**
> A: Is this your dog?
> B: **Yes, it is. This is Rex.**

Listening (SB page 14)

1 **1.28–1.31** Students now listen to situations in which they hear the people from the other pictures. The first time, they match the conversations wtih the pictures.

> 1 c   2 b   3 a   4 d

2 Now students match the sentences to the conversations.

> It's our dog. 4
> Oh, they're my keys! 1
> I'm Canadian. 2
> Is this your car? 3

1.28–1.31

Conversation 1

A: Bye

B: Bye

A: Oh …

C: Come over here. What are these?

A: Oh, they're my keys!

C: OK.

Conversation 2

A: Passport! What's your name?

B: Smith, Jean Smith.

A: Where are you from?

B: I'm Canadian. I'm from Vancouver.

A: OK.

B: Thank you.

Conversation 3

A: Is this your car?

B: Er … Yes, it is.

A: What's the number?

B: Um … JGK 869D.

A: Where are you from?

B: I'm Polish. I'm from Warsaw.

A: What's your address?

B: The Royal Hotel.

A: OK, thank you.

B: Thank you!

Conversation 4

A: Open, please! Are these your bags?

B: Yes, yes they are.

A: Where are you from?

B: We're French. We're from Lyon.

A: What's that?

B: It's our dog.

A: OK, thank you.

B: Thank you!

Grammar (SB page 15)

Ask students to read the examples, then write the following chart on the board and ask students to help you complete it.

I	*my dog*
you	*your car*
we	*our keys*

Note: third person forms are dealt with in Unit 3.

1 Students transform the sentences according to the prompt. Look at the example together, then give students time to work individually and then check in pairs.

1 your	2 my	3 our	4 your

2 Here students complete the sentences with an appropriate possessive adjective.

1 your	2 Our	3 my	4 your

3 **1.32–1.33** Students listen and check their answers.

Ⓖ Grammar focus

Show students the icon. Write *page 106* on the board and ask them to find it. Show students the part of the language summary on subject pronouns and possessive adjectives.

You can use exercises 5 and 6 on page 107 for:

a) extra practice now

b) homework

c) review a couple of lessons from now.

The answers are on page 116 of the Teacher's Book.

TEACH GLOBAL THINK LOCAL **Extra activity**

Before working on numbers 11–20, it's probably a good idea to do a quick review of numbers 1–10. Options for this include:

- anagrams: write numbers jumbling the letters (eg *vefi*) and ask students to write them correctly
- phone numbers: ask students to write three phone numbers which are important to them; they then dictate them in pairs
- numbers quiz: ask some simple questions about things in the room, eg *How many students? 7; books? 10; English people? 1*

Vocabulary (SB page 15)

1 The activity helps students build on their existing knowledge of numbers. Ask students to complete the numbers individually and then check in pairs.

2 **1.34** Listen to check. Stop the recording after each number to check the spelling.

eleven
twelve
thirteen
fourteen
fifteen
six**teen**
se**ven**teen
eighteen
nine**teen**
twenty

3 🔘 **1.35–1.38** Students listen and complete the missing information.

🔘 **1.35–1.38**

1 A: What's your address?
   B: **18** Oxford Road.
   A: What's your postcode?
   B: **L13** 3PQ.
2 A: What's your address?
   B: **20** King Street.
   A: What's your postcode?
   B: BS**17** 5TW.
3 A: What's your address?
   B: **14**b London Road.
   A: What's your postcode?
   B: M**16** 1A.
4 A: What's your address?
   B: **15** Park Street
   A: What's your postcode?
   B: NW**11** 4PT.

Writing and Speaking (SB page 15)

Here the students focus on a short dialogue asking about personal details.

1 Ask students to look at the picture. The picture on page 15 is an enlarged detail from picture (a) on page 14. Draw a question mark on the board and try to elicit some questions the police officer could ask. Look at the activity and read the model with students. Ask them to continue.

2 🔘 **1.39** Students listen and check.

Is this your car?
What's the number?
What's your name?
What's your address?
Where are you from?
OK, thank you.

---

3 Students write their own answers to the questions. Monitor as they work.

4 Pairwork. Students practise the conversation. You may like to ask some students to perform for the class.

Global voices

These lessons in *Global* are designed to provide students with exposure to authentic speakers of English from both native and non-native English backgrounds. In this unit

we extend the theme of nationalities.

Warm up (SB page 16)

Read the nationalities with students. Ask them to write the name of the country. Do the first one together as an example.

American:	United States	Saudi Arabian:	Saudi Arabia
Scottish:	Scotland	Spanish:	Spain
French:	France		

TEACH GLOBAL THINK LOCAL **Extra activity**

Check understanding by asking students to tell you the name of a famous person or place in the five countries.

Listening (SB page 16)

1 🔘 **1.40–1.44** Listen to the extracts and match the person with their country.

1	Pilar:	Spain
2	Al-Mutasem:	Saudi Arabia
3	Marc:	France
4	Dorothy:	Scotland
5	Mireille:	United States

---

2 Listen again for the places.

🔘 **1.40–1.44**

1 My name is Pilar, I am from Spain. Uh, from **Madrid**.
2 My name is Al-Mutasem Billa and my surname is Alam. I come from Saudi and I'm from a city, it's called **Jeddah**.
3 So, my name is Marc, I come from France. More specifically, from a city called **Lyon**.
4 My name's Dorothy Robertson. I'm from **Alloa**, Scotland.
5 My name's Mireille Yanow. I'm from **Diamond Bar**, California, in the United States.

Language focus: question words (SB page 16)

Read the *Language note*, then ask students to complete with the correct question word.

---

1 What   2 Where   3 What

Speaking (SB page 16)

Students personalise the question words by asking other people in the class. Note the expressions *Can you spell that?* And *Can you repeat that?* on the board to remind them.

Global review

These activities can be used at home but are designed to be used in class with students working together in pairs.

Aim: to review the language of the unit.

Tips:

- Encourage students to work together.
- Allow them to look back through the unit or consult their notes.
- In feedback, elicit more examples or the reason why an answer is correct.

Vocabulary (SB page 17)

1

Country	Nationality
Brazil	Brazilian
Britain	British
China	Chinese
France	French
Japan	Japanese
Poland	Polish
Portugal	Portuguese
Russia	Russian
Spain	Spanish
United States	American

2, 3 🔊 1.45

1 United States
2 China
3 France
4 Britain

4

1 thirteen
2 nineteen
3 fifteen
4 eighteen

5 🔊 1.46

12, 17, 20, 13, 19, 14, 11, 15, 16, 18

Grammar (SB page 17)

1

Subject pronouns: he, I, it, she, they, we, you
Possessive adjectives: my, our, your

2, 3 🔊 1.47

1 My
2 my
3 She's
4 are
5 He's
6 are
7 Our
8 is
9 he's

Listen again (SB page 17)

The *Listen again* text in this unit comes from the *Listening* section on page 14 with the conversation between an immigration officer and a passenger. Here, students listen again to become aware of redundant words.

1 🔊 1.48

A: Passport! ~~Hello.~~ What's your name, ~~please~~?
B: ~~My name's~~ Smith, Jean Smith.
A: ~~And~~ where are you from ~~Ms Smith~~?
B: I'm Canadian. I'm from Vancouver, ~~British Columbia~~.
A: OK, ~~thanks~~.
B: Thank you. ~~Goodbye~~.

2

1 c
2 a
3 b

Them & Us

Coursebook

Unit 3	Language	Texts	Communicative skills
Part 1 SB page 18	Pronunciation Linking words Grammar Possessive adjectives (2)	Reading and Vocabulary *1000 Families*	Speaking Describing a family Writing Describing a family
Part 2 SB page 20	Vocabulary Family Grammar Possession Questions with *be*	Listening and Speaking Family numbers Reading and Listening *A family photograph*	Speaking Your family Functional language Introducing people
Global reading SB page 22	A website Reading about familes and friends Writing about yourself		
Global review SB page 23	Family members Possessive adjectives *my*, *his*, *her*, *their* Writing about your family Reference words		

Additional resources

eWorkbook	Interactive and printable grammar, vocabulary, listening and pronunciation practice Extra reading and writing practice Additional downloadable listening and audio material
TB resource CD	Communication activity worksheets to print and photocopy
Go global Ideas for further research	**Them** Ask students to use the internet to find TV programmes and films that contain family words in their names, eg *Big Brother* (TV programme), *Sister Act* (film). **Us** Ask students to use the internet to find information about the people in a famous family from their country, draw the family tree and come ready to tell the class.

Part 1

Lead-in

Before reading about three families from different countries, recap vocabulary on countries and nationalities.

Take in some flags from countries seen in Unit 2. (Make your own flashcards or download from the internet.) First elicit and drill the name of the country and nationality. Then turn the flags face down and see if individual students can remember the country. Then give each student a flag, get them to mingle and ask each other *A: Is it Russia? B: Yes / No* to identify the flags the other students have.

Reading and Vocabulary (SB page 18)

In the texts, three people from different countries introduce the members of their families. The pictures all come from a book called *1000 Families*.

1 Ask students to look at the pictures and guess where the families are from. Read the yellow box about the book *1000 Families*.

Background note

German photographer Uwe Ommer started work on his *1000 Families* project in 1995 and spent four years photographing families in 130 countries. This work culminated in the publication of the book in the year 2000.

Read the three texts while students follow or ask them to read silently. On the board write *family*. Show the example *mother* in the first text and ask students to underline the other family words.

mother	wife	husband
father	daughter	baby
sister	mother	son

2 Pairwork. Students look at the pictures and decide if the family words are male or female.

brother M	daughter F	wife F
mother F	sister F	son M
husband M	father M	

3 1.49 Listen and repeat.

1.49	
Male	**Female**
brother	sister
father	mother
husband	wife
son	daughter

4 First check the collective vocabulary *children* (= sons and daughters) and *parents* (= mothers and fathers). In some languages the masculine word is pluralised (eg in Spanish *children* is *hijos* – literally *sons*; *parents* is *padres* – literally *fathers*), so highlight these words. Working individually, students decide if the sentences are true or false. Allow time for pairs to check together before class feedback.

1 T	2 T	3 T	4 F (she's a mother)	5 T

Mixed ability

Early finishers can write one or two additional *True / False* sentences to read to the class later.

5 Students personalise the vocabulary by deciding which words apply to themselves. Start by saying which words apply to you and then ask students to do the same in pairs before asking a few students to tell the class.

Pronunciation (SB page 18)

Pronunciation note

The exercise focuses on word linking, in this case the link between a consonant sound and the following vowel. While student *production* of such features of connected speech is not essential, it is very important that they become used to word linking in order to aid *understanding* of naturally spoken English.

1.50 Play the recording, pausing after each pair and ask students to repeat. Give students time to continue practising together before hearing some individuals pronounce the word pairs. Read the *Language note* and check the pronunciation. Pay special attention to *woman* / ˈwʊmən/, *women* /ˈwɪmɪn/.

Speaking (SB page 18)

In this activity Student A first reads a description of a family while B listens and selects from three drawings. The students then change roles.

Ask students to form AB pairs. Write *Student A – page 96* and *Student B – page 100* on the board and tell them to turn to the correct page. Hold up your book. Say *Student A read, Student B listen and choose the family*. As students start working, monitor to help.

Extra activity

For an additional activity, ask students to invent a description of one of the other families. They can either say it directly for their partner to guess or write it first and then read to the class.

Grammar (SB page 19)

Recap Unit 2 by writing on the board the subject pronouns and possessive adjectives:

I   my dog

you   your car

we   our keys

Elicit the third person forms by saying *Palani?* (or the name of a male student in the class), *Venus?* (or a female student), *Alla and Yakov?* (or two students from the class) and add to the board:

he ♂   his family

she ♀   her mother

they ♂♂ ♂♀ ♀♀   their children

Ask the students to read the examples and grammar notes. Note that English only has one third person plural form, unlike other languages which may have separate masculine and feminine forms.

1 Do the first one as an example and then let students continue working individually before checking.

> ### Language note
>
> A common mistake is for students to place a possessive adjective according to the gender of the *following* noun, eg ~~This is my brother and her wife.~~
>
> Use arrows to indicate that the possessive adjective is determined by the possessor as follows:
>
> This is my brother and his wife.

1 his	2 their	3 her

2 Here, the students have to determine the correct possessive adjective by identifying the subject.

It may help to make this process explicit with this diagram:

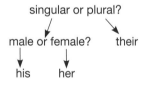

Students complete the sentences.

1 Their	2 his	3 Her

3 In this exercise, students discriminate between use of a subject pronoun or a possessive adjective. Ask the students to look at the picture, guess where the girl is from and which family members they can see.

Students complete the activity.

> This is Flore, her / **she's** 11. Her / **She's** from France. This is his / **her** family. This is his / **her** father, he / **his** name's Thomas. This is his / **her** mother. This is her brother Didier, his / **he's** 6.

> ### TEACH GLOBAL / THINK LOCAL **Extra activity**
>
> Students can get confused here. If so, go back to the grammar rules and note on the board:
>
> Subject pronoun (*she, they ...*) + verb
>
> Possessive adjective (*her, their*) + noun
>
> Write:
>
> 1 *They / Their are American.*
>
> 2 *Sara is he / his sister.*
>
> Ask students to choose the correct form.

G Grammar focus

Show students the icon. Write *page 108* on the board and ask them to find it. Show students the language summary on subject pronouns and possessive adjectives (2).

You can use exercise 1 on page 109 for:

a) extra practice now

b) homework

c) review a couple of lessons from now.

The answers are on page 116 of the Teacher's Book.

Writing (SB page 19)

1 Ask students to look at the picture of Dao and her family. On the board write *brother, father, mother, sister*. Ask *Who's Arthit?* and elicit the answer (*brother*). Look at the *Useful phrases* and drill the pronunciation. Ask students to work in pairs to decide about the other family members.

Sawat:	mother
Lek:	sister
Arthit:	brother
Bichai:	father

2 Write the first sentence from the Flore text on the board. Erase *Flore* and *11*. Write in *Dao, 12*.

Ask students to continue transforming the text into a description of Dao. It's important to provide a structured approach to writing before expecting students to produce a text independently. Monitor to help.

> ### TEACH GLOBAL / THINK LOCAL **Writing extra**
>
> Either in class or for homework, ask students to think about a person in their family, and supply a picture if possible. Ask them to write a similar description.

Part 2

Lead-in

To develop students' sensitivity to word stress and lead into this lesson, write the following countries on the board: *Australia, Brazil, China, Gambia, Germany, Japan, Morocco, Portugal, Sweden, South Africa*, and also the stress patterns as follows:

Oo oO Ooo oOo oOoo

Ask students to work in pairs to categorise the countries according to the pronunciation. (If they have difficulty, get them to focus first on the number of syllables or tell them how many words are in each group.)

Oo China, Sweden

oO Brazil, Japan

Ooo Gambia, Germany, Portugal

oOo Morocco

oOoo Australia, South Africa

Listening and Speaking (SB page 20)

1 Before students open their books, write on the board: *South Africa 4, Sweden 2, Gambia 8*. Ask the students what the numbers mean (if they're stuck say some family words as a clue). Ask them to open their books and read the introductory information. Ask them how many people are in a typical family in their country.

2 💿 **1.51–1.55** Play the recording for students to note the numbers. Write answers *4, 9, 2, 3, 6* on the board with a question mark beside each answer. Elicit the question, if necessary replaying the recording, and read the *Language note* with students.

💿 **1.51–1.55**

1 Louise, Australia

 A: How many people are in your family?

 B: **Four**.

2 Sulayman, Gambia

 A: Sulayman, how many people are in your family?

 B: In my family? **Nine**.

3 Torsten, Germany

 A: Torsten – what about your family? Is it big?

 B: No, only **two** – me and my wife.

4 Noriko, Japan

 A: How many people are in your family?

 B: **Three**.

5 Hasna, Morocco

 A: So Hasna, how many people are in your family?

 B: **Six**. My mother and father, my sister and her husband. My niece – that's my sister's daughter, and me.

---

3 Read the example conversation and drill the question, before asking a few stronger students to reply. Then ask students to stand (or turn and speak to others nearby) and ask and answer the question.

Extra activity

Before moving on, do a quick review of family vocabulary. Options include:

* giving the male word and asking students to come up with the corresponding female word (eg *brother → sister*)

* writing the words in pairs (eg *b _ _ _ _ _ _ / s _ _ _ _*) and asking students to complete

* giving students one minute to write all the family vocabulary they can remember and comparing in pairs.

Vocabulary (SB page 20)

1 💿 **1.56** Introduce the word *niece* (and *nephew* which is needed in exercise 2); drawing a family tree will help clarify this. Read the family vocabulary and then play the recording of Hasna for students to circle the words they hear.

mother; father; sister; husband; niece; daughter

2 💿 **1.57** Look at the family tree. Play the recording and ask students to repeat. If you have a monolingual class, you could ask them to translate some of the family words.

Alternative procedure

As a more engaging alternative, you might choose to extend family vocabulary using your own family tree and bringing in photos of your own family members.

Vocabulary extra

To help remember and personalise the vocabulary, you could ask students to write their own family members on the tree.

If your students are ready for more vocabulary, you could focus on the prefix *grand-* and the suffix *-in-law* and show them how these can be used in English to generate more vocabulary (eg *grandson, daughter-in-law*).

Grammar (SB page 20)

1 Read the note and practise the pronunciation. On the board write *My mother's brother is my ...* and try to elicit *uncle*. Then ask students to do the exercise.

Language note

The *'s* used to show possession is pronounced just like a plural. Students may use the *of* form, eg ~~the brother of my wife~~, but this is not usual when the first noun refers to, or names, a person (eg we say *my wife's cousin* but *the time of my class*) as is normal when describing possession (eg *John's book, my sister's house*).

1	my mother's mother: my grandmother
2	my father's sister: my aunt
3	my sister's husband: my brother-in-law
4	my sister's son: my nephew
5	my aunt's daughter: my cousin

2 Students now use the possessive *'s* to write explanations of the vocabulary as in the example. Ask students to work individually and then check their answers in pairs before class feedback. Point out that more than one answer is possible.

1	my brother's wife / my wife's sister / my husband's sister
2	my mother's father / my father's father
3	my mother's brother / my father's brother
4	my husband's mother / my wife's mother
5	my sister's son / my brother's son

G Grammar focus

Show students the icon. Write *page 108* on the board and ask them to find it. Show students the language summary on possessive *'s*.

You can use exercise 2 on page 109 for:

a) extra practice now

b) homework

c) review a couple of lessons from now.

The answers are on page 116 of the Teacher's Book.

Speaking (SB page 20)

Demonstrate the activity with people from your family as a whole class activity. Then show students the example conversation. Put students into pairs or threes and ask them to do the same while you monitor.

Reading and Listening (SB page 21)

In this activity students listen to people talking about a family picture.

1 🔊 **1.58** First, ask students to look at the picture, say where they think they are and give ideas about the relationships between the people. Then write the names *James* and *Lucy* on the board and check who is the man and who is the woman. Students read as they listen and label the picture.

James is on the left of the picture, Lucy is on the right.

2 Students now read the text more closely to answer the questions. Check in pairs before whole class feedback.

1	F (He's in London.)
2	T
3	T
4	T
5	F (She's his cousin.)

TEACH GLOBAL THINK LOCAL Vocabulary extra

For extra practice, ask students to close their books. Then give them one minute to write down all the family words they can remember from the conversation.

family, sister, brother, wife, married, single, cousin

Grammar (SB page 21)

Ask students to read the examples. Then ask them to go back to the conversation and find another example of a *Yes / No* question. (*Is she Australian? No, she isn't.*)

TEACH GLOBAL THINK LOCAL Grammar extra

To consolidate, write *Are you from London?* And elicit the answers *Yes, I am. / No, I'm not.*

Ask students to continue writing similar questions and answers for *he, she, we* and *they.*

1 Look at the example or write it on the board and ask students to order it. Students continue working individually before feedback.

1	Is the family at a party?
2	Is James in London?
3	Are James and Lucy in Sydney?
4	Are Christopher and Lucy married?

2 Students answer the questions, following the example.

1	Yes, it is. (see *Language note* below)
2	Yes, he is.
3	No, they aren't.
4	No, they aren't.

Language note

Note that *family* is a collective noun. We say *a family*, so *the family is at a party*, but when we are referring to the family members we often use a plural verb. At this level you may prefer to keep to the singular form.

3 For further practice, ask students to look at the smaller picture and choose the correct options in the conversation.

> A: OK. So who's this?
>
> B: That's my sister Clare and her husband Jed.
>
> A: *Jed is* / **Is Jed** English?
>
> B: No, **he isn't** / *he not*. He's Irish.
>
> A: And *are this* / **is this** their daughter?
>
> B: No, that's our cousin Danielle.
>
> A: *Are* / **Are they** here in Manchester?
>
> B: No, they **aren't** / *isn't*. They're in Dublin.

4 💿 **1.59** Listen and check.

Ⓖ Grammar focus

Show students the icon. Write *page 108* on the board and ask them to find it. Show students the language summary on questions with *be*.

You can use exercise 3 on page 109 for:

a) extra practice now

b) homework

c) review a couple of lessons from now.

The answers are on page 116 of the Teacher's Book.

Functional language (SB page 21)

This section focuses on introducing people.

To set the scene, either write the word *party* on the board or download some pictures of parties from the internet.

1 Read the words in the box and ask students to repeat them. Ask students to read the conversations and complete them, using the words.

2 💿 **1.60** Listen and check.

> 💿 **1.60**
>
> 1 A: Juliet, this **is** Nigel. He's **from** Canada.
>
>   B: Hello Nigel. Nice to meet **you**.
>
> 2 A: Naomi, this is my **brother** Lee.
>
>   B: **Hi** Lee.

3 Ask students to form pairs and practice the conversations. After a few minutes, ask them to close their books and continue practising.

4 Explain that you're going to have a party in the classroom. You could put on some suitable background music. Ask students to stand up in their pairs and then go and introduce their partner to other students in the room. Mingle to help and correct. Stronger students can be encouraged to ask additional questions.

Global reading

The *Global reading* pages encourage students to approach different text types and develop the ability to read for pleasure. Here the text is similar to a social networking website (eg Facebook, MySpace, LinkedIn).

TEACH GLOBAL THINK LOCAL Lead-in

Try to elicit the names of things we read. If possible, take in some real-life objects (eg a book, a newspaper) to help.

1 Ask students to look at the four options and then decide which is the source of the text on page 22.

> c A website

2 Ask students to read the website to themselves, then read it again to the class, before asking students to answer the questions.

> 1 T
>
> 2 F (She's from Rome.)
>
> 3 F (Her brothers are Luigi and Paolo Cerase.)
>
> 4 F (She's in London.)
>
> 5 T
>
> 6 T
>
> 7 T

3 Using Isabella's text as a model, students write a similar paragraph about themselves.

TEACH GLOBAL THINK LOCAL Mixed ability

Stronger students or early finishers can be encouraged to swap texts and correct each other's work.

As an alternative, ask students to write their texts omitting their name. Display the work and get the class up to read the texts and identify who wrote each one.

Global review

These activities can be used at home but are designed to be used in class with students working together in pairs.

Aim: to review the language of the unit.

Tips:

- Encourage students to work together.
- Allow them to look back through the unit or consult their notes.
- In feedback, elicit more examples or the reason why an answer is correct.

Vocabulary (SB page 23)

> **1** female: sister, daughter, cousin, niece, aunt ...
> male: brother, son-in-law, nephew, uncle ...
> grand: grandson, granddaughter, grandfather
>
> **2** c

Grammar (SB page 23)

> **1** 1 I 2 My 3 Her 4 He 5 Their
> **2** Students' own answers.

Listen again (SB page 23)

The *Listen again* texts in this unit come from the *Reading and Listening* and *Grammar* sections (page 21) on talking about pictures.

Here students listen again to work on reference words.

> **1** 🔊 **1.61**
>
> 1 James
> 2 James's
> 3 James's wife
> 4 Christopher and Lucy
>
> **2, 3** 🔊 **1.62**
>
> A: OK. So who's this?
> B: That's my sister Clare and her husband Jed.
> A: Is Jed English?
> B: No, **he** isn't. **He**'s Irish.
> A: And is this **their** daughter?
> B: No, that's **our** cousin Danielle.
> A: Are **they** here in Manchester?
> B: No, they aren't. They're in Dublin.

Big & Small

Coursebook

Unit 4	Language	Texts	Communicative skills
Part 1 SB page 24	Vocabulary Numbers 20–100 Grammar *There is / There are*	Vocabulary and Reading *Shopping in numbers*	Pronunciation and Speaking schwa /ə/ Writing Describing a hotel
Part 2 SB page 26	Vocabulary and Speaking Prices Reading and Vocabulary Adjectives	Reading and Vocabulary *A small shop near my house*	Vocabulary and Speaking Saying and talking about prices Functional language In a shop Writing and Speaking A shop near your house
Global game SB page 28	Describing what you can see in a mall Answering questions about a mall		
Global review SB page 29	Places in a town, numbers 20–100, adjectives for describing shops *There is / There are* More practice of adjectives to describe shops		

Additional resources

eWorkbook	Interactive and printable grammar, vocabulary, listening and pronunciation practice Extra reading and writing practice Additional downloadable listening and audio material
TB resource CD	Communication activity worksheets to print and photocopy
Go global Ideas for further research	**Big** Ask students to write four or five sentences about the biggest mall in the world or in their country. **Small** Ask students to find the price of five different products in a shop near their home.

Part 1

Vocabulary (SB page 24)

TEACH GLOBAL THINK LOCAL **Lead-in**

Review the numbers from 1–20. Say *one* and ask students to continue counting round the class. Then write the numbers 2 to 9 in a column on the board and ask different students to spell them as words. Write these next to the numbers. Now add a second column, as below, with the numbers 12–19. Again, ask students to spell them, and write them as words. Now add the numbers 20 to 90 in a third column and write *twenty* next to 20. Underline the similarities between the words *twelve* and *twenty*. Point out that *two* also starts with *tw* but is pronounced differently. Tell students they are going to learn to say the numbers from 20 to 100.

2	two	12	twelve	20	twenty
3	three	13	thirteen	30	
4	four	14	fourteen	40	
5	five	15	fifteen	50	
6	six	16	sixteen	60	
7	seven	17	seventeen	70	
8	eight	18	eighteen	80	
9	nine	19	nineteen	90	

1 Students write the words next to the numbers in the exercise.

2 🔘 **1.63** Play the recording to check answers. Then ask students to call out their answers and write the words on the board next to the corresponding number. When checking 100, explain that we say *a* or *one* before *hundred*, and *two hundred* for 200, etc. Now point out that, like *twelve* and *twenty*, the numbers 30 to 90 are very similar in spelling to the *teen* numbers, and end in *-ty*. Underline the similarities: *thirteen - thirty*, etc.

Play the recording and ask students to repeat each number. Mark the stress on the words on the board and check that they stress the first syllable. Drill any numbers that they find difficult.

O o
thirty

20:	twenty /ˈtwenti/
30:	thirty /ˈθɜːti/
40:	forty /ˈfɔːti/
50:	fifty /ˈfɪfti/
60:	sixty /ˈsɪksti/
70:	seventy /ˈsevnti/
80:	eighty /ˈeɪti/
90:	ninety /ˈnaɪnti/
100:	a /one hundred /ə ˈhʌndrəd/, /wʌn ˈhʌndrəd/

3 Write *fifty* + *seven* = on the board and elicit and write the answer *fifty-seven*. Draw attention to the hyphen, and then ask students to do the exercise individually. Write the numbers from the exercise on the board as they work. To check answers, invite different students to write an answer on the board. Finally, model the numbers for students to repeat. For hyphenated numbers, make sure they either stress both words equally or the second word a little more.

50: fifty	7: seven	57: fifty-seven
30: thirty	9: nine	39: thirty-nine
60: sixty	1: one	61: sixty-one
24: twenty-four		
82: eighty-two		
33: thirty-three		

4 Students match the numbers with the words.

23:	twenty-three
46:	forty-six
89:	eighty-nine
32:	thirty-two
64:	sixty-four
98:	ninety-eight

5 🔘 **1.64** Students listen and write the numbers they hear as words.

1	forty-two
2	twenty-seven
3	eighteen
4	sixty-four

🔘 **1.64**

1	My house number is 42.
2	I'm 27 years old.
3	There are 18 people in the class.
4	My grandmother is 64 years old.

TEACH GLOBAL THINK LOCAL **Extra activity**

Play the recording for exercise 5 again. After each sentence, ask students what they heard, and write the sentence on the board. Students then write four similar sentences and read them to a partner, who writes down the number, then shows it to them to check.

Vocabulary and Reading (SB page 24)

This text contains facts and figures about the Cevahir shopping mall in Istanbul, Turkey.

Lead-in

Write *Where am I?* on the board and mime the following places: *in a car, a car park, a shop, a restaurant, a cinema, a supermarket*. Give students any new words. Then draw a large building (a shopping mall) on the board. Say *The car park, shop, restaurant, cinema and supermarket are in here. What is it?* Don't tell them the word, but accept *shopping mall* or *centre* if they know it.

1 **1.65** Ask students to look at the pictures and the words. Point out that *car park* is two words in English (*parking* is used in some European languages), and that *shop* is a place and *shopping* an activity. Also explain that *shopping mall* is American English and that the British English term is *shopping centre*. Now play the recording and ask students to repeat the words. Give extra practice where needed, eg saying only two syllables in *restaurant /ˈrestrɒnt/* or the *a* sounds in *car /kɑː(r)/, park /pɑːk/* and *mall /mɔːl/*.

🔊 **1.65**

a   supermarket

b   restaurant

c   car park

d   shopping mall

e   cinema

f   shop

---

2 Ask students the question. If the answer is yes, ask *Where is it?, What's its name?* and *What's in it?* to review words from exercise 1. Also ask *Do you go to the shopping mall? When?*

3 Before students read, point to the pictures again. Use them to teach *screen* (in the cinema) and *floor* (in the shopping mall), using gesture if necessary. Then tell students they are going to read about a shopping mall in Istanbul, Turkey. They should read and complete the text with the numbers. At this stage they should guess the numbers.

4 🔊 **1.66** Students listen and check their answers. Ask *Is the mall big or small?* and gesture to clarify the meaning of the adjectives. Ask *Why?* and encourage them to refer to numbers in the text. Then focus students on the *Language note*. Explain that *many* is the same as *a lot of*. Point to the text and say *The mall is big. Look. There are many interesting shops.*

🔊 **1.66**

In this mall there are **6** floors for shopping and a big car park with **4** floors for cars. There are many interesting shops and there's a big supermarket. But it's not just for shopping: there are **48** restaurants and a cinema with **11** screens.

Grammar (SB page 25)

Here the focus is on *There is* and *There are* to describe things.

Read through the examples one by one. After the first two ask *Where?* and establish that they refer to the text on page 25. Then see if students can answer the two questions about the shopping mall. At this stage they can just say *yes* or *no*. Look at the rules with students and then return to the short answers, explaining how these are formed for plural and singular questions.

Alternative procedure

Students close their books. Write the first examples on the board like this:

There _____ a big supermarket.

There _____ 48 restaurants.

Can students complete them? If not, ask students to find them in the text on page 25. Ask why we use *is* or *are* and explain as necessary. Next, write the two questions on the board:

_____ _____ a cinema?

_____ _____ any banks?

Can students complete them? Explain how we form singular and plural questions and short answers. Point out the use of *any* in plural questions.

1 Students read the six sentences about a shopping mall. They decide which four are grammatically incorrect and correct them. Point to the example to show how the exercise works, or write the example on the board and ask students to correct it. Students should work individually and then compare answers in pairs.

Sentences 1, 2, 3 and 6 are incorrect. The corrected sentences are:

1   There **are** two floors.

2   There**'s** one cinema.

3   There **are** six floors for shopping.

6   There **are** many people.

---

2 Students underline the correct words in the questions.

1	Are there
2	Is there
3	Is there
4	Is there
5	Are there

TEACH GLOBAL THINK LOCAL **Extra activity**

In pairs, students ask and answer the questions in exercise 2 about their local area using short answers.

G Grammar focus

Show students the icon. Write *page 108* on the board and ask them to find it. Show students the language summary on *There is / are*.

You can use exercises 4, 5 and 6 on page 109 for:

a) extra practice now

b) homework

c) review a couple of lessons from now.

The answers are on page 116 of the Teacher's Book.

Pronunciation and Speaking (SB page 25)

Here the focus is on weak forms in unstressed words and syllables.

1 🔵 1.67 Students read the three sentences and tell you which letters are underlined (*a, e, u*). Point out that these are all vowels. Students listen to the sentences. Tell students the underlined sounds are pronounced /ə/. Draw the phonetic symbol on the board. Demonstrate that to make the sound, you relax your mouth and tongue. Tell students that many vowel sounds are pronounced /ə/ when they are not stressed. Say the sentences again, exaggerating their stress pattern to make this clear. Then play the recording again for students to repeat.

2 Tell students they are going to work in pairs and talk about two other shopping malls. Ask students to form AB pairs. Write *Student A – page 96* and *Student B – page 100* on the board and tell them to turn to the correct page.

Students first complete the questions with *Is there* and *Are there*. Monitor them as they work to check answers. They then take it in turns to ask each other questions about the other person's shopping mall and note the answers in the table. When they finish, ask them to compare their tables to check that their answers are correct.

Writing (SB page 25)

1 Focus students on the information about the Allstar Hotel. Explain that you want them to write some sentences about the hotel using *There is / are*, using the text about the shopping malls on page 25 to help them, if necessary. Check students' work as they do this. When they finish, ask them to compare their sentences in pairs and to consult you if there are any differences. Finally, invite a few students to read their sentences to the class and give feedback as necessary.

Part 2

Vocabulary and Speaking (SB page 26)

TEACH GLOBAL THINK LOCAL **Lead-in**

Write the following symbols on the board in a column: $, £, €, and ask students what they are. Write *Symbol* above the column. Teach the words *dollar*, *pound* and *euro* if students don't know them, and write them next to the symbols under the heading *Currency*. Then ask which countries people use them in (see the Background note) and write these next to the currencies under the heading *Countries*. Can students add to the table?

1 🔘 **1.68** Ask students how they think we say the prices in the exercise. Don't say if they're right or not. Play the recording so that students can check their answers, and then play the recording again for students to repeat. Point out that we say *dollar(s)*, *pound(s)* or *euro(s)* after the number before the decimal point, and then just say the number after the decimal point, eg $4.50 is said *four dollars fifty*.

Background note

The dollar ($) is the currency in many countries around the world, including the US, Australia, Canada, the Caribbean Territories, Hong Kong and Singapore. The pound sterling (£) is the currency of the UK. The euro (€) is the official currency in the majority of countries in the European Union.

2 🔘 **1.69** Students listen to the conversations and circle the prices they hear. Note that in the last conversation they don't hear *pounds*, just *six forty-nine*. Explain that it is common not to say the currency if the price includes pence or cents.

1 a	2 c	3 c	4 b

 1.69

1 A: How much is this?

B: £24.

2 A: How much is the camera?

B: $99.

3 A: Excuse me.

B: Yes.

A: How much is this pen?

B: That's €1.30 please.

4 A: Hello.

B: Hi.

A: How much is this book, please?

B: Let's see – er, £6.49.

A: Thanks.

3 Ask students to write four prices of their own. Encourage them to use different currencies. Now put students in pairs. One student tells their partner their prices. Their partner should write them down and then show them to the other student to check. Students then swap roles and repeat. Monitor their pronunciation of both numbers and currencies as they do this, giving feedback as necessary.

4 Focus students on the example conversation. Explain that we use the question *How much is ...?* to ask for the price of something, and *It's ...* to say the price. Say the question and ask students to repeat. Next, point to the pictures and prices. Say each of the words and ask students to repeat them. Ask a student *How much is the cola?* Then point to the milk and indicate that the student should ask you a similar question. Answer the question. Finally, put students in pairs, point to the sample conversation and pictures and say *Now you* to indicate that they should ask and answer the same question about the things in the pictures.

5 Before the class, find the exchange rate from dollars to the local currency. Write the exchange rate on the board: *$1 = (amount in local currency)*

Ask *How much is the cola in your currency?* Now ask *How much is a cola here? Is the price the same?* Finally, use the local price for a cola to help teach the words *cheap* and *expensive*.

Look at the example conversation with students and check they understand it. Then put students in pairs and ask them to compare the prices of the things in the pictures with prices in their country. When they finish, invite different pairs to tell the class if they think each of the prices is the same, cheap or expensive when compared to local prices.

Functional language (SB page 26)

This section focuses on shopping expressions.

1 Here students look at a conversation in a shop. Point to the conversation and explain that a *shop assistant* work in a shop and a *customer* buys things. Ask students to complete the conversation with the words in the box. Then choose two students and ask them to read it, taking a role each. Does the class agree with their answers? Don't say which answers are correct at this point.

2 🔘 **1.70** Play the recording to check answers. Using gestures, establish that we say *here you are* when we give something to another person.

1.70

A: **Hello**.

B: Hi. **How much is** the magazine?

A: $3.00, please.

B: Here you are. Thanks.

A: **Thank you**. Goodbye.

B: **Bye**.

3 In pairs, students practise the conversation, changing roles when they finish. Go round the class and monitor their speaking. When they finish, give help with any aspects of pronunciation that are causing problems.

TEACH GLOBAL THINK LOCAL Alternative procedure

When students finish their initial practice of the conversation, ask them to close their books and to help you to reconstruct the conversation on the board. Rub out five of the words and replace them with lines and ask students to practise the conversation again. When they change roles, rub out five more words, including *magazine* and the price if still there.

4 Working in different pairs, students make a similar conversation about the things in the pictures on page 26. Demonstrate the activity with a student if necessary. If you used the *Alternative procedure* above, replace the remaining words on the board with lines after they've made one or two conversations. If some pairs finish faster, tell them to repeat the conversation about things in the class, using the *Useful phrases*.

Reading and Vocabulary (SB page 27)

Here, students read and listen to four people talking about a shop near their house.

TEACH GLOBAL THINK LOCAL Lead-in

Ask students the question *Are there any shops near your house?* If students don't understand, write the question on the board and say *two or three or five minutes from your house* to clarify the meaning of *near*. If students say *yes*, ask *Is it big or small?* and *What's in the shop?* If they mention any shop names, write these on the board.

1 **1.71–1.74** Tell students they are going to read and listen to four people talking about a shop near their house. Tell them not to worry about any new vocabulary at the moment. When they finish, ask *Are there any shops near your house?* Then students read again and match the four pictures a–d to the texts 1–4.

1 c   2 b   3 a   4 d

2 Ask students to complete the pairs of opposite adjectives with adjectives from the texts. They should use the pictures above the pairs of words to help them. When they finish, ask them to compare answers with a partner.

3 **1.75** Students listen and check their answers to exercise 3. Then they listen again and repeat the pairs of words. Give extra practice on words that your students find difficult, eg the *ie* in *(un)friendly*, the three (not four) syllables in *interesting*, and the vowel sound in *cheap*. Look at *small* in texts 2, 3 and 4 with students. Explain that adjectives come before nouns (*small shop*) and after *is/are* (*my house is very small*).

good; friendly; small; open; interesting; old; cheap; expensive

4 Put students in pairs and ask them to underline the adjectives you can use to describe the things. Check that students know what the things are first. Students might want to use *unfriendly* to describe a café. Make it clear this is possible, but that the word really refers to the people who work in the café.

1   good, friendly
2   open, small
3   boring, closed, new
4   boring, cheap
5   old, interesting

Writing and Speaking (SB page 27)

1 Tell students to think about a small shop near their house and to make some notes about it, including its name and adjectives to describe it.

2 Ask students to write a short description about the shop using their notes and the descriptions in the *Reading and Vocabulary* section to help them. Monitor their work as they do this, giving help as needed.

3 Put students in small groups. Tell students they are going to tell the other students about their shop. Explain that they can either read their description or talk about their shop without looking at their descriptions. The other students in the group should ask questions about the shop when they finish, eg *Are the people friendly? Are there lots of things to buy?*

Global game

This game is designed to give students the opportunity to use and consolidate language from the unit.

1 Put students in pairs and focus on the picture of the mall and the example sentences. Then tell them to say as many other sentences about the mall as they can. Ask them to write their sentences, and give them a time limit to complete the task. This could be five minutes but you may want to allow less with stronger classes. At the end of the time limit, find out which pairs wrote the most sentences.

2 **1.76** Students continue to work in pairs. Tell them they are going to listen to ten questions about the mall. After each question, you are going to stop the recording and pairs should discuss their answer and write it down. Before they listen, review the questions *How much is …?* for prices, and *How many …. ?* to ask about the number of things.

At the end, ask which pair had the most answers right, and if any pairs included the answer to all the questions in their sentences in exercise 1.

---

1 There are five restaurants.
2 No, there isn't.
3 There are three banks.
4 It's £45.
5 It's 73p.
6 Yes, there is.
7 Yes, there is.

🔘 **1.76**

1 How many restaurants are there in the picture?
2 Is there a hotel?
3 How many banks are there?
4 How much is the CD player?
5 How much is milk?
6 Is there a car park?
7 Is there a music shop?

Global review

These activities can be used at home but are designed to be used in class with students working together in pairs.

Aim: to review the language of the unit.

Tips:
- Encourage students to work together.
- Allow them to look back through the unit or consult their notes.
- In feedback, elicit more examples or the reason why an answer is correct.

Vocabulary (SB page 29)

1
cinema
bank
restaurant
hotel

2–4 Students' own answers.

5
1 closed
2 cheap
3 expensive
4 unfriendly
5 interesting

Grammar (SB page 29)

---

1 a
2 b
3 b
4 a

Listen again (SB page 29)

The *Listen again* text in this unit comes from the *Reading and Vocabulary* section on page 27 in which four people talk about a small shop near their house. Here, students listen again to work on adjectives.

1, 2 🔘 **1.77–1.80**
1 good, friendly
2 open
3 small
4 interesting, expensive

3 Students' own answers.

UNIT 5 Work & Play

Coursebook

Unit 5	Language	Texts	Communicative skills
Part 1 SB page 30	Grammar *There isn't / There aren't* Vocabulary and Speaking Jobs	Reading *VSO* Listening Describing jobs	
Part 2 SB page 32	Vocabulary and Speaking Sports Grammar and Pronunciation *Like*	Listening Talking about sports Reading and Speaking *The Human Race*	
Global voices SB page 34	Listening to people talking about sports they like Questions Asking about a partner's likes and favourite things		
Global review SB page 35	Jobs and sports vocabulary *There is / There are* and expressing likes and dislikes Writing about your work, national sport and likes and dislikes More practice of linking words together		

Additional resources

eWorkbook	Interactive and printable grammar, vocabulary, listening and pronunciation practice Extra reading and writing practice Additional downloadable listening and audio material
TB resource CD	Communication activity worksheets to print and photocopy
Go global Ideas for further research	**Work** Ask students to find the word for three jobs not covered in the Student's Book and the name of the corresponding workplace. **Play** Ask students to find out about the most popular sports in a country not covered in the Student's Book.

Work & Play

Part 1

Reading (SB page 30)

This text is about the international organisation VSO.

Background note

VSO is an international development organisation that works through volunteers to fight poverty in developing countries. It was founded in the UK in 1958.

TEACH GLOBAL THINK LOCAL Lead-in

Put students in pairs and focus attention on the pictures on page 31. Ask them to write two sentences about each one – one with *There is / are* and one about the country. Write on the board *Maybe it's in ...* to help them. Invite some pairs to read out their sentences. Do people agree about the countries? Now write *VSO* on the board and ask students if they know what it is. Point to the volunteers in the photos and say *He / She works for VSO*. Tell students they are going to read about VSO.

1 Ask students to read the introduction to the text about VSO and look at the pictures. When they finish, teach *organisation* by giving examples of ones students will recognise and ask *Where is the organisation from?* (It's British, so from the UK.) Then ask what students think *poor* means. Use gesture to clarify meaning as you ask *With a lot of money, or a little money?* Also explain that a *volunteer* works for little or no money. Next, focus students on the pictures of VSO volunteers and check that these make the meaning of *hospital*, *school*, and *farm* clear. Students now complete the sentences with the countries in the box.

A volunteer in a **hospital** in Malawi.

A VSO volunteer in a **school** in Guyana.

A volunteer on a **farm** in Kenya.

2 🔊 **2.01** Students listen and read more about VSO and choose the best title for the text. Tell them not to worry about any new vocabulary at this point, but make sure they understand the titles before they read.

The best title is 'Working for VSO'.

3 Put students in pairs and ask them to decide if the sentences about the text are true or false. Teach *fun* in question 5 before they do this. Tell them you want them to find the place in the text that gives them each answer.

1 F (VSO is a British organisation.)

2 T

3 F (There aren't any volunteers in North Africa.)

4 F (It's a South American country.)

5 F (There's time for fun.)

TEACH GLOBAL THINK LOCAL Reading extra

Write *over* and *only* on the board, and ask students to find them in the text. Clarify their meaning and then get students to complete these sentences using the text:

There are over ... in ...

There's only one ... in ...

4 Ask a student the main question. When they answer *Yes* or *No*, ask *Why?* and help them to express their answer. Write on the board: *Because ...* and explain that we use this word to give a reason or explanation. Now look at the *Useful language* with students and review the adjectives. Tell students you want them to prepare their answer to the questions, and then to ask and answer them in small groups. Monitor them as they do this, picking up on problems as necessary. Finally, find out if most people in the class think working for VSO is interesting or not, and what their main reasons are.

Grammar (SB page 30)

Here the focus is on *There isn't* and *There aren't*.

Draw students' attention to the examples and explain that they come from the text on VSO. Read through the rules with students and clarify that we use *a* before singular nouns and *any* before plural nouns.

1 Students underline the correct words in the sentences. Suggest they do this individually first, and then compare with a partner.

1 aren't

2 isn't

3 aren't

4 aren't

2 Students complete the sentences with *There isn't* or *There aren't*.

1 There aren't

2 There isn't

3 There aren't

4 There isn't

3 Ask students *Are the sentences in exercise 2 true for you?* Go through each sentence and, with the students help, write the true version of any false sentences on the board. For the moment, avoid *some* if they want to correct questions 1 and 3 unless you are confident your students will know this word.

G Grammar focus

Show students the icon. Write *page 110* on the board and ask them to find it. Show students the language summary on *there isn't / aren't*.

You can use exercise 1 on page 111 for:

a) extra practice now

b) homework

c) review a couple of lessons from now.

The answers are on page 116 of the Teacher's Book.

Listening (SB page 30)

Here students listen to six people talking about their jobs

1 **2.02–2.07** Tell students they are going to listen to six people talking about their jobs. Ask *How many people work for VSO?* When checking answers, ask if students can remember their names. (Ingrid and Julie).

> Two people work for VSO.

2 Students listen again and match the names to the sentences. Ask students to read through the sentences first and check that their meaning is clear. Note that each speaker says more than appears in the sentences on page 30; students should listen for the place where each speaker works (**bold** in the audioscript below.)

> 🔊 **2.02–2.07**
>
> **Jim**
> I work **in a shop**, it's a small shop. It's open every day. It's OK, but it's a bit boring.
>
> **David**
> I work **outdoors** on a farm. It's a good job, but it's a difficult job too.
>
> **Ingrid**
> I work for VSO, I'm a volunteer and I work in China. I'm a teacher, I work **in a school**. There are 12 teachers in the school. There isn't a lot of money but it's a very interesting job.
>
> **Maria**
> I work **in a restaurant**. It's a cheap restaurant and it's very popular! There are a lot of people every day so it's very busy!
>
> **Richard**
> I work for a big company in the centre of town. There are 150 people in the company. I work **in an office**. There are 19 people in the office with me. They're very friendly.
>
> **Julie**
> I'm a volunteer for VSO. I work **in a hospital**. It's a good job, but it's very busy.

3 Students listen again and underline the correct words. Finally, focus students on the *Language note* and how we use *I work ...* .

Jim:	boring
David:	difficult
Ingrid:	interesting
Maria:	busy
Richard:	friendly
Julie:	busy

TEACH GLOBAL THINK LOCAL **Listening extra**

In stronger classes, students in pairs could try to choose the correct words before they listen again, and then listen to check their answers.

Vocabulary and Speaking (SB page 31)

1 Ask students to turn to page 104 and to match the pictures to the jobs. When they finish, practise saying the jobs by asking students to listen to you and repeat them, paying attention to word stress.

TEACH GLOBAL THINK LOCAL **Mixed ability**

Ask students if they know the names of any other jobs and write these in a list on the board.

2 Focus students on the table and ask them to read it. Draw attention to the use of *a* before the job in the sentence *I'm a student*. Then use the *Language note* to clarify the meaning of *unemployed* and *retired*, and drill both words to practise their pronunciation. Now ask students to choose one of the tasks, A or B. They either tick the true sentence about themselves, or they choose a job from those on page 104 and tick the true sentence about that job. The options here allow students not to talk about their work situation if that's a sensitive issue.

3 Students speak to five other people in the class and make a note of their answers. If practical, arrange the class into groups of six to do this. Draw their attention to the example conversation to help them, especially the use of *And you?*

4 Students decide if the sentences are true or false for the people in their group. Teach the word *nobody*, meaning 'no people', before they do this. After noting their answers, ask students to compare with their group. Do they all have the same answers?

TEACH GLOBAL THINK LOCAL **Speaking extra**

Ask groups to talk in their groups and to correct any false sentences in exercise 4. Then ask them to write three more sentences about their group. They should ask more questions to find out the new information. Finally, ask groups to tell the class their sentences.

Part 2

Vocabulary and Speaking (SB page 32)

1 Ask students to look at the pictures and write the missing vowels to complete the names of the sports. They then compare answers with a partner. Ask if they have the same answers before you check them with the class.

> swimming
>
> running
>
> table tennis
>
> cricket
>
> basketball
>
> American football
>
> football

2 **2.08** Students listen and repeat the sports. Write these on the board and mark the stress, which is generally on the first syllable of each word. Also note that *table* in *table tennis* is stressed more than *tennis*, and that in *American football*, the second syllable of *American* is stressed, and both words are given equal emphasis. Point out, too, that the final *e* of *table* is silent.

3 Focus students on the bar chart of national sports. Working in pairs, students guess the sports 1–4 from the sports in exercise 1. Tell them to use the countries to help them decide, and draw attention to the example conversation. Write *I think ...* and *What do you think?* on the board before they talk and explain that they are used to give and ask about an opinion. Drill the pronunciation of the question, but don't give a grammatical explanation of how the question is formed at this point. When students have finished, invite some pairs to tell the class their answers, and see if others agree. Don't confirm answers at this stage.

4 **2.09** Students listen and check their answers.

> **2.09**
>
> 1 In most of South America, Africa and Europe, **football** is the national sport.
>
> 2 In India, Pakistan and Australia, **cricket** is the most popular sport.
>
> 3 In the United States the national sport is football – **American football**.
>
> 4 In China, **table tennis** is very popular.

5 Working in pairs, students ask and answer the questions. Give students time to read through the questions and deal with any queries they have before they start talking. When pairs finish, discuss the questions with the class so that students can share their knowledge if they come from different countries, or try to agree if they all come from the same country.

Listening (SB page 32)

Here students listen to two people talking about sports.

Students close their books. Ask them to tell you the sports names they studied in exercise 1 of *Vocabulary and Speaking*, and to dictate their spelling as you write them on the board. Point to the sports one by one and ask *Do you like (sport)?* Use gestures, eg thumbs up and down, or happy and sad faces, to clarify the meaning of *like*. Find out whether a majority of class members like or don't like each sport.

1 Go through the meaning of each symbol. Start by explaining what *like* means, either through gesture or by saying *It's good*. Then explain that *love* means 'like a lot', and that *I don't like it* is the negative form of *I like it*. Also tell them that *it* is a pronoun and refers to the sport (basketball, etc.). Students write the symbols in the box for each picture. When they've finished, call out the name of a sport and invite different students to tell you what they think of it. Work on pronunciation as they do this, and drill any problem phrases as necessary.

2 **2.10** Tell students they are going to listen to two students talking about football and swimming. Ask them to look at the table and explain that they need to tick the man and the woman's opinions of the two sports.

> The woman likes football and she loves swimming.
>
> The man thinks football is OK and he doesn't like swimming.

3 Students listen and write the conversation in the correct order. Check answers and tell students that they will study the language in this conversation in the grammar section.

> **2.10**
>
> A: Do you like football?
>
> B: Yes, I do. And you?
>
> A: Well, it's OK.
>
> B: What about swimming, Steve? Do you like swimming?
>
> A: No, I don't.
>
> B: Really? I love it.

Grammar and Pronunciation (SB page 33)

Here the focus is on questions with *like* and short answers.

Focus students on the example question and tell students it comes from the conversation in *Listening* on page 32. Read through the rules with them and check that they understand how the auxiliary *do* is used to form the question. However, don't give a detailed grammatical explanation at this point. The idea is to introduce this example of the present simple as a lexical chunk.

1 Students underline the correct words in the conversation, working individually at first and then comparing in pairs. Ask pairs to try and agree on their answers, and then invite a pair to read out their version of the conversation. Do other students agree? If not, ask them to give their answers before giving the correct ones. Refer to the rules to clarify any doubts.

> like; do; Do you like; I don't; I like

2 Students write words to complete the questions following the prompts in brackets. Look at the example for the first question to make sure this is clear.

3 Students write their answers to the questions. Remind them to use one of the short answer forms in the examples at the top of the section.

4 ⊘ 2.11 Ask students to read the sentences which come from *Listening* on page 32. Point to the lines that link two of the words in each sentence and play the recording. Ask students to notice how the two words connect in each case. Play the sentences again one by one. Point out how *Do you* becomes one word, as if it was written *D'you*. *Yes, I* is also said as if it was one word. In the case of *No, I* the words are connected with a /w/ sound.

5 Students listen again and repeat the sentences. Give plenty of practice here, as this is a key feature of pronunciation that will help students to understand natural spoken English.

6 Working in pairs, students ask and answer questions 1–4 from exercise 2. Remind them to link words at the start of their questions and answers.

TEACH GLOBAL
THINK LOCAL **Mixed ability**

Fast finishers could extend their speaking by asking similar questions about other things. Tell them to see if they can find four things in common. They could tell the class about these when everyone has finished using *We both like …*

G Grammar focus

Show students the icon. Write *page 110* on the board and ask them to find it. Show students the language summary on *like*. You can use exercise 2 on page 111 for:

a) extra practice now

b) homework

c) review a couple of lessons from now.

The answers are on page 116 of the Teacher's Book.

Reading and Speaking (SB page 33)

1 In pairs, students ask each other the question *Do you like running?* When they finish, find out if the class in general likes or doesn't like running.

TEACH GLOBAL
THINK LOCAL **Alternative procedure**

Ask a student *Do you like running?* When he / she has answered, ask students to ask the same question in pairs, and, when they have finished, to ask other people. Does the class in general like running? Now ask *Do you love running?* If anyone answers yes, find out about their running habits. Ask *Do you run in races?* Write *race* on the board and explain its meaning.

2 Write the word *race* on the board and ask students what they think it means. Focus them on the picture and say *This is a race* to clarify or confirm its meaning. Now ask students to read the information about the race and to answer the questions. Before they start, explain that *special* means *different* or *unique*.

Background note

The 'Nike + Human Race 10k' was first held in 2008 in 25 cities around the world to raise money for The UN Refugee Agency. In 2009, the event was held in 30 cities. Events were organised in smaller locations too so that around a million people participated in both years.

---

1 It's called 'The Human Race'.

2 It's in many cities or you can run where you live.

3 It's 10 kilometres.

4 It's special because you can run at home and because 1 million people around the world run in it.

---

3 Put students in AB pairs. Refer As to page 97 and Bs to page 101. Tell each student to read about another race and then to tell their partner about it. They should ask you about anything they don't understand in their texts. Encourage students to try and do the speaking task without referring to the text if this is feasible with your students. If not, students can refer to the text for support.

4 Working in the same pairs, students ask each other if there are any important races in their country and talk about them. Suggest they talk about other races round the world if this isn't very generative. Before they speak, write the following prompts on the board to help them.

It's a (number) km race.

It's in (month).

It takes place in …

It's for …

When ready, invite some pairs to report back to the class on the races they talked about.

UNIT 5 Work & Play

Global voices

These lessons in *Global* are designed to provide students with exposure to authentic speakers of English from both native and non-native English backgrounds. In this unit we extend the theme of sport.

Warm up (SB page 34)

1 💿 **2.12** Students listen and repeat the names of the sports in the pictures. Point out the stress patterns – on the first syllable in all the sports except *capoeira*.

Background note

Capoeira is an Afro-Brazilian sport that combines martial arts and dance performed to music by two players at a time. It is often played outdoors and its popularity is growing around the world.

2 Students look at the sports in the box and find sports to match the definitions. Review *indoors* and teach *alone* before they do this. Then ask them to work individually before comparing with a partner.

Sports you play with a ball: basketball; football; golf; tennis

Sports you normally do indoors: basketball; dancing; judo; swimming

Sports you normally do with one other person: capoeira; dancing; judo; tennis

Sports you normally do alone: golf; motorbike racing; running; ski-jumping; swimming

TEACH GLOBAL THINK LOCAL Extra activity

In pairs, students take it in turn to mime a sport. The other person has to say its name. The person guessing should close their book to encourage them to remember the sport's name.

Listening (SB page 34)

Here students listen to five people talking about sports.

1 💿 **2.13–2.17** Students listen to five people answering the questions *Do you like sport? What's your favourite sport?* and write the speaker's number next to the phrases. Before they listen, ask some students in the class the questions to check that their meaning is clear.

a 4   b 3   c 5   d 2   e 1

💿 **2.13–2.17**

1 Mireille, US
I love sports. Well, some sports I like. I like watching football and I like swimming.

2 Christina, Germany
Yes, I do. My favourite sport is capoeira. It's a kind of Brazilian dance.

3 Francesco, Italy
Well, I mean, yes, quite a bit. Not too much, but yes. I like motorbikes, so I like racing.

4 Jolanta, Poland
Not football. I like ski-jumping the most.

5 Eva, Switzerland
I do like sport, but not too much, not everything. I'm not a very sporty person in general. But what I do like doing is dancing.

2 Students listen again and write the speakers' favourite sports from the list in *Warm up* exercise 2.

1 football, swimming
2 capoeira
3 motorbike racing
4 ski-jumping
5 dancing

Language focus: questions (SB page 34)

Ask students to read the *Language note*. It reminds them that questions starting with *do* normally have *Yes / No* answers, and that *Wh-* questions ask for information. They then underline the correct answer for each question.

1 Yes, it's OK.
2 Opera – I love opera.
3 Well, yes, but not too much.
4 Chinese food.
5 Yes, I do, they're great.

Speaking (SB page 34)

In pairs, students ask and answer the questions from the *Language focus* section. Monitor them as they do this to check that their answers are appropriate.

Global review

These activities can be used at home but are designed to be used in class with students working together in pairs.

Aim: to review the language of the unit.

Tips:

- Encourage students to work together.
- Allow them to look back through the unit or consult their notes.
- In feedback, elicit more examples or the reason why an answer is correct.

Vocabulary (SB page 35)

> 1 restaurant; office; shop; outdoors; home; hospital
>
> 2 retired; unemployed
>
> 3 1 basketball
>   2 tennis
>   3 football
>   4 cricket
>   5 swimming
>   6 running

Grammar (SB page 35)

> 1 I work in a school, it's a small school. **There is** one head teacher and **there are** 5 teachers. It's a school for girls. **There are** 80 girls in the school. The girls are from 5 to 11 years old. **There aren't** any boys. I like my job, **there isn't** a boring day - every day is busy and interesting!
>
> 2
>
> 3 I don't like cricket.
>
> 4 I like football.
>
> 6 You think swimming is OK.
>
> 7 You love cricket.
>
> 8 You don't like football.
>
>   The sentences are pairs, so sentences 1–4 begin with *I* and 5–8 begin with *You*.
>
> 3
>
> 1 do
>
> 2 I love it
>
> 3 It's OK.
>
> 4 I don't

Writing (SB page 35)

Students complete the sentences about themselves, their work, the national sport in their country and their likes and dislikes.

Listen again (SB page 35)

The *Listen again* text in this unit comes from the *Listening* on page 30 in which five people talk about their jobs. Here students listen again to work on word linking.

> **1–3** 2.18
>
> Students' own answers.
>
> **4** 2.19
>
> I‿work‿outdoors‿on‿a farm.
>
> It's‿a‿good job, but‿it's‿a‿difficult job too.

Day & Night

Coursebook

Unit 6	Language	Texts	Communicative skills
Part 1 SB page 36	Functional language Telling the time Grammar Present simple	Listening and Vocabulary Daily routine / *have* and *go* Reading *A day in my life*	Writing A day in the life of ...
Part 2 SB page 38	Vocabulary and Pronunciation The time Word stress Extend your Vocabulary *good* + time of day Grammar Present simple negative	Reading and Listening *24/7 Services*	Speaking and Vocabulary Your favourite time of day Functional language Giving an opinion
Global reading SB page 40	Rating answers to a question posted on a website Discussing ratings with a partner Matching answers on a website to comments		
Global review SB page 41	Revision of the time and daily routines More practice of the present simple for describing routines Choosing short answers to questions Ordering phrases to make complete sentences		

Additional resources

eWorkbook	Interactive and printable grammar, vocabulary, listening and pronunciation practice Extra reading and writing practice Additional downloadable listening and audio material
TB resource CD	Communication activity worksheets to print and photocopy
Go global Ideas for further research	**Day** Ask students to find out what the time is in the capital city of four countries in four different continents. **Night** Ask students to list five different places where they live that are open 24 hours a day.

Part 1

Functional language (SB page 36)

This section focuses on telling the time.

TEACH GLOBAL THINK LOCAL **Lead-in**

Review the numbers from 10–60. Write *10–60* on the board and say *four nine*. Ask a student to say the number (*forty-nine*). Then say *Now you* to indicate that the student should say two other numbers and invite a classmate to say the full number. Point to the board if they say a number outside the range indicated. Keep going until students are comfortable using these numbers. Then look at your watch or mobile. Ask *What's the time?* and let students try to tell you. This highlights the need to learn how to tell the time.

1 Point to a watch or clock and tell students they are going to learn one way to tell the time. Focus them on the digital clocks and ask them to match the times to the clocks. When checking, point out that you say the numbers either side of the decimal point, and if the number after the decimal point is between 01 and 09, you say *oh* for 'zero'. If students know the other way to tell the time (*twenty past six*, *twenty-five to six*, etc.), acknowledge this and tell them they will learn this soon.

1	06.20
2	05.35
3	11.30
4	03.00
5	07.05
6	04.45

2 ● 2.20–2.23 Students listen and write the times they hear. Tell them that they will hear the times in different contexts.

> ● **2.20–2.23**
>
> 1 It's **six o'clock**. This is David Barnes with the news on Radio Cardiff.
>
> 2 The train on Platform 4 is the **10.20** for London. 10.20 for London on Platform 4.
>
> 3 At the third stroke it will be **nine fifty five** precisely.
>
> 4 A: Excuse me. What's the time?
>
> B: Let's see – it's **two thirty**.
>
> A: Sorry?
>
> B: Two thirty.
>
> A: OK. Thank you.

3 ● 2.24 Students listen again to number 4 and put the lines of the conversation in the correct order.

TEACH GLOBAL THINK LOCAL **Alternative procedure**

In pairs, students put the conversation in order before listening, and listen again to check their answers.

4 Ask students to write five different times in their notebooks. In pairs, students then practise similar conversations using these times.

TEACH GLOBAL THINK LOCAL **Speaking extra**

In multilingual classes, students could ask each other about the time in their countries. Write on the board *What's the time in ...?* to help them.

Listening and Vocabulary (SB page 36)

Here students listen to someone describing their daily routine.

1 ● 2.25 Focus students on the pictures and times. Tell them they are going to hear someone talking about when they do the different activities, but that some of the times are incorrect. Students listen and tick the correct times. If students have trouble picking out the times, either pause the recording at the end of each sentence, or read the description yourself, pausing as necessary.

> 7.00 and 1.00 are correct

> ● **2.25**
>
> I have a shower at **7.00** and then I have breakfast at about **7.30**. I go to work at **8.15**. I have lunch at **1.00**. When I finish work I go to the gym – that's at about **6.15**. After that I go home – at about **7.30**. We have dinner at **8.00** and go to bed at **11.00**.

2 Students listen again and correct the incorrect times. Pause the recording to give them time to write their answers. Then ask them to compare in pairs. If they don't agree, play the recording again to see who is right.

7.00 ✓	8.00 8.15	6.30 6.15	8.30 8.00
7.20 7.30	1.00 ✓	7.45 7.30	11.30 11.00

3 Students listen again and complete the expressions with *have* or *go*. Read through the expressions before they do this, using the pictures to clarify meaning, and pause the recording to give them time to write their answers.

1	have a shower	5	go to the gym
2	have breakfast	6	go home
3	go to work	7	have dinner
4	have lunch	8	go to bed

Mixed ability

If you have stronger students who you think may already know some of the vocabulary, ask them to complete the expressions before they listen again.

After checking answers, practise pronouncing the expressions. Point out the stress on the first syllable of *shower*, *breakfast* and *dinner*. Then focus students on the *Language note* and how we use *at* and *about* with times. To reinforce this, play the recording again and stop after each time. Ask *at* or *at about*?

4 Ask two or three students the question *What time do you have / go ...?* about the activities in exercise 3. Students then write sentences like the example about activities that they do.

5 🔘 **2.26** Students listen and repeat the conversation. Remind them that *do you* is pronounced as one word (*d'you*) and point out the linking between *at* and *about*.

6 In pairs, students ask each other the question *What time do you ...?* about the activities in exercise 3 and note their partner's answers. They don't write complete sentences at this point.

Reading (SB page 37)

This text is about a typical day in the life of two different people.

1 Ask students to read the title and the introduction. Make sure they understand *engineer* and *office worker*, and remind them that Malawi is a country in Africa. Divide students into As and Bs. One student reads about Nelson and the other about Linda, and complete the times in the table for that person.

He / she ...	Nelson	Linda
has breakfast at	5.30	7.30
goes to work at	7.00	8.15
has lunch at	12.30	12.30
goes home at	5.00	3.30
has dinner at	6.00	6.00
goes to bed at	10.00	11.30

2 Students underline *has* or *goes* for each phrase in the table. After checking answers, practise the pronunciation of *has* and *goes*, as individual words and then in the complete sentences.

3 Working in pairs, students tell each other the times that Nelson or Linda do things, and complete the table for them. Then they look at the times and comment on which are the same and different. Review the meaning of *the same* and *different* and draw their attention to the example conversation to help them. When they finish, write *start work* and *finish work* on the board. Ask *The same or different?* Students should read the text again if necessary to find out when Nelson and Linda do these things. (Note that the text doesn't explicitly say when Nelson finishes work, but we know he goes home at five o'clock.)

Grammar (SB page 37)

Here the focus is on the form and meaning of the present simple.

Ask students to look at the three examples and read through the rules with students. Highlight the fact that the verb is the same as the infinitive for all persons except *he*, *she* and *it*, when it ends in *-s* or *-es*, and remind them of the third person forms of *have* (*has*) and *go* (*goes*).

Alternative procedure

Students close their books. Write the following gapped sentences on the board with times that are true for you:

I ____ breakfast at (time).

Nelson ____ breakfast at 5.30.

I ____ to work at (time).

Linda ____ to work at 8.15.

In pairs, students try to complete the sentences. Tell them to look back at exercise 2 in Reading for help with the sentences about Nelson and Linda.

1 Students write the correct form of the verb to complete the sentences. Ask them to do this individually and then compare in pairs. Can they agree on all answers?

1 have
2 works
3 start
4 has
5 finish
6 starts
7 go

2 In pairs, students look at their notes from *Listening and Vocabulary* exercise 6 and write sentences about their partner. If they don't have notes, they should ask their partner questions about their daily activities. Focus on the example to make the activity clear, and monitor them as they work to check the third person singular form. When they finish, invite some students to read out their sentences. Their partner should say if they are correct or not.

G Grammar focus

Show students the icon. Write *page 110* on the board and ask them to find it. Show students the first two parts of the language summary on the present simple. You can use exercise 3 on page 111 for:

a) extra practice now

b) homework

c) review a couple of lessons from now.

The answers are on page 116 of the Teacher's Book.

Writing (SB page 37)

1 Ask students to look again at the *Reading* text and to find the words in bold – *and*, *after that* and *then*. Read through the *Language note* with students to explain their use.

Language note

If necessary, highlight the fact that we use *after that* and not *after* to say what happens next. Students might use *after* because one word is used in their language in this context.

2 Ask students to think about a friend or someone in their family and to write about a typical day in their life using *and*, *then* and *after that*. Monitor to help.

3 Working in pairs, students compare their descriptions. Are they the same or different? Ask pairs to find one thing that is the same and one that is different, and to tell the rest of the class.

Part 2

Vocabulary and Pronunciation (SB page 38)

TEACH GLOBAL THINK LOCAL Lead-in

Write *12.30* on the board. Ask *What's the time?* Students should answer *twelve thirty*. Ask if they know a different way to say this time and write *half past twelve* on the board. Draw a clock face, mark the time on it, and shade in the right half. Use this to explain the meaning of *half* and *past*. Draw an arrow round the outside of the clock from 12 to 6 to reinforce the meaning of *past*, and from 6 to 12 for *to*. Do the same with 3 and 9 to introduce *a quarter* and *to*, and then write *12.15* on the board. Students tell you two ways to say this time.

1 Focus students on the diagram showing another way of telling the time and explain how it works. Then ask them to tick the correct times in the exercise. When checking answers, see if the class agrees before giving the right answer for each one.

1 ✓	2 ✗	3 ✗	4 ✗	5 ✓	6 ✓	7 ✓	8 ✗

2 Students correct the incorrect times in exercise 1, individually first before comparing with a partner.

> 2   a quarter to seven
>
> 3   five past eight
>
> 4   ten o'clock
>
> 8   ten to ten

3 **2.27** Students listen and repeat the times in exercise 1, paying attention to the stress. Focus them on the example to demonstrate what the stress pattern is for the times.

> **2.27**
>
> 1   half past two
>
> 2   a quarter to seven
>
> 3   five past eight
>
> 4   ten o'clock
>
> 5   a quarter to nine
>
> 6   two o'clock
>
> 7   ten past ten
>
> 8   ten to ten

4 Ask students to write six times, three in one way and three in the other, as in the example. Working in pairs, students take it in turns to say a time. The other student has to say the time in the other way.

Extra activity

The new way of telling the time may prove difficult for some students. For extra practice, ask what the time is at regular intervals during this and subsequent classes.

Speaking and Vocabulary (SB page 38)

1 Ask students to look at the pictures and say when the different times of the day (morning, afternoon, evening and night) start and finish for them. Make it clear there is no correct answer here. Next, students compare their ideas with a partner. Focus them on the example conversation to help them, and read through the *Language note* to clarify the meaning of *am* and *pm*. When they finish, discuss opinions about when the different parts of the day start and finish.

Language note

The meaning of *morning*, *afternoon*, *evening* and *night* varies from one person to another. For most people, *morning* is from when you get up to when you have lunch, and *afternoon* starts after lunch. *Afternoon* often ends when you finish work, have dinner, or when the sun goes down. *Evening* or *night* start when afternoon ends, but for some people, *night* is after the *evening*, when it is time to go to bed.

2 In groups, students talk about their favourite time of the day. Draw attention to the question in the rubric and the example sentence to help them.

Speaking extra

Invite groups to tell the class what they found out about each other's preferences. Write on the board:
(Name) and (name)'s favourite time of the day is ...

Extend your vocabulary (SB page 38)

Read through the explanation with students. It's important to emphasise that *Good night* is a way to say goodbye, and that you say *Good evening* to say hello politely at night. Students then do the exercise.

1 Good afternoon
2 Good night
3 Good morning
4 Good evening

Vocabulary extra

Introduce and explain the meaning of *midday* and *midnight*.

Reading and Listening (SB page 39)

The text is about services that are offered 24 hours a day. Students listen to four people talking about 24/7 services.

Lead-in

Write *24/7* on the board. Can students guess its meaning or what the numbers refer to?

1 Students complete the sentences with the words in the box.

24/7 means 24 **hours** a day, 7 **days** a week.

2 Students read the text about 24/7 services and find three examples of each thing. (There are in fact four examples of places where people work and four expressions that mean 24/7.) When they finish, go through the answers and check the meaning of any words or phrases.

Jobs: doctor; nurse; taxi driver

Places where people work: hospital; supermarket; taxi; call centre

Expressions that mean 24/7: round the clock; all day, every day; at all hours; day and night

3 🔘 2.28–2.31 Focus students on the four pictures and ask them to name each place where the people work. Then say they are going to listen to four people talking about the places. Students number the pictures in order.

1 d   2 c   3 a   4 b

🔘 **2.28–2.31**

1 I phone my bank's **call centre** at night. I don't have time to phone in the day and at night it isn't so expensive.
2 I like my job because it's just me and my **car**. And I like working nights. There's no traffic. My wife doesn't like it because I work all night and come home in the morning.
3 I don't work normal hours, I work nights in a **hospital**. I like my job, but we don't have time to see other people. All my friends are nurses too!
4 My **supermarket** doesn't close at night. 24-hour shopping? I think it's great. You don't spend hours in the shop. There's no one there – it's very quiet.

Grammar (SB page 39)

Here, the focus is on the negative form of the present simple.

Look at the example sentences with students and read through the explanation. Make sure it's clear that *don't* or *doesn't* are used to make the present simple negative and that the main verb is an infinitive and doesn't change. Conjugate *have* on the board for all persons and highlight the third person forms.

1 Students complete the sentences from *Reading and Listening* exercise 3 with the negative form of the verb in brackets. Ask students to compare answers with a partner when they finish.

2 **2.32** Students listen and check their answers.

> **2.32**
>
> 1 My wife **doesn't like** it because I work all night.
> 2 I **don't work** normal hours.
> 3 I like my job, but we **don't have** time to see other people.
> 4 My supermarket **doesn't close** at night.
> 5 You **don't spend** hours in the shop.

3 Students write some sentences about themselves using affirmative and negative verbs in the present simple. You could write a selection of verbs on the board to help them, eg *like, work, have, go, start, finish, spend, close.*

4 Students work in pairs and read their sentences to each other. For each sentence, the other student should say a version of the sentence that's true for them, or say *That's true for me too.* Write this expression on the board.

G Grammar focus

Show students the icon. Write *page 110* on the board and ask them to find it. Show students the third part of the language summary on the present simple negative. You can use exercises 4 and 5 on page 111 for:

a) extra practice now

b) homework

c) review a couple of lessons from now.

The answers are on page 116 of the Teacher's Book.

Functional language (SB page 39)

This section focuses on giving opinions.

1 **2.33** Write the gapped sentence on the board and invite students to finish it. Write their suggestions on the board. Then play the recording. Students write what speaker 4 in *Reading and Listening* exercise 3 says.

> 24-hour shopping? I think it's **great**.

2 Focus students on the words we use to give an opinion. How many of them coincide with their suggestions? Students match the words with the symbols. They could do this in pairs if the words are unfamiliar to them.

+++	great, fantastic
++	good
+	OK
x	bad
xx	terrible

3 Tell students they are going to work in pairs and give their opinion on working and shopping. Refer As to page 97 and Bs to page 101. Students ask their questions, listen to their partner's opinion, and then react with their opinion. Write prompts on the board to clarify this:

A: What do you think of ...?

B: I think it's ...

A: Yes, me too. / Really? I think it's ...

At the end, ask pairs how many of their opinions are the same.

Global reading

The *Global reading* pages encourage students to approach different text types and develop the ability to read for pleasure. This text is from a website where you can ask questions to other internet users.

1 Ask students to look at the page from a website and to choose the best way to complete each sentence. Give them time to read the questions and ask about anything they don't understand before they start.

> 1 b   2 a

2 Students read Jan's question and the answers and decide who has a good answer by completing the answer ratings with one to five stars. Check that they understand the phrase *the clocks go back one hour* before they start reading.

> **TEACH GLOBAL THINK LOCAL** **Alternative procedure**
>
> Dictate Jan's question and ask students for their answers. Help them to express these, as this will help them understand the text.

> Students' own answers.

3 In pairs, students compare their answer ratings to see if they agree. Draw attention to the example conversation to help them. When they finish, find out if there's a general class consensus on the rating for each answer. Also find out if students discovered anything new from reading the text.

4 Ask students to read Jan's comments and ask about anything they don't understand. Then tell students the comments are not in order. They should write her comments under the correct answers.

> **Jan's answers**
>
> To Mr X: Me too! I love my bed.
>
> To Roger: No problem Roger! That's OK.
>
> To Ruth: I know. That's a problem for me too.
>
> To Pete: That's very interesting, Pete. Now I understand about the different countries.
>
> To Maxie: Hi! Lots of information here. Thank you.
>
> To Lily from London: Well that's a very good thing. Thanks!

Global review

These activities can be used at home but are designed to be used in class with students working together in pairs.

Aim: to review the language of the unit.

Tips:

- Encourage students to work together.
- Allow them to look back through the unit or consult their notes.
- In feedback, elicit more examples or the reason why an answer is correct.

Vocabulary (SB page 41)

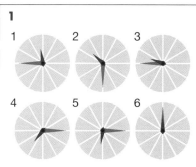

1

2

1   half past two: 2.30

2   a quarter past eleven: 11.15

3   ten to four: 3.50

4   twenty-five past six: 6.25

5   twenty-five to seven: 6.35

6   a quarter to ten: 9.45

3

go; home; to bed; to the gym; to work

have: a shower; breakfast; dinner; lunch

Grammar (SB page 41)

1

Text 1

Jamie is a farmer in New Zealand. He works on a sheep farm and his day **starts** very early. He **has** a coffee and **starts** work at 6 o'clock. He then **has** breakfast at about 7.30. He **starts** work again at 8.15.

Text 2

I don't **have** lunch with Bev; we **have** lunch outdoors at 1 o'clock. I **go** home at 6.00. After that, I **have** dinner with Bev - at about 7.00. We **go** to bed at 10.30.

2

1   do

2   does

3   doesn't

4   don't

Listen again (SB page 41)

The *Listen again* text in this unit comes from the *Reading and Listening* on page 39 in which four people talk about 24/7 services. Here, students listen again to reconstruct one or two sentences by each speaker.

---

1 🎧 **2.34–2.37**

The complete sentences are:

1 I don't have time to phone in the day and at night it isn't so expensive.

2 I like my job because it's just me and my car.

3 I like my job, but we don't have time to see other people.

4 I think it's great. You don't spend hours in the shop.

UNIT 7 Places & People

Coursebook

Unit 7	Language	Texts	Communicative skills
Part 1 SB page 42	Vocabulary Places in nature Direction words Grammar and Speaking Question words	Listening and Reading *UNESCO World Heritage sites* Reading *Great Smoky Mountains National Park*	Writing A place you know
Part 2 SB page 44	Vocabulary People you know Grammar Present simple questions	Reading *On safari*	Speaking A person you know well
Global game SB page 46	Carrying out language-based tasks as part of a board game		
Global review SB page 47	Places in nature and people you know Verb + noun / preposition phrase collocations More practice of question words		

Additional resources

eWorkbook	Interactive and printable grammar, vocabulary, listening and pronunciation practice Extra reading and writing practice Additional downloadable listening and audio material
TB resource CD	Communication activity worksheets to print and photocopy
Go global Ideas for further research	**Places** Ask students to go to the UNESCO World Heritage Site website and find three World Heritage sites in their part of the world. **People** Ask students to find the name of five animals you can see on a safari in Tanzania.

Part 1

Vocabulary (SB page 42)

TEACH GLOBAL THINK LOCAL ### Lead-in

Students have their books closed. On the board, draw the outline of a well-known place in nature, eg Mount Everest, the Niagara Falls or somewhere more local. Ask: *What's this?* Encourage students to speculate in English using *Is it ...?* and *I think it's ...* and give clues if necessary. Find out if they know its name in English if appropriate, but don't teach any geographical words now. The idea is to introduce the theme and make students aware of the geographical words they do and don't know. Invite some students to come to the board and sketch other places for their classmates to speculate about. Then students open their books. Can they point to where the places are on the map?

1 🔘 **2.38** Focus students on the map and the pictures and ask them to listen and match pictures a, e, f and g with the phrases in the box. Tell them they will hear all the phrases that label the pictures and not just the ones in the exercise. Students could work in pairs to do this if the target vocabulary is likely to be new.

> 🔘 **2.38**
>
> a **a mountain in the US**
> b a lake in Kenya
> c a forest in Slovakia and Ukraine
> d a desert in Jordan
> e **a river in China**
> f **an island in Australia**
> g **a national park in Spain**

2 🔘 **2.39** Play the recording of the words in bold in the box. Students listen and repeat the words. Focus on word stress (it's on the first syllable in all words) and point out that the *s* in *island* /ˈaɪlənd/ is silent.

TEACH GLOBAL THINK LOCAL ### Extra activity

To give more practice with the new vocabulary, students play a game in small groups. One person says the name of a well-known place in nature (in their own language if necessary) and the others have to say what type of geographical feature it is.

3 Introduce the word *compass*. Point to the compass and ask students to repeat the directions *north*, *south*, *east*, *west* after you. Then tell students to look at the map and decide if the sentences are true or false.

Language note

When we use direction words to describe the location of one place to another, we say *north / south / east / west of*, eg *France is north of Spain.* As the Earth is round, this is relative to the position of the speaker; the world map on page 42 has Europe at the centre and directions are relative to there. An Australian map, for example, shows Australia at the centre and so the US is east of Australia if the speaker is in Australia.

> 1 T
> 2 F (It's west of Australia.)
> 3 F (It's east of Kenya.)
> 4 T
> 5 T
> 6 F (It's east of Australia.)

TEACH GLOBAL THINK LOCAL ### Extra activity

Students write some more sentences about the world map or about their own country, some of which are true and some false. They then exchange their sentences with a partner, who has to decide which ones are true and false.

Listening and Reading (SB page 42)

Here students listen and read about UNESCO World Heritage sites.

Background note

UNESCO, the United Nations Educational, Scientific and Cultural Organisation, was established in 1945. An international treaty allowing the creation of World Heritage sites was accepted by the United Nations in 1972.

1 🔘 **2.40** Write the title of the text on the board and ask students if they know what UNESCO is. You could use the information in the *Background note* to tell your students something about it. Do they know what a World Heritage site is? Tell them to read and listen to the text to find out. They should also tell you which place on the map is not one.

> The desert in Jordan is not a World Heritage site.

2 Students underline the correct answers, referring again to the text to help them if necessary. Before they start, point out that although there is no clear answer as to the number of countries in the world, there are at least 193.

> 1 Yes, it does.
> 2 No, it doesn't. (It has over 170 natural sites and over 670 cultural sites.)
> 3 Yes, it does. (It has 43.)
> 4 Yes, it does. (It has 15.)

3 Ask students if their country has any World Heritage or other important sites. If so, ask if they are cultural or natural sites, and where they are. In multilingual classes, encourage students to tell their classmates about sites other students might not be familiar with.

Reading (SB page 43)

1 Students read the questions about the Great Smoky Mountains National Park and match them to the answers. Check they understand the questions before they do this. Read through the information box about seasons with them and provide pronunciation practice by modelling each of the seasons for students to repeat. Point out that the *n* in *autumn* /ɔːtʌm/ is silent.

> 1 d   2 b   3 e   4 a   5 f   6 c

2 **2.41** Students listen and check their answers. Ask them if they think this is an interesting place to visit.

> **2.41**
>
> A: What's the name of the site?
>
> B: Great Smoky Mountains National Park.
>
> A: Where is it?
>
> B: It's in the south of the US – Tennessee and North Carolina.
>
> A: How much is it?
>
> B: Nothing! The park is free.
>
> A: Wow, and when is it open?
>
> B: It's open all day, every day.
>
> A: What are the main attractions?
>
> B: The park is great for walking. There are over 500 km of walks. The mountains are very popular and the fishing is good too!
>
> A: When is a good time to visit?
>
> B: Well, it's very busy in the summer. Spring and fall are seasons to visit. And the trees are beautiful in the fall.
>
> A: Great. Thanks!

Language note

The speakers use discourse markers *Wow* and *Well*. These do not add anything to the meaning of the sentences but keep the conversation flowing and show that the speakers are listening to each other.

Grammar and Speaking (SB page 43)

Here, the focus is on question words.

Focus students on the example questions and read through the explanation with them. By now these question words should be familiar, as they have met them all in previous units. Point out that short answers to *Wh*-questions can be single words or short phrases, and that long answers give more information and are sometimes expressed in complete sentences.

1 Students complete the questions about another UNESCO World Heritage site with the words in the box. Tell them to look at the answers to help them when they are doing this.

> 1 What
>
> 2 Where
>
> 3 What
>
> 4 When
>
> 5 How much

2 Put students in AB pairs. Refer As to page 97 and Bs to page 101. Explain that pairs should ask and answer the questions about each other's sites and write their partner's answers. When they finish, they should decide which of the two sites they like best. Invite some pairs to tell the class which site they like best. Do both of them like the same site? Find out if there is a general class preference for one of the sites.

ⓖ Grammar focus

Show students the icon. Write *page 110* on the board and ask them to find it. Show students the first part of the language summary on question words. You can use exercise 6 on page 111 for:

a) extra practice now

b) homework

c) review a couple of lessons from now.

The answers are on page 116 of the Teacher's Book.

Writing (SB page 43)

1 Students think of a place that they know and write their answers to the questions. Read through the questions with students first and check they understand that the answer to the last one could be a season or a month. Also point out that their choice doesn't have to be a natural place. It could be a museum, for example.

2 Students work in groups. They read each other's descriptions and decide which place they would like to visit.

Alternative procedure

Students could stick their descriptions on the walls of the class and then go round the class reading other students' descriptions in order to choose the place they would most like to visit. You could take a class vote to see which three places are the most popular.

Extra activity

Instead of reading each other's descriptions, students could ask and answer the questions about their places in pairs, and then swap pairs and repeat the activity as many times as is practical in your class. They could then decide which place they would most like to visit.

Part 2

Vocabulary (SB page 44)

Lead-in

If you think your students will know some of the words in the diagram, write the name of five people with different roles in your life on the board. Include a family member in order to review family relationships. Ask students to speculate about who the people are. Write on the board *Is he / she your ...?* to help them, and encourage students to tell each other any words they know. As they speculate, provide any words they need to use, but don't write these on the board.

1 **2.42** Focus students on the pictures and the diagram. Use the pictures to help teach the meaning of the new words, and then ask students to complete the diagram with the words *study*, *work* and *personal life*. Next, students listen and repeat all the words in the diagram. Pause the recording after each one to give students time to repeat them. Because of their spelling, words like *colleague*, *friend* and *neighbour* might need extra practice. Finally, point out how the words *friend* and *mate* combine with another word. Write *class + mate* on the board and ask students what word they make (*classmate*). Do the same for *flatmate*, *boyfriend* and *girlfriend*.

> **2.42**
>
> Work: my boss; a colleague
>
> Study: my teacher; a classmate
>
> Personal life: my flatmate; a friend; a neighbour; my girlfriend; my boyfriend

2 Students work in pairs. Student A says a word from exercise 1. Without looking at their book, Student B says the category that Student A's word is from. Then they swap roles and repeat. If necessary, demonstrate this with a student to make the activity clear.

Reading (SB page 44)

Students read about a company called Wild Things that organises safaris in Tanzania.

Lead-in

Focus students on the pictures that accompany the text on page 45. Can students guess what the relationship is between the people? Ask them to look at the title of the text. Does this help them? (They all work together.) If students don't know the word *safari*, explain what a safari is (see *Background note*).

UNIT 7 Places & People

Background note

The word *safari* comes from Swahili, an east African language that is official in Kenya and Tanzania. In Swahili, safari means 'journey'. In English, a safari is a holiday, especially in Africa, in which people travel to watch, photograph or hunt wild animals.

1 Ask students to look at the picture above *On safari* and read the short text about the company Wild Things. When they finish, check students have understood by asking what the connection is between the people in the pictures (they all work for the same company, Wild Things), and what Wild Things does (it organises safaris). If students are not familiar with the word *safari*, explain what people do on one.

2 Students read texts 1–6 about Salim's life. Then they look at the five underlined sentences and choose the one that describes each picture a, b and c. Check that the pictures make the meaning of the sentences clear, and review the word *alone* if necessary.

> a I'm a driver and a tour guide for Wild Things.
> b I take the visitors to three or four different National Parks.
> c At the weekends I go out with my friends.

3 Ask students to read the questions and check their meaning is clear. Point out that the *do* in the question *What do you do?* is used to ask about a person's job. In contrast, the *do* in *What do you do in your free time?* is used to ask about activities in general. Ask students to match the questions to Salim's answers in the text.

> Where do you work? 3
> What do you do? 1
> What time do you start work? 4
> Who do you live with? 5
> What do you do in your free time? 6
> Where are you from? 2

Grammar (SB page 45)

Here the focus is on present simple questions.

Focus students on the example questions and read through the explanations with them, pointing out that we use *does* with a third person singular subject. Highlight the form of questions, ie *question word + do / does + subject + infinitive* and write this on the board. Also remind students how we form questions with *be*. Write on the board *question word + am / are / is + subject* to remind students that we don't use *do / does* in these questions.

1 Students put the words in the correct order to make questions.

Pronunciation note

It's important for students to see that while adding -s or -es to form the third person singular form of a verb doesn't normally change the pronunciation of the verb, it does in the case of *do*. Model the pronunciation of *do* /duː/ and *does* /dʌz/, and get students to practise the two forms in isolation and then in the context of the questions.

> 1 What does she do?
> 2 Where does she work?
> 3 Who does she work with?
> 4 What time does she start work?

2 Students read the information about Cathy from Wild Things and answer the questions in exercise 1. Explain what a sales officer does and check that students understand *headquarters*.

> 1 She's a sales officer.
> 2 She works in the office at the Wild Things headquarters in Dar es Salaam.
> 3 She works with three colleagues, Tina, Tanya and Mariam.
> 4 She starts work at 9.00am.

3 Students write four questions using the words in the table. Suggest that they write one question for each question word, and explain that there are at least two possible questions for each of the question words.

> What time do you have breakfast / go to work / go to bed / study English?
> Where do you have breakfast / work / study English?
> When do you have breakfast / go to work / go to bed / study English?
> Who do you work with / live with?

4 Invite different students to read out their questions to see if they are appropriate, and make sure that all the different questions students have written are checked. Then practise pronouncing the questions by asking students to repeat a selection of them after you. Remind students that *do you* is pronounced as one word (*d'you*) and draw attention to the stress and intonation patterns in the questions. Finally, students ask and answer their questions in pairs.

Ⓖ Grammar focus

Show students the icon. Write *page 110* on the board and ask them to find it. Show students the second and third parts of the language summary on present simple questions. You can use exercises 7 and 8 on page 111 for:

a) extra practice now

b) homework

c) review a couple of lessons from now.

The answers are on page 117 of the Teacher's Book.

Speaking (SB page 45)

Ask students to write the name of one person they know well from *Vocabulary* exercise 1. Tell students they could talk about a family member if this would be easier for them. Then put students in pairs. They should ask their partner questions about their person, using the notes and the example conversation to help them. You could provide extra support by inviting students to suggest questions for the prompts before they start talking. When they finish, invite some pairs to repeat the activity in front of the class and give feedback as needed.

Global game

This game is designed to give students the opportunity to use and consolidate language from this unit and from previous units.

1 Students are going to play a board game, so you will need enough dice and counters for students to be able to play in small groups. If you don't have counters, suggest that students use different coins.

2 Focus students on the playing board and tell them that they are going to play the game in small groups. Look first at the *Useful language* phrases in the centre of the board. Check students understand these and practise pronouncing them as they will need to use them while playing.

3 Then explain the rules. Players take it in turns to roll a dice, move a counter or coin to the corresponding square, and then follow the instruction on the square to complete a task. The other members of the group have to decide if the player has carried out the task successfully. If they agree that he or she has done so, the player can stay on the square. If not, the player has to go back to where they were. Now, the next player has a turn. The game continues until one player reaches the middle of the board. If the other members of the group cannot decide if a player has carried out the task successfully, they should consult you for a final decision.

4 As groups play, monitor the tasks. Give immediate feedback where practical, but also note any problems to deal with at the end of the game with the whole class. When groups finish, suggest that they play again, or, if some groups finish at around the same time, that students form new groups and play again.

Global review

These activities can be used at home but are designed to be used in class with students working together in pairs.

Aim: to review the language of the unit.

Tips:

- Encourage students to work together.
- Allow them to look back through the unit or consult their notes.
- In feedback, elicit more examples or the reason why an answer is correct.

Vocabulary (SB page 47)

1
1 mountain
2 forest
3 desert
4 island
5 river
6 national park
7 lake

2
1 neighbour
2 colleague
3 teacher
4 girlfriend
5 classmate

3
spring; summer; autumn; winter

4
1 **have** breakfast, a shower (lunch, dinner, etc)
2 **go** to the gym, to my English class (to a shopping centre, to bed, etc)
3 **start** my day, work (school, a conversation, etc)
4 **study** English, Chinese (Italian, Spanish, etc)
5 **like** Brazilian music, football (American football, coffee, etc)

Grammar (SB page 47)

1
1 Who?
2 How much?
3 What time?
4 How much?
5 Where?
6 When?
7 What time?
8 Where?
9 Who?
10 When?

Listen again (SB page 47)

The *Listen again* text in this unit comes from *Reading* exercise 2 on page 43, in which two people talk about the Smoky Mountains National Park. Here, students listen again to work on question words.

1–3 💿 **2.43**
What; Where; How much; when; What; When

In & Out

Coursebook

Unit 8	Language	Texts	Communicative skills
Part 1 SB page 48	Vocabulary and Speaking Food Pronunciation Consonant clusters	Reading and Speaking *Eating in, Cuban style*	Functional language Offering
Part 2 SB page 50	Vocabulary and Pronunciation Days of the week Extend your Vocabulary *classes* Grammar Adverbs of frequency	Listening and Reading Going out in London	Writing Eating out
Global voices SB page 52	Listening to people talking about what they eat and drink at home Language focus: *every* Speaking about what you eat and drink at home		
Global review SB page 53	Food and places to go out Describing eating habits and how often you do other things More practice with making, accepting and refusing offers		

Additional resources

eWorkbook	Interactive and printable grammar, vocabulary, listening and pronunciation practice Extra reading and writing practice Additional downloadable listening and audio material
TB resource CD	Communication activity worksheets to print and photocopy
Go global Ideas for further research	**In** Ask students to find out which types of food from other countries they can eat in restaurants where they live. **Out** Ask students to visit the *Time Out* website and find one restaurant they would like to eat at in three different cities.

Part 1

Vocabulary and Speaking (SB page 48)

Lead-in

Draw what you had for breakfast this morning on the board (or your last meal if you didn't have breakfast). Say *This is my breakfast* and invite students to tell you what the food is by pointing to things and asking *What's this?* Don't explicitly teach any new words at this point as the activity serves to establish the theme. Students could do the same activity in pairs.

1 Focus students on the spider diagrams and explain that they show things people eat and drink for lunch or dinner. The pictures should make the meanings of *drinks*, *dessert* and *main course* clear, but give further explanation if not. Ask students to complete the diagrams with the words in the box. They have met *coffee* and *tea* in previous units, but encourage them to try and match the other words to pictures without help as some of the other words are cognates in some languages. Put them in pairs to do the activity if necessary.

2 **2.44** Students listen and check their answers. Play the recording again for students to repeat the words, pausing if necessary to give them time to do this. Some words might be tricky for students, so give plenty of practice. Point out the weak vowels in *vegetables* (which has three syllables and a silent second *e*) /ˈvedʒtəbəlz/, *potatoes* /pəˈteɪtəʊz/, *pasta* /ˈpæstə/ and *water* /ˈwɔːtə(r)/.

 2.44

Main course:

potatoes

meat

fish

cheese

rice

eggs

vegetables

pasta

Drinks:

juice

tea

coffee

water

Dessert:

fruit

cakes

ice cream

---

3 Students write which food and drink from exercise 1 they have for breakfast, lunch and dinner. Focus them on the example so that they understand what to do.

4 Students compare their answers to exercise 3 in pairs and find out what's the same and what's different. Write the following question prompt on the board to help them do this: *What do you have for ...?* When pairs finish, ask some to tell the class what they found out. Write on the board: *We have (food / drink) for (meal). (Name) has (food / drink) for (meal) and I don't have (food / drink).*

5 Working in different pairs if practical, students ask and answer the questions. Practise pronouncing the questions first, and then focus on the example answer to help them before they start talking. When they finish, you could take a class vote to find out what the class's favourite main course, dessert and drink is.

Pronunciation (SB page 48)

1 **2.45** The pronunciation point here is consonant clusters, which can be difficult for students if they don't occur in their first language(s). Ask students to listen and repeat the words, being careful with the underlined sounds. Invite individual students to say each of the words to see which ones create problems, and give extra practice with these.

2 Students work in pairs. They take it in turns to point to a word. Their partner says the word and they say *Good!* or *Try again!* depending on how well their partner pronounced it. Then they change roles.

Extra activity

If consonant clusters are difficult for your students, find other examples for them to practise. Some words that have come up in previous units are *picture*, *bank*, *Spain*, *Portugal*, *children*, *basketball*.

Reading and Speaking (SB page 49)

Students read about a type of restaurant in Cuba called a *paladar*.

Background note

Cuba has had small, privately owned restaurants for a long time, but they were illegal until the early 1990s. Their name comes from a popular Brazilian soap opera in which a poor woman manages to open a restaurant called 'Paladar'. In Portuguese, *paladar* means taste or flavour.

1 Focus students on the picture and ask what they can see in it. If they recognise that it's a restaurant, ask where it is. If they don't know, ask them to look at the title of the text. Now students read the text and find out what is special about paladar restaurants.

> Paladar restaurants are special because they are in a family home and the family cooks the food.

2 Students read the text again and decide if the questions are true or false.

> 1 T
>
> 2 F (The family cooks Cuban food.)
>
> 3 F (A maximum of 12 people eat in the restaurant.)
>
> 4 F (Tourists and Cuban people like these restaurants.)
>
> 5 T

3 Students work in pairs to ask and answer the questions. Read through the questions with students first and check that they understand them. Then give them a little time to think about their answers. Tell them they can make notes if they are not confident about speaking yet.

When students finish speaking, invite some pairs to tell the class what their partner told them. In multilingual classes, talk about whether there are restaurants in family homes where students come from, and if so, how they work and what type of food you can eat in them. Finally, find out if most students like eating at home or in restaurants, and why.

4 Put students in pairs. Refer As to page 97 and Bs to page 101. Explain that pairs should read about eating at home in Italy or Peru and then tell each other about it. As they listen to their partner, they should circle the food and drink that people have there in the table provided. In stronger classes, encourage students to try and remember the information in the description and not to refer to the book unless they really need to.

When they finish, tell them to show each other the completed tables to check answers. If anyone in your class is familiar with eating at home in Italy or Peru, ask them if they can tell the class anything else about mealtimes. If not, ask which way of eating at home is more similar to their own country, and why.

TEACH GLOBAL
THINK LOCAL **Extra activity**

Refer students to the world map on page 42. In pairs, ask students to see if they know where Cuba, Italy and Peru are. Check answers, and if your students come from different countries, invite them to show other students where they come from on the map.

Functional language (SB page 49)

This section focuses on expressions for offering food and drink.

1 Ask students to read the conversation and to tell you who the people are (they are friends) and what the situation is (one person is at the other person's home).

Make sure this is clear, and then ask students to complete the conversation with the words in the box. Suggest they do this in pairs if you think your students will find this difficult. Finally, invite a pair of students to read out the conversation. Do other students agree with their answers? If not, ask what they put, but don't say who has the right answers.

2 ● 2.46 Students listen and check their answers. Ask if they think B likes the cake? Ask them to say why or why not. (This should be clear from the way B talks about it.) Then check the meaning or function of any new words and expressions. *Would you like ...?* should be treated as a lexical chunk, used to offer things, and shouldn't be analysed grammatically. Look at the different ways this question is used in the conversation.

> ● **2.46**
>
> A: Would you like something to drink?
>
> B: Yes, please. Do you **have** apple juice?
>
> A: Sure. Here you are.
>
> B: **Thank you**.
>
> A: Would you like something to **eat**?
>
> B: What's that?
>
> A: It's Battenberg. It's a type of cake. Would **you** like to try some?
>
> B: OK. Mmm – it's delicious.
>
> A: Would you like some more cake?
>
> B: Um, **no** thanks.

3 ● 2.47 Students listen and repeat the five phrases from the conversation. As they practise pronouncing the phrases, focus on intonation and stress patterns. Also point out linking in *Would you, Do you* and *It's a* and the weak form of *to* and *of* in *something to drink* and *type of cake*.

4 In pairs, students practise the conversation.

TEACH GLOBAL
THINK LOCAL **Extra activity**

As in Unit 4, you could give extra practice here by writing the conversation on the board as students are practising it, and then asking students to close their books. Rub out four or five words, and replace them by lines. Students practise the conversation again. Continue until there are no words left on the board, just lines. This will help students to memorise the new phrases in the conversation.

5 Write the phrases on the board and elicit ways to complete them. Suggest students look back at the conversation for initial ideas, but encourage them to think of other options too. Now ask students to write two endings for each phrase, and invite some students to read out their ideas. Write some of these on the board and focus on *a* and *some* after *Would you like …?* Point out that we use *a* to mean *one* for things you can count and *some* for things you can't count.

Possible answers

Would you like a sandwich?

Would you like some water?

Do you have potatoes?

Do you have coffee?

It's a type of dessert.

It's a type of cheese.

Language note

With stronger students, you might want to introduce the concept of countable and uncountable nouns here, and teach how we use *a*, *some* and *any*. This language is taught explicitly in *Global Elementary*, but you could explain that we use *a* before a singular countable noun, and *some* and *any* before uncountable and plural nouns. Point out that we normally use *any* in questions, but that *some* is often more natural in the question *Would you like …?* To practise this language point, ask students to complete these phrases with countable and uncountable nouns:

Would you like a …?

Would you like some …?

Do you have a …?

Do you have any …?

6 Students work in pairs. They imagine that Student B is at Student A's house and have a conversation like the one in exercise 1, using the phrases in the *Useful phrases* box to help them. Give ongoing feedback, and then comment on any common problems with the whole class. Students should now repeat the conversation with a different partner. Invite some pairs to act out their conversation for the whole class when they finish.

Part 2

Vocabulary and Pronunciation (SB page 50)

Lead-in

Days of the week are a vocabulary set that some students might know, so ask students *What day is it today?* If they know, ask if they can name other days of the week.

1 🔊 **2.48** Students number the names of the week in the correct order. Ask them to do this in pairs if you know that they would find it difficult to do this alone. Then play the recording for students to check their answers. Point out that in English, days of the week always start with a capital letter – this is not the case in all languages.

---

1 Monday

2 Tuesday

3 Wednesday

4 Thursday

5 Friday

6 Saturday

7 Sunday

---

2 Students listen again and repeat the words. Pause the recording if they need extra time to mark the stress. Point out that the stress is on the first syllable in all the words, that the *d* in *Wednesday* is silent and that *Monday* rhymes with *Sunday*.

Extra activity

If students have diaries with them, they could practise the days of the week by asking each other questions about when different special days occur during this year and / or next year, depending on when your class takes place – their birthdays, festivals, etc. Write on the board *When's … this / next year?* and *It's on (day of the week)* to help them do this and make it clear they are not expected to talk about dates here.

3 Students write their answers to the questions. Read through the questions with them before they do this to check their meaning is clear, especially the phrase *go out with your friends and family*. Also teach *because* so that students can follow up each question with why and give their reasons.

4 Students work in pairs and compare their answers to the questions. Practise the pronunciation of the questions before they do this.

5 Establish the meaning of *weekend* – two consecutive days in a week when many people don't work – and ask students which days are the weekend in their country. In multilingual classes, take time to listen to all their answers so that students can learn from each other.

Then students work in pairs to guess which countries in the box have their weekends on which days. Finally, look at the *Language note* with students and highlight the use of the prepositions *at* and *during*. Teach or remind them that we use the preposition *on* with a particular day.

> 1 Egypt and Saudi Arabia
> 2 Jordan
> 3 Poland

Listening and Reading (SB page 50)

Students read and listen to four people talking about going out in London.

Background note

The original *Time Out* magazine was first published in 1968 and tells you about films, concerts and other free-time events in London. *Time Out* now produces versions of its magazine for other cities and countries around the world, including Barcelona, Beirut, Jakarta, New York, Sydney, Tel Aviv, Abu Dhabi, Bahrain, Bali, Dubai and Singapore.

1 🔊 **2.49–2.52** Focus students on pictures a–f at the top of the page and check that they understand the meaning of the places written under them. Tell them that they are going to listen to four people talking about going out in London. Students listen to the people and decide which place in the pictures they do not talk about – that is, none of the four speakers mentions this place.

> They do not talk about restaurants (c).
>
> Charlie and Danny both talk about food; Charlie refers to *hamburgers* as fast food; Danny mentions *hamburgers*.

2 Ask students to look at the text on page 51. Ask if students know what *Time Out* magazine is, and tell them the information contained in the *Background note*.

Students read the text and match the speakers to the places. Explain that some pictures match more than one speaker.

After checking answers, ask students if they are similar to one of the speakers and if so, why. Finally, draw attention to the quotation under the text. Ask students to read it, and the information about it, and discuss what it means. In monolingual classes, you could ask students to agree on a translation for the quotation. Does the quotation apply to a city that they know?

> Andrea: b
> Ben: d, f
> Charlie: e
> Danny: a, e, f

Extend your vocabulary (SB page 50)

Focus students on the example sentence and ask what they think evening classes are. Do your students go to evening classes? Is *this* class an evening class? Now look at the words in the box and check that students understand them all. Ask students to complete the sentences with the words, individually first before comparing with a partner. Finally, ask students if they go to any of the classes. If so, on what day and at what time? Where are the classes?

> 1 language
> 2 art
> 3 cookery
> 4 computer
> 5 music

Grammar (SB page 51)

Here the focus is on adverbs of frequency.

Read through the examples with students and point out that they come from the texts about going out in London. Explain that the words in bold are adverbs of frequency, and tell you how often or frequently a person does something. Now read the explanation and highlight the word order with *be* and other verbs. This is a key aspect of this grammar, so to draw attention to it, you could ask students to find and underline the verbs in the sentences.

1 Students write the missing letters to complete the adverbs. Tell them that they can find all the words in the grammar box. Now focus on their meaning. To do this, point out the percentages beside the words. If this isn't completely clear, you could refer to days of the week. Write on the board. *I … have coffee for breakfast.* Explain that adding *always* means seven days a week. Adding *never* means on no days. *Usually* means five or six days, and *sometimes* means two or three days. Now practise pronouncing the adverbs. Some of the sounds, eg the first *a* in *always* and the *s* in *usually*, will be difficult for some nationalities. Point out the weak vowel sound in *never* and *us<u>ua</u>lly*.

> always
> usually
> sometimes
> never

2 Students underline the best adverb to make true sentences about the four people in the *Listening and Reading* section.

1	usually
2	always
3	always
4	sometimes

3 Students add *always*, *usually* and *sometimes* to the questions. Make it clear that they can decide which adverb to use, though some adverbs are more natural than others in some of the questions (see the suggested answers). Invite different students to read out their questions to check word order, and then practise pronouncing the questions.

Suggested answers

1 Do you **sometimes / usually / always** go to the cinema during the week?

2 Do you **sometimes / usually / always** go to the theatre with your family?

3 Do you **always** go to your English classes?

4 Do you **sometimes** go to cafés?

5 Do you **sometimes / usually / always** eat fast food for dinner?

4 In pairs, students ask each other their questions from exercise 3. Before they do this, run through possible answers and write these on the board: *Yes, I do. / No I don't. Yes, sometimes / usually / always. No, never.* You could ask one or two students the questions to show how the answers work. When they finish, invite some pairs to tell the class their partner's answers.

G Grammar focus

Show students the icon. Write *page 112* on the board and ask them to find it. Show students the language summary on adverbs of frequency. You can use exercises 1–3 on page 113 for:

a) extra practice now

b) homework

c) review a couple of lessons from now.

The answers are on page 117 of the Teacher's Book.

Writing (SB page 51)

1 Students read the text about eating out and find five spelling mistakes.

> I **usually** go out to eat on **Thursday** night. I sometimes have **Italian** food – I love pizza and spaghetti! My favourite **restaurant** is called Luigi's. I also eat a lot of **Chinese** food because I like rice. I never eat meat, I don't like it ...

2 Students choose one of the tasks for their writing. Read through the tasks so students are clear what they involve and where they can find a model to support their work. As they write, go round and monitor their work, paying particular attention to the use of adverbs of frequency.

TEACH GLOBAL THINK LOCAL Extra activity

When students finish their writing, ask them to exchange their work with a partner, and to find two or three things in common. Invite some pairs to tell the class about these things.

Global voices

These lessons in *Global* are designed to provide students with exposure to authentic speakers of English from both native and non-native English backgrounds. In this unit we extend the theme of food.

Warm up (SB page 52)

1 Students look at the pictures and complete them with the words from the box.

1	sushi
2	chicken, lamb

Listening (SB page 52)

Here, students listen to people from Italy, Saudi Arabia and Japan talking about the food they eat and drink at home.

1 **2.53–2.57** Students listen to five people answer the question *What do you eat and drink at home?* and tick the food or drink in the table that they talk about.

	Katerina, Italy	Abdul, Saudi Arabia	Ryusuke, Japan	Omar, Saudi Arabia	Francesco, Italy
rice		✓		✓	
pasta			✓		✓
coffee	✓				
sushi			✓		
chicken		✓		✓	
pizza			✓		

 2.53–2.57

Katerina, Italy
I always, always every day have breakfast at 8 o'clock in the morning with my family, coffee is very important to wake us up and also some biscuits and some croissant with marmalade.

Abdul, Saudi Arabia
I eat dinner sometimes, but the main meal for me is lunch which is rice with lamb or chicken.

Ryusuke, Japan
I usually have er … dinner – for example I eat pasta and pizza and also Japanese traditional food such as sushi, Japanese omelettes and so on.

Omar, Saudi Arabia
Usually I like to eat rice. We eat it for lunch time. It's so simple – rice and chicken, lamb and some vegetable with it.

Francesco, Italy
Well, we're Italian so usually we eat pasta – that's the best thing we can find in Italy.

2 Students listen again and decide if the sentences are true or false.

1	T
2	F (It's lunch.)
3	F (He has pasta or pizza for dinner.)
4	F (He usually has rice for lunch.)
5	F (He usually has pasta.)

Language focus: *every* (SB page 52)

Ask students to read the *Language note*. Point out that *every* is used before words like *day, Friday, morning, weekend,* and that the phrase normally comes at the end of the sentence. Now students put the words in the correct order in the exercise.

1	I eat with my family every Sunday.
2	She goes to salsa classes every week.
3	We eat fast food every Friday.
4	I drink coffee every morning.
5	Do you eat pasta every day?

Speaking (SB page 52)

In pairs, students ask each other the question *What do you eat and drink at home?* and try to use adverbs of frequency, *every* and *a type of* in their answers if appropriate. Draw attention to the example conversation to help them, and give them time to prepare their answers if this would make the activity more successful.

Global review

These activities are designed to review the content of the unit. They can be used at home but are designed to be used in class with students working together in pairs.

Aim: to review the language of the unit.

Tips:

- Encourage students to work together.
- Allow them to look back through the unit or consult their notes.
- In feedback, elicit more examples or the reason why an answer is correct.

Vocabulary (SB page 53)

In exercise 1, let students try the exercise first and then give them the defining words in the wrong order if they need help – *place/meal, food/drink, work/place, snack/Italian, drink/dessert*.

1

1 *Café* is different because it's a place / it isn't a meal.

2 *Rice* is different because it's a food / it isn't a drink.

3 *Office* is different because it's a workplace.

4 *Sandwich* is different because it's a snack / it isn't Italian.

5 *Tea* is different because it's a drink / it isn't a dessert.

2

1 breakfast

2 café

3 fruit

4 language

5 dessert

3

Monday: 1

Wednesday: 3

Saturday: 6

Sunday: 7

Thursday: 4

Friday: 5

Tuesday: 2

4

Students' own answers.

Grammar (SB page 53)

1

1 coffee

2 ice cream

3 a sandwich

4 rice

2

1 I always have breakfast at 8 o'clock.

2 They never do their English homework.

3 Do you usually have breakfast at home?

4 She is sometimes late for work.

5 This is always a busy restaurant.

Listen again (SB page 53)

The *Listen again* text in this unit comes from the *Functional language* on page 49 in which two friends talk about food. Here students listen again and put the conversation in order.

In exercise 3, make it clear to students that the extra words are not incorrect, and that the conversation is correct with and without them.

1–3 2.58

A: It's Battenberg. It's a ~~special~~ type of cake. Would you like to try some? 7

A: Would you like some more cake? 9

A: Would you like ~~to have~~ something to eat? 5

A: Sure. Here you are. 3

A: Would you like ~~to have~~ something to drink? 1

B: Yes, please. Do you have apple juice? 2

B: Thank you ~~very much~~. 4

B: Um, no thanks. ~~I'm fine~~. 10

B: What's that ~~there~~? 6

B: OK. ~~Thanks~~. Mmm – it's delicious. 8

Here & There

Coursebook

Unit 9	Language	Texts	Communicative skills
Part 1 SB page 54	Vocabulary Rooms and furniture Grammar Prepositions of place	Reading and Listening *Living underground*	Speaking Giving opinions
Part 2 SB page 56	Vocabulary and Speaking Types of transport Grammar Imperatives Pronunciation Sentence stress	Reading and Vocabulary *48 hours in Vancouver*	Functional language Making recommendations Writing 48 hours in ...
Global reading SB page 58	Reading about forms of transport Deciding on suitable forms of transport for people		
Global review SB page 59	Rooms and furniture in a house *in, next to, on, under* Writing sentences to describe a room Beginnings and endings of sentences		

Additional resources

eWorkbook	Interactive and printable grammar, vocabulary, listening and pronunciation practice Extra reading and writing practice Additional downloadable listening and audio material
TB resource CD	Communication activity worksheets to print and photocopy
Go global Ideas for further research	**Here** Ask students to find photographs of three unusual houses on the internet, and to prepare to discuss why they find them interesting. **There** Ask students to find out about another city they would like to visit, and to come with information and pictures, if possible, to describe their cities in class.

Part 1

Lead-in

Tell students that you are going to draw a picture of something and that they need to guess what it is. Start drawing a house slowly, line by line, part by part. You can make it more tricky by doing the details first rather than the outline, and by not drawing the obvious, eg a round window, not a square one.

Vocabulary (SB page 54)

1 Focus students on the picture of the doll's house. Ask them to work in pairs to point to the rooms and say the name of each.

a	bathroom
b	bedroom
c	living room
d	kitchen

2 💿 **2.59** Students listen and repeat. Pay particular attention to any problematic words, containing tricky sounds, eg *kitchen* /ˈkɪtʃən/ and *bathroom* /ˈbɑːθˌruːm/. To focus on this language further, students draw four bubbles in their books, one for each room. Then randomly dictate house objects they should know, eg *bed*, *shower*, etc. Students write each word in the appropriate circle.

3 💿 **2.60** Draw attention to the small pictures around the main picture of the house. Students listen and repeat the names of the rooms and the furniture in them.

> 💿 **2.60**
> Bathroom: shower; bath; washbasin; toilet; door
> Bedroom: bed; lamp
> Living room: sofa; armchair; TV, bookshelf
> Kitchen: cooker; fridge; sink; table; chair; window

4 Read out the example given, asking students to say if this is true or false. Then students do the same with the five sentences, working individually initially, then checking in pairs.

1	F
2	T
3	F (There is one sofa and an armchair.)
4	T
5	T

5 Write *In the classroom there is / there are ...* on the board. Elicit a possible ending. Put students in pairs and give them four minutes to write as many complete sentences as possible. Emphasise the limited time limit, to add a competitive element. Hear some examples at the end and

put any useful vocabulary which comes up on the board, eg *board*, *light*.

Language note

For your own interest, note that increasingly nowadays fluent speakers use *there is* even with a <u>plural</u> noun, eg *There's two sofas in the living room.*

Writing extra

If your students would benefit from extra practice, find two pictures of rooms in magazines – if possible of the same room, eg a living room. Photocopy them and put students in pairs. Students should write five sentences to describe the living room, including one false one. (If students need help here, put them in A and B pairs at this writing stage, then regroup to mixed pairs.) Students then give their partner their statements and picture. Their partner spots the false statement.

Reading and Listening (SB page 55)

1 Students first read the information under the *Living underground* heading and decide whether it's hot or cold (it's hot).

2 💿 **2.61** Tell students they are going to find out why Merv lives in an underground house. Ask students if they think they know the answer before listening.

> It is very hot outside. The house never gets too hot or cold.

> 💿 **2.61**
> G'day! I live in Coober Pedy. This is a town in South Australia. It's in the desert and it's very hot in the summer! I live in an underground house. An underground house is great because it's never very hot or very cold. Come on in!

3 💿 **2.62** Refer students to the picture of the doll's house on page 54. Tell them they should tick the things that they hear. Give an example, showing a tick (✓) on the board.

> The following which Merv mentions appear on page 54:
> kitchen: fridge, cooker, table, chairs
> living room: chairs, sofa, lamps
> bathroom: shower

> 💿 **2.62**
> This is the kitchen. We have a fridge and a cooker of course. We eat in here so there's a table and chairs too. The living room is next to the kitchen, with a sofa, more chairs ... There are lots of lamps because there are no windows. And this is the bathroom. We have a shower but no bath. It's fun living in an underground house!

9 Here & There

Background note

Coober Pedy is a small town of 3,500 inhabitants in the outback of South Australia, about 1,000 kilometres from Adelaide. It is the world's largest opal mining centre but is also well known for its accommodation: many people live underground, often in converted mines. In winter (April to October) the daytime temperature is pleasant at 16–20 °C, but in summer (November to March), it is 35–45 °C in the shade. The nights can be very cool. This is a semi-desert area, with dust storms.

Grammar (SB page 55)

Students close books. Write the two example sentences on the board, with the prepositions omitted:
I live _____ an underground house.
The living room is _____ _____ the kitchen.

Elicit the missing words and write the word *preposition* on the board too. You can translate this word into students' first language, if possible and appropriate. Read out the two rules, giving examples from the classroom to help clarify what they mean.

1 Focus students on the pictures of the cats, and the preposition. Then ask them to refer to the pictures of Merv's house and to complete the sentences. Do the first example together. Take whole class feedback.

1	in
2	on
3	under
4	next to

2 **2.63** Let students look at the two pictures of the bedrooms. In pairs let them describe the pictures to each other before listening.

Then ask students to listen to Merv and find out which bedroom is his. Play the recording and if necessary, replay it before feedback.

Picture 2

> **2.63**
>
> And this is the bedroom. We have a bed of course, and a small table next to the bed. There aren't any windows but there's a lamp on the table. Oh and our cat is under the bed!

3 Put students in AB pairs. As turn to page 98, Bs to page 102. Be prepared to stage this activity carefully. Ask students to read exercise 1 and check where they are going to draw their furniture, in plan A or B. Give them a two-minute time limit and monitor to check students are on task. Then ask the As to describe their rooms to the Bs, who listen and draw in the blank plan. Give an example first, eg *The TV is next to the window*. Then they swap roles. Finally, students compare their drawings with their partners' originals.

G Grammar focus

Show students the icon. Write *page 112* on the board and ask them to find it. Show students the rest of the language summary on prepositions of place.

Speaking (SB page 55)

Ask students: *Does Merv like living underground?* Give students a couple of minutes to read the task. Ask a strong student to be A; you, the teacher, are B. Model the task for the class. Particularly with stronger students, give reasons why you would (not) like a particular place. Then students work in groups to discuss.

TEACH GLOBAL THINK LOCAL **Extra activity**

Bring in about 12–14 objects from home and arrange them on your desk, possibly on a tray, eg a cup, a spoon, a key, etc. Students should know all or most of the words; write any new ones up. Put some of the items *next to* each other, *under*, *on*, *in* etc, eg the key in the cup. Students come up and memorise the objects and their position for two minutes. Then cover up the objects with a shawl or sheet.

Ask students to first write all the items down. Take feedback, then ask about eight questions, eg *Where is the key?* Students write down the answer in each case, eg *It's in the cup*. In whole class feedback, put students into teams of two or three to confer. Award points for correct answers (both linguistically and factually).

Part 2

Vocabulary and Speaking (SB page 56)

1 Write up *Different types of transport* on the board. Hold up the book and point at the pictures. Ask *What are these?* to elicit the different types. Students then work in pairs to discuss the question given.

2 **2.64** Students listen and repeat. At the end, ask which one was different, writing up *on foot*. Read out the *Language note* in the book. Ask a student who you know walks or cycles to their lesson: *How do you come to class?* Answer: *by bike / I ride a bike* or *on foot / I walk*.

 2.64

by train

by bus

on foot

by bike

by car

by plane

TEACH GLOBAL THINK LOCAL Extra activity

As preparation for exercise 3, prepare six possible answers to the six questions eg:

Most people go by car.

By bus.

We go by plane.

To the river.

Yes, in the summer time, with my brother.

I like to go by train.

Write these answers on the board, jumbled. Students in pairs match the answers to the questions.

---

3 Before students ask each other three questions, let different students ask you the questions. Give interesting answers in each case, trying also to give simple reasons why, if appropriate. Students then work in pairs. Early finishers can ask the remaining questions. Monitor and take feedback on any problem areas or points of interest.

Reading and Vocabulary (SB page 56)

1 Write up *Vancouver* on the board, and ask students if they know anything about it. Warn students they will have only two minutes to read (signal the text here) and find out who the information is for. Take feedback after they have read the text.

It's for tourists.

Background note

Vancouver is a busy city on the west coast of Canada, just north of the United States. It has a population of around 600,000 people (Canada's 8th city) and is a vibrant port. Tourism is one of its biggest industries, as well as forestry, and the film and software industries. Vancouver is a multicultural city, attracting people from around the world, both to live and visit. It is very beautiful, surrounded by forests, the ocean and mountains. There are plenty of parklands within the city itself too.

2 Tell students they will now read the text more carefully to answer the questions. When they have finished reading, let students compare answers in pairs before taking whole class feedback. You could also teach the expressions *Would you like to go here? What would you like to do or see there?*

Children: Stanley Park

Shopping: Chinatown

Art: Museum of Anthropology

Sports: Stanley Park

General idea of city: Vancouver Lookout

Relax: Chinese Garden in Chinatown

---

3 Students work alone to fill in the missing words. For stronger students, you could see if they can remember without looking at the text, at least initially.

---

1 fantastic   2 fascinating   3 close

---

4 This exercise focuses further on the meaning of the words. Let students work alone before checking answers in the whole class.

---

1 close to   2 fascinating   3 fantastic

Note that *close* is followed by *to* + noun, but *near* does not need *to*, eg *the hotel is near (to) the centre*.

TEACH GLOBAL THINK LOCAL Reading extra

This text contains lots of useful phrases which you could highlight to students. Students close their books. Write the four jumbled sentences below on a handout or on the board. Use a capital letter to highlight the first word. Students order them in pairs. Monitor and assist less strong students by showing the second and third words in each sentence to help. Students check with the text.

1 *city centre park the is to lovely This close*

2 *place the all is great It a for family*

3 *garden tired relax the When Chinese in are beautiful you*

4 *the one of and eat many in restaurants wonderful markets in the Go shopping*

Grammar (SB page 57)

Write the three examples on the board as follows:

Go   the city.
Don't forget   shopping.
See   to visit Chinatown.

Students match the two parts of each sentence correctly. Tell students that this form is called the *imperative*, writing this up on the board. Then read out the other general rules, with students following.

1 Ask students to re-read the Vancouver text and underline examples of the imperative. Tell students there are eleven examples. Take feedback, putting (some of) them on the board.

See the city
Visit the Vancouver Lookout for fantastic 360° views of the city, mountains and the Pacific Ocean.

Visit Chinatown
Don't forget to visit Chinatown - it's a fascinating place to visit. **Go shopping** in the markets and **eat** in one of the many wonderful restaurants. When you're tired, **relax** in the beautiful Sun Yat Sen Chinese Garden.

See a museum
Take the bus to the Museum of Anthropology near the University. The museum has 13,000 examples of art from many cultures. The totem poles are fantastic.

Go for a bike ride
Stanley Park is a major tourist attraction. This lovely park is close to the city centre. It's a great place for all the family: there's Vancouver Aquarium and a miniature train for children, a forest with all types of animals and birds, and sports such as golf and tennis. **Rent** a bike – it's a very good way to see the park.

---

2 Students read and complete the text individually.

3 **2.65** Students listen and check their answers

🔘 **2.65**

Gastown is the old part of Vancouver. **Go** for a walk in the historic streets, **have** lunch at the Water Street Café, **go** shopping or **visit** its museums and galleries. It's a fantastic place.

Language note

Students will meet more functions of the imperative at higher levels, eg for giving orders and rules, warnings, instructions. Generally speaking, students find this form conceptually easy. The imperative can only be used in this way where the unspoken subject is *you*, either singular or plural.

G Grammar focus

Show students the icon. Write *page 112* on the board and ask them to find it. Show students the language summary on imperatives. You can use exercises 4–6 on page 113 for:

a) extra practice now

b) homework

c) review a couple of lessons from now.

The answers are on page 117 of the Teacher's Book.

Pronunciation (SB page 57)

1 🔘 **2.66** Tell students to underline just one word in each phrase. Take feedback, then replay the recording. Students repeat.

Go for a <u>walk</u>.

Have a <u>coffee</u>.

Take the <u>bus</u>.

Visit the <u>park</u>.

Pronunciation note

When working on pronunciation, make sure that students do not come across as rude, ie they sound as if they are giving orders rather than recommendations. This sometimes happens if they overstress the verb (see exercise 1). Model clearly, softening the expressions with your intonation and facial expression.

---

2 Write several situations on the board, eg *Your partner is too hot* or *Your partner is tired*. Elicit an example, eg *Open the window!* Students then work alone to write one imperative phrase for each situation. Stronger students can write two recommendations.

Functional language (SB page 57)

This section focuses on making recommendations.

1 Let students read the sentences, and then elicit other possible matches for *Eat the local fish*, eg *It's fantastic*. Then students work in pairs to match the others. Take feedback.

---

1 b, c, d

2 a, b, d, e

3 a, d, e

4 a, d, e

5 b, d, e

---

2 Draw students' attention to the *Useful language* expressions. Elicit an example first. Ensure that there is a follow-on comment, eg *It's really beautiful*, by prompting with *Why?* Then students think of their own town or country. Give students a few minutes to write these down. Monitor and assist at this stage. Then students work in pairs to give their recommendations.

Writing (SB page 57)

1 Encourage students to use the same title as the Vancouver text: *48 hours in (city)* and to use at least three sub-headings, as in the example text. Write the framework up on the board. Remind them of the two language areas: imperatives and adjectives. As they are writing, monitor and assist, providing dictionaries if possible. Early finishers can write a little more. Encourage stronger students to include some recommendations with *Don't …*

2 Ask a stronger student to read out one of their paragraphs; ask him / her two questions about what they have written (write two question marks on the board as you do so, to focus students). Then students read their partner's work silently, before asking two or more questions in the same way.

Global reading

The *Global reading* pages encourage students to approach different text types and develop the ability to read for pleasure. This text is a set of travel directions.

1 Elicit the names of the two biggest airports near London: *Gatwick* and *Heathrow*. Tell students they are going to find out about how to get from Gatwick to central London. Students look at the pictures and complete the missing headings. After feedback, highlight to students what the text genre is (a leaflet informing visitors how to get to the capital).

By train	By taxi	By car	By bus

2 Tell students that they are going to read the text, but not to worry if they do not understand every word. Most of the answers simply require students to scan the text for numbers.

Transport	train	taxi	car	bus
Journey time	30 mins	55–70 mins	60–75 mins	60 or 90 mins
Price	Express class: £17 / £29 1st class: £25/£48	£75–£100	special £8 charge	Easy Bus: from £2 National Express: £7.60
Frequency	every 15 mins	–	–	EB: every 20 mins NE: every 60 mins

3 Tell students which form of transport you would use, if you were going to spend one week in central London with your family. Give reasons why. Then students work in pairs to make recommendations to the five visitors to Gatwick, and give reasons. Students should just talk and remember, not write. Take feedback.

Possible answers

1 Bus, because it's cheap.

2 Taxi, because it's very quick and takes up to five people.

3 Train, because their hotel is near Victoria Station.

4 Taxi, because it's quick and he / she hasn't got time to change money so can pay by credit card.

5 Rented car, because he / she wants to travel around.

---

4 Ask students to tell their partner which form of transport they prefer generally. Encourage students to give reasons.

Global review

These activities can be used at home but are designed to be used in class with students working together in pairs.

Aim: to review the language of the units.

Tips:

- Encourage students to work together.
- Allow them to look back through the unit or consult their notes.
- In feedback, elicit more examples or the reason why an answer is correct.

Vocabulary (SB page 59)

1

1 K   2 B   3 B   4 K   5 K   6 B   7 K

2

Picture a

3

1 next to

2 in

3 on

4 under

4

1 b   2 c   3 a

Grammar (SB page 59)

1

No, unless you like hot weather!

2

Go shopping; have a coffee; eat the local street food; rent a bike; relax under the trees; Visit Hanoi in the spring or autumn

---

Listen again (SB page 59)

The *Listen again* text in this unit comes from *Reading and Listening* on Coober Pedy on page 55. Here students listen again to practise listening intensively.

1, 2 2.67

1 b   2 d   3 c   4 a   5 e

Ancient & Modern

Coursebook

Unit 10	Language	Texts	Communicative skills
Part 1 SB page 60	Grammar *Was / were*	Reading and Speaking *Ancient civilisations* Listening and Writing Life in the past	
Part 2 SB page 62	Vocabulary and Listening Adjectives Pronunciation Stress and intonation Grammar *Was / were* negatives and questions	Vocabulary and Listening Cairo	Speaking Asking about a trip (1)
Global game SB page 64	Answering questions on Units 9 and 10 Choosing the odd one out *Wh-* questions		
Global review SB page 65	Adjectives Making questions Writing an email about a real or imaginary trip *was, were, wasn't, weren't*		

Additional resources

eWorkbook	Interactive and printable grammar, vocabulary, listening and pronunciation practice Extra reading and writing practice Additional downloadable listening and audio material
TB resource CD	Communication activity worksheets to print and photocopy
Go global Ideas for further research	**Ancient** Ask students to find out about another ancient civilisation, to discuss in the next lesson. **Modern** Ask students to read about another holiday destination, and to write a fictitious postcard from there to their classmates, using the information they find.

Part 1

Lead-in

Bring in some pictures of famous historical sites, eg Taj Mahal, The Pyramids, The Great Wall, Petra, Machu Picchu, Parthenon, etc. Try to find about six different places. Get pictures from the internet by doing an image search, using the relevant key words in each case. Put up the pictures around the room. Students in pairs walk around and examine the pictures, saying if possible what each place is, where it is and why it is famous. Take feedback when students have finished, holding up each picture in turn and eliciting ideas.

Reading and Speaking (SB page 60)

This text gives factual information about two ancient civilisations: the Maya and Khmer.

1 Write up the three questions on the board. Check the words *famous historical sites*, giving and / or eliciting examples. Write one example on the board. Put students in groups of three, in mixed nationality groups if appropriate for the mini discussion and point out the *Useful phrases* expressions.

Take feedback on any points of interest. Be sure not to overcorrect here, allowing students to make mistakes if their message is clear.

2 Focus students on the two pictures representing the Maya and Khmer civilisations. Elicit from students any facts that they already know, eg where they are, how old they are, etc. Divide the class into As and Bs, with As on one side of the room and Bs on the other. As read about the Khmer, Bs the Maya.

3 Put students into smaller groups of three or four within their A and B groups. Together they choose the four most interesting facts from their text. Refer students to the example language, modelling it with a strong student first. Tell students that they have one minute to try and memorise the facts.

4 Now put students in mixed AB pairs. Students tell each other their four interesting facts, from memory if possible, particularly for stronger students. For fun, you could ask them to put four things on the table, to represent each of their four facts, eg a pen top, a rubber, a coin, a pencil. They move one of their items, every time they give one fact to their partner.

Reading extra

Draw two big empty bubbles on the board. Write the heading *Adjectives* over one, and *Nouns* over the other. Elicit an example of a noun in the text (do not include proper nouns, ie names of places). Ask students to work in pairs to find seven words in the text for each bubble, eg *modern, different* (adjectives); *temple, roads* (nouns). Monitor and check if they have appropriate answers and clarify words as appropriate. This exercise encourages students to re-read the text and raises awareness of parts of speech. It also expands vocabulary.

Grammar (SB page 61)

Ask students to read the three sentences in the grammar box. Ask students if they can remember which civilisation each sentence refers to. Write *was* and *were* on the board. Students re-read each sentence and think about why *was* or *were* is used in each case. Elicit suggestions, if necessary in their L1, in a monolingual class. Ask useful concept questions, eg *Is this present or past*? *Why is it 'were'*?

Ask students to read and follow as you read out the rules underneath.

1 Tell students they are going to find out some more information about two cities from the Maya and Khmer civilisations. Do the first example together, then let students work alone to complete the gaps with *was* or *were*. Monitor and assist where necessary, helping students with the target language. Let students compare answers in pairs.

> Angkor **was** a major city in Khmer times and is now a UNESCO world heritage site. It **was** the capital of the Khmer empire and there **were** a million people in Angkor. There **were** over 100 temples. It was **also** the location for the film *Tomb Raider.*
>
> Tikal **was** an important Mayan city. It **was** the political and economic capital of the region. There **were** many important temples and beautiful buildings. Some of the temples **were** in the film *Star Wars.*

2 🔊 **2.68** Students listen and check their answers.

Language note

Was and *were* are high frequency grammar words, not key content words carrying the message. Therefore, when they are spoken within sentences they are often reduced to a weak form, eg *Angkor was* /wəz/ *a major city. There were* /wɜː/ *many important temples.*

You could highlight this to your students if appropriate.

Ⓖ Grammar focus

Show students the icon. Write *page 114* on the board and ask them to find it. Show students the first part of the language summary on the past simple with the verb *be*, positive, singular and plural.

You can use exercise 1 on page 115 for:

a) extra practice now

b) homework

c) review a couple of lessons from now.

The answers are on page 117 of the Teacher's Book.

Listening and Writing (SB page 61)

1 **2.69** Focus students on the picture. Elicit what the civilisation is and any extra information they know. Students listen to find out.

> **2.69**
>
> **Ancient Egypt** was very important from 3150 to 35 BC.

2 **2.70** First, give students time to read the notes through, before playing the recording.

> **TEACH GLOBAL**
> **THINK LOCAL** **Extra activity**
>
> Many of the words in the notes appear in the texts on page 60. You could ask students to find these words before listening to the complete recording.

If your students are not confident listeners, let them compare answers in pairs before whole class feedback. Monitor to see if they have the correct answers and if necessary, re-play the recording.

> fantastic architects
>
> agriculture – important
>
> typical food – bread and vegetables
>
> no symbols for numbers 2–9
>
> animals – important

> **2.70**
>
> Ancient Egypt was very important from 3150 to 35 BC. The ancient Egyptians were fantastic architects and there were many wonderful pyramids and temples.
>
> Agriculture was very important and the typical food for normal Egyptians was bread and vegetables.
>
> We have examples today of Egyptian writing and numbers. There were symbols for numbers one and ten, but no symbols for numbers two to nine.
>
> Animals were very important to Egyptian families and many families had a pet. Cats were very popular.

3 Task A is easier as the information is provided in skeletal form. Do the first point together, writing up on the board: *Ancient Egypt was very important from 3150 to 35 BC*. Elicit from the notes in exercise 2, prompting them by saying *fantastic architects*. Write up the whole sentence: *They were fantastic architects*. Then students continue alone, expanding the other notes in the same way.

If students want to choose task B, they may need to do some research, so you could assign this as homework.

> **TEACH GLOBAL**
> **THINK LOCAL** **Writing extra**
>
> Depending on your students' interests and where they come from, ask them to think of their own town or village. Write up on the board: *My town 300 years ago* (or choose a relevant year for their context). They can then write about the following areas, as in the texts on the Maya, the Khmer and the Egyptians: typical food, agriculture, religion(s), roads, architecture and any other points of interest. This task would also suit stronger students.

Part 2

Vocabulary and Listening (SB page 62)

TEACH GLOBAL THINK LOCAL **Lead-in**

If you can, bring in 2–5 postcards of different places. Show students the pictures and try to elicit the place. Ask students *Does the place sound nice / not so nice / both? Which place would you like to go to?* Then read some sentences (invent if necessary) from the back of each one (use clear intonation and expression to aid understanding), eg *This place is fantastic! The food here is really good and the beach is wonderful.*
The place is beautiful but the hotel is really noisy ... It does not matter here if one or two words or grammar structures are above the level, as long as students understand the general idea.

1 Students put the words in the appropriate box.

+	–
delicious	awful
fanastic	noisy
wonderful	terrible

2 Students add their own example. Stronger students can write more. If some interesting words are being added, brainstorm and add them to the board, but keep the pace fast at this stage.

TEACH GLOBAL THINK LOCAL **Extra activity**

To engage students with the topic of Cairo, put students into two or more teams, and ask the questions below. They should work alone initially, then confer with their team.

Where is Cairo exactly? (Egypt)

What river is it on? (The Nile)

What's the main language? (Arabic)

Give another important city in the same country. (eg Alexandria)

What's the currency? (Egyptian pounds)

Which sea is near to Cairo? (Red Sea or the Mediterranean)

How big is Cairo? (nearly 7 million in the city)

Handle feedback as a competition, awarding points for correct answers.

3 Focus students on Jackie's holiday pictures. They point out the things that they can see in pairs.

Everything can be seen in the pictures.

4 🔘 **2.71** Tell students that they will hear Jackie talking about her holiday to a friend. They should number the photos in the order that she talks about them.

The correct order is: b, f, h, i, a, g, c, d, e

🔘 **2.71**

A: So Jackie, you were in Cairo last month. What was that like?

B: Fantastic, Mike! Here, have a look at my photos.

A: OK, oh so was this **your hotel**?

B: Yes, it was. It was the first modern hotel in Cairo. It was great! The hotel was next to the **Egyptian museum**, the one with King Tutankhamen inside. That was wonderful!

A: Was the **food** good?

B: Yes, it was. It was delicious. This was my first meal in Cairo. There was rice, meat, vegetables and bread in lots of different bowls.

A: Wow, the **Pyramids**!

B: Yes, they were fantastic, of course. Look at **me on the horse**! It was very old and slow! There weren't any other tourists because I was there very early in the morning – and it was cold! It wasn't hot in January in the morning! OK, so this was **Ali, my guide**.

A: Ali, right. So, were the people nice?

B: Well, Ali was very nice – all the Egyptians were very friendly.

A: Cairo's a very big city. Was the **traffic** bad?

B: Oh yes, that was terrible. There were so many cars, and buses and taxis. The **taxis** were awful – they weren't expensive but they were very hot and very slow. It was really noisy too. But at night **the river Nile** was really beautiful.

A: So, a good trip?

B: Oh yes!

5 Before listening again, let students read the adjectives and nouns. Demonstrate the activity by eliciting a possible adjective which goes with *hotel*, eg *modern*, *wonderful*, etc. Play the recording for students to match the others. In feedback, get students to put the word in a sentence, according to Jackie's description, thereby revising *was* and *were*, eg *The hotel was modern*.

1 c	2 d	3 a	4 b	5 e	6 g	7 f	8 h

Pronunciation (SB page 63)

1 **2.72** Demonstrate the activity first. Students listen and underline the stress.

> **2.72**
>
> 1 That was <u>won</u>derful.
> 2 It was de<u>li</u>cious.
> 3 They were fan<u>tas</u>tic.
> 4 They were very <u>friend</u>ly.
> 5 That was <u>te</u>rrible.
> 6 The taxis were <u>aw</u>ful.
> 7 It was really <u>noi</u>sy too.

2 Tell students they will now focus on the whole sentence, not just the word. Drill the sentences chorally and individually, as appropriate. Then put students in pairs and ask them to read a sentence out each in turn, until they have repeated all of them.

Language note

Many of these adjectives are extreme adjectives, eg *fantastic*, *delicious*, *awful*. All of them are likely to be said by the speaker with clear feeling, when discussing personal experiences, as here. A speaker will naturally emphasise the adjective in such cases.

Make sure that students use their voices effectively to show that they do indeed feel negative or positive. In English, the movement of the voice in these cases is quite considerable, using a wide pitch range. Students may feel a little uncomfortable at first, but encourage them to sound natural and interested.

Grammar (SB page 63)

Read aloud the examples and general rules about grammar, with the students following. Write on the board:

was + not = wasn't /wɒzənt/
were + not = weren't /wɜː(r)nt/

Drill these, saying them first of all within their example sentences, then isolating them for students to copy.

1 Elicit where you think Jackie went shopping in Cairo. Students might know something about the bazaars, markets or souvenir shops. Find the first word together. Students then complete the task individually.

2 **2.73** Students listen and check their answers in pairs before whole class feedback.

> There **were** many places to go shopping in Cairo. My favourite place **was** Khan al-Khalili market. It **was** fantastic! I **was** there in the afternoon and it was very noisy. There **were** many things to buy and they **weren't** very expensive. There **were** lots of coffee shops, but they **weren't** very big. They were usually small and friendly. The Arabic coffee was delicious! There was only one problem – there were lots of streets and I **wasn't** sure how to find my hotel!

3 Write on the board *No, I wasn't. I was with my sister.* Try to elicit the question. Then students match the questions to the answers in pairs.

4 **2.74** Students listen and check.

> 1 c
> 2 e
> 3 a
> 4 d
> 5 b

> **2.74**
>
> A: Were you with your family?
> B: No, I wasn't. I was with friends.
> A: Was it an expensive trip?
> B: No, it wasn't. It was cheap.
> A: Was the weather good?
> B: Yes, it was. It was sunny every day.
> A: Were you there in summer?
> B: No, I wasn't. I was there in winter.
> A: Were there any problems?
> B: No, there weren't. It was a great trip!

G Grammar focus

Show students the icon. Write *page 114* on the board and ask them to find it. Show students the rest of the language summary on the verb *be*, the negative and question forms.

You can use exercises 2 and 3 on page 115 for:
a) extra practice now
b) homework
c) review a couple of lessons from now.
The answers are on page 117 of the Teacher's Book.

Speaking (SB page 63)

1 Divide students into As and Bs. As refer to page 98, and Bs page 102. Tell them they are going to read about a lovely holiday they went on. Give students 90 seconds to memorise the facts.

Tell students they have to give full answers, eg *Where were you?* Answer: *I was in Bangkok*. Bs cover their answers, then As ask the questions, noting down Bs answers. Then they swap roles and Bs ask the questions.

2 This task allows students to personalise the new language.

Model the activity. Tell students that you are thinking of your last trip somewhere. Smile as you are doing this, and put on a 'thinking face'. Students use the prompts to ask you questions. Make your responses interesting!

Particularly with less strong students, allow them time to write down the questions on their own, using the prompts. Remember to also give students a moment to think about their own trip.

3 Put students in pairs to ask and answer their questions. Monitor and take notes on any problems, for feedback at the end. Early finishers could work with a different pair.

TEACH GLOBAL THINK LOCAL **Extra activity**

For further practice and some fun, start students off with the sentence starter: *I went to London and the weather was horrible*. Students then try to carry on with a *noun + adjective* sentence. You may need to prompt with ideas, eg *hotel*, *Big Ben*, *the Queen*, *the people*, *the food*, *the parks*, *the shops*, *the tea*. Students should try and remember each sentence, in a memory game. Each student first repeats what has gone before, then adds their own sentence, eg:

Student A: *I went to London and the weather was horrible.*

Student B: *I went to London and the weather was horrible. We were in a lovely hotel.*

Student C: *I went to London and the weather was horrible. We were in a lovely hotel. The shops were busy.*

If you have a large class, split the class into two or three groups, with a strong student acting as a 'teacher' in each one. Put less strong students nearer the beginning of the game, where the recall challenge is lower.

Global game

The aim of this game is to review some of the ideas and the language from Units 9 and 10 in a fun, cooperative way. It is designed rather like a British pub quiz. Part 1 reviews Unit 10, and Parts 2 and 3 cover Units 9 and 10.

Divide the class into teams, ideally with two or three students in each team. Try to separate them physically, to give a competitive feel. Then explain the rules of the game or write them on the board or on a handout:

Your holiday starts tomorrow! But you can't go on holiday without the objects on the page, which you have to win as a team.

On the CD there are questions in three different parts. Listen to the questions in each part. Discuss the answers with your group and note your answers in the space.

After each section, I will give you the correct answers.

If you have four answers in the section correct, you win the object.

Follow it up with check questions, eg *Do you answer the questions alone? Who gives the questions? Who gives the answers and when? What happens if you get four of the questions right in a section? Which objects do you need to win to go on holiday?*

🔘 **2.75** Play each section, and after each one give students a few minutes to decide on the right answer. Do not let them refer to earlier pages in the unit. Be prepared to play the recording once more if required. Then give the answers.

Once the game has ended, take the scores for each group. If they have managed to win the suitcase, camera and passport, give them two minutes to decide where they are going to go for two weeks! Take feedback.

Part 1 answers

1 Buddhism & Hinduism

2 rice and fish

3 20

4 vegetables

5 Star Wars

Part 2 answers

1 *awful* is a negative adjective, the rest are positive.

2 The shower is in the bathroom, but the fridge, the cooker and the table are in the kitchen.

3 *friendly* is a positive adjective, the rest are negative.

4 Monday, Friday and Thursday are days of the week. The weekend consists of two days.

5 *was* is the only verb in the past. *rent*, *go* and *see* are all infinitive forms.

Part 3 answers

1 In January, Jackie was in Cairo. (U10)

2 In Angkor, Cambodia. (U10)

3 Merv's house was in Coober Pedy, Australia. (U9)

4 Stanley Park was in Vancouver, Canada. (U9)

🔘 **2.75**

Part 1: Remember Unit 10

1 What was the religion of the Khmer?

2 What was the typical food for the Khmer?

3 How many days were in the Mayan month?

4 What was the important food for the Mayans?

5 What film was made in Tikal?

Part 2: Odd one out

1 wonderful, fantastic, awful, delicious

2 fridge, cooker, table, shower

3 terrible, friendly, noisy, awful

4 Monday, Friday, weekend, Thursday

5 rent, was, go, see

Part 3: Where was ...?

1 Where was Jackie in January?

2 Where was the film *Tomb Raider* made?

3 Where was Merv's underground house?

4 Where was Stanley Park?

---

10 Ancient & Modern

Global review

These activities are designed to review the content of the unit. They can be used at home but are designed to be used in class with students working together in pairs.

Aim: to review the language of the unit.

Tips:

- Encourage students to work together.
- Allow them to look back through the unit or consult their notes.
- In feedback, elicit more examples or the reason why an answer is correct.

Vocabulary and Pronunciation (SB page 65)

<table>
<tr><td colspan="4">1</td></tr>
<tr><td colspan="4">1 delicious</td></tr>
<tr><td colspan="4">2 great</td></tr>
<tr><td colspan="4">3 friendly</td></tr>
<tr><td colspan="4">4 busy</td></tr>
<tr><td colspan="4">2</td></tr>
</table>

	●•	•●•	●••
wonderful			✔
delicious		✔	
terrible			✔
noisy	✔		
fantastic		✔	
awful	✔		
beautiful			✔
friendly	✔		

Reading (SB page 65)

b Yes, but there were good and bad things.

Grammar and Writing (SB page 65)

1

1 Was the weather good?

2 Was the traffic bad?

3 Was the hotel expensive?

4 Were the people nice?

2, 3 Students' own answers.

Listen again (SB page 65)

The *Listen again* text in this unit comes from the *Grammar* section on Jackie's trip to Cairo on page 63. Here students listen again to focus on *was(n't) / were(n't)* in short answers.

1, 2 🎧 2.77

Mike:	Were you with your family?
Jackie:	No, I **wasn't**. I was with friends.
Mike:	Was it an expensive trip?
Jackie:	No, it **wasn't**. It was cheap.
Mike:	Was the weather good?
Jackie:	Yes, it **was**. It was sunny every day.
Mike:	Were you there in summer?
Jackie:	No, I **wasn't**. I was there in winter.
Mike:	Were there any problems?
Jackie:	No, there **weren't**. It was a great trip!

3, 4

Students listen and repeat, then practise the conversation in exercise 1.

Life & Times

Coursebook

Unit 11	Language	Texts	Communicative skills
Part 1 SB page 66	Vocabulary Years and life events Grammar Past simple Pronunciation Regular past simple	Reading & Listening *DNA: Fact or fiction?* *The DNA Man*	Writing A biography / autobiography
Part 2 SB page 68	Vocabulary Dates Grammar Past simple negative	Reading *Around the world in 2004*	Speaking Talking about last year
Global voices SB page 70	Listening to people talk about important years for them and why *because* Talking about important years for each other		
Global review SB page 71	Significant life events Months and years Regular and irregular past simple verbs *at*, *in*, *on*, *to*		

Additional resources

eWorkbook	Interactive and printable grammar, vocabulary, listening and pronunciation practice Extra reading and writing practice Additional downloadable listening and audio material
TB resource CD	Communication activity worksheets to print and photocopy
Go global Ideas for further research	**Life** Ask students to use the internet to find out about an inventor they admire, or someone who made an important discovery, to talk about in the next lesson. **Times** Ask students to find five significant events from the preceding year, and to compare their lists of events with each other in the next lesson.

Part 1

Vocabulary (SB page 66)

TEACH GLOBAL THINK LOCAL **Lead-in**

As a lead-in to the topic put some different world events (just the name on a piece of paper) and stick them up around the room. Students walk around in pairs and write them in order of when they happened. Alternatively, just put them on the board randomly. Events could include: *the First World War, the first man on the moon, the discovery of America, the first TV, the invention of the telephone,* etc. Correct order: *America (1492), Bell's first telephone call (1876), First World War (1914–18), Commercial TV (1941), first man on the moon (1969).* Choose events your students will be familiar with. Listen to how students are saying the years.

1 🔘 **3.01** Students work in pairs to first look at the dates and try to pronounce them. Then they listen and repeat. Pause the recording and assist as necessary, drilling chorally and individually.

2 Students again predict how to say the years, working with a different partner this time. •

Pronunciation note

When pronouncing *2012*, fluent speakers might pronounce them differently. You can either say *two thousand (and) twelve* or *twenty twelve*. American speakers often omit the *and* in dates.

3 🔘 **3.02** Students listen and number the dates in exercise 2 in order, writing *1, 2,* etc in the space provided.

1	1976
2	2005
3	1967
4	1908
5	1998
6	2012

4 Give students time to write down five years. Put them in pairs or threes for them to dictate to each other. They should then check with each other's written version. Monitor as they are doing this and assist as appropriate, either immediately or in delayed feedback.

TEACH GLOBAL THINK LOCAL **Extra activity**

If you did the *Lead-in*, go back at this point and ask them for the years. Note that there is disagreement over some of the dates in the *Lead-in* (telephone and television). You could research these further yourself or ask students to do this.

5 Students look at the pictures and label them using the vocabulary in the box. Do the first example together. Take feedback as students need to be comfortable with this vocabulary in order to do the following task. Many of the expressions have come up earlier in the book so should not pose problems.

a	buy a house
b	go to university
c	start work
d	have children
e	go to school
f	retire
g	have granchildren
h	get married

6 Students work alone to put the events in order for their country. Put them in mixed nationality pairs, if possible, for them to compare their orders. The order given here is a possible order for the UK.

| e, b, c, a, h, d, g, f |

Reading and Listening (SB page 66)

1 🔘 **3.03** Write *DNA* on the board. Ask students if they know what this means, and if they know anything about it. Students read the fact box on page 67 and identify the false sentence. Hear some suggestions from students before listening, then play the recording to check who was right.

| Sentence 4 is false. The DNA of brothers and sisters is only 50% the same, not 100%. |

 3.03
DNA: Fact or fiction?
1 DNA means *deoxyribonucleic acid.*
2 DNA is in all plants and animals.
3 The police use DNA in their work.
4 The DNA of brothers and sisters is 50% the same.
5 People use DNA to test food and wine.

2 Ask students if they know the scientist(s) who discovered DNA. Students read to find out more about Crick. Set a time limit of three minutes, then close books and ask students if they can recall any of the information in pairs.

3 🔘 **3.04** Ask students what information is missing in the text *The DNA Man* (the dates). Students listen and fill in the missing years. If necessary pause the recording and replay (part of) it.

1	1916
2	1940
3	1949
4	1951
5	1954
6	1962
7	1976
8	2004

Language note

PhD is an abbreviation for 'Doctor of Philosophy'. A doctorate is a high-level degree awarded for original research.

4 Students order the events in Crick's life. This task requires students to read the text as a whole more closely. It also exposes them more to language that they are going to focus on shortly (the past simple). Let students work alone, before checking their answers in pairs.

The correct order is:
1 He studied in London and Cambridge.
2 He had his first child.
3 He had two daughters with his second wife.
4 He started working with James Watson.
5 He won the Nobel prize.
6 He worked in California.
7 He died.

Grammar (SB page 66)

Look at the sentences with students. Ask *Is this information about Crick about his past or present? Can you remember what happened in 1954?* Write up the answer on the board, drawing students' attention to the past form, using colour to highlight: *He **finished** his PhD in 1954.* Do the same with the second sentence and then read the points underneath.

1 Tell students to look at the text again and to count the number of verbs in bold they see, using *studied* as an example. Ask *What are the last two letters?* Answer: *ed*. Students write the examples down and also the infinitive, as in the example. Write these examples on the board and highlight the fact that *y* changes to *i*, using colours.

studied	study
continued	continue
started	start
finished	finish
died	die

2 Focus students on the underlined verbs, and point out that they are formed differently from those they looked at in exercise 1. Students write the past form of the infinitive, referring to the text to help them.

1	met
2	went
3	was born
4	got
5	had
6	won

3 Divide students into AB pairs. As turn to page 98 and Bs to page 102. Explain that student A is going to talk about Marie Curie, and B about Jane Goodall, writing the names of these two scientists on the board. Let students look at the notes in exercise 1 for a minute, then ask a confident students to model the first example. Explain to students that they each have two tasks: to make complete sentences about their own scientist; then to listen to their partner and fill in the other table with the important dates.

G Grammar focus

Show students the icon. Write *page 114* on the board and ask them to find it. Show students the first part of the language summary, the table on the past simple in the affirmative.

You can use exercises 4 and 5 on page 115 for:
a) extra practice now
b) homework
c) review a couple of lessons from now.
The answers are on page 117 of the Teacher's Book.

TEACH GLOBAL THINK LOCAL Extra activity

Give students two minutes to re-read the text and tell them to try and remember the years. Put up all the infinitive forms on the board randomly. (If you have a weaker group, put up the past simple forms of regular verbs only.) Challenge students in pairs, books closed, to try and remember the events from Crick's autobiography, including the dates!

This activity revises the past forms, as well as dates.

Pronunciation (SB page 67)

1 🔊 **3.05** Ask students to close their books. Elicit the past forms of the three verbs: *finish, die, start,* writing them on the board. Ask students to say the past forms in their own minds, silently. Then students listen to how the ending is pronounced. Play the recording. Focus in on the extra syllable in *started*. Drill the three past forms.

2 🔊 **3.06** Stronger students can try to predict the verbs with an extra syllable, like *started*. Then they listen and check.

continued
ended ✓
liked
listened
lived
repeated ✓
visited ✓
worked

3 Students say the verbs after you or the recording. With a stronger group, you could briefly highlight some of the rules regarding pronunciation.

Pronunciation note

If the infinitive ends in a /t/ or /d/ sound, then an extra syllable is needed, eg *needed, started*. You probably do not need to provide further details at this level.

For your own interest, or if you have strong or curious students, if the infinitive ends in an unvoiced consonant, such as /p/, /ʃ/, /s/ or /k/, then the ending is pronounced as a /t/, eg *hoped, washed, missed, walked*. If the infinitive ends in a voiced consonant or vowel sound, then the ending is pronounced as a /d/, eg *loved, enjoyed*.

Writing (SB page 67)

Ask students to decide which task they would prefer to do: A or B. (Assign tasks yourself if more appropriate.) Neither of the tasks requires research – in A it is personal, in B the information is provided. Remind students of the Crick biography to give an idea of length, particularly if they choose B, the biography of Tim Berners-Lee.

As students will work at their own pace, you may wish to give this for homework.

If you do the task in class, ask early finishers to check their writing for past forms. Then let those who have finished read each other's work, and check it for how clear it is, and if the past forms are correct.

Part 2

Vocabulary (SB page 68)

TEACH GLOBAL THINK LOCAL **Lead-in**

Revise dates by asking students to stand in two parallel lines, both facing away from the board. The line nearest and parallel to the board is A. There should be an equal number of As to Bs. A students should stand so that they can 'write' on their partner's back. (Their partners are those in line B.) Write a year on the board, eg *1973*. Students in line A turn around quickly to read it, then write the date silently on their partner's back with their finger. B students must not look at the board. B students shout out the year as soon as they know it. Write 6–8 more dates, one at a time, swapping the AB lines half way. Record the ongoing score to find the quickest pair.

If physical contact is culturally inappropriate for your context, write the years in the air with your finger, from the front of the class. Students shout out the year, then do the same 'writing in air' activity in pairs.

1 🔊 **3.07** Students listen to the recording and number the months in order. If you have a stronger group, you could ask them to do the exercise without listening and then play the recording to check.

1	January	7	July
2	February	8	August
3	March	9	September
4	April	10	October
5	May	11	November
6	June	12	December

2 Say *January*, and elicit where the stress is (first syllable). Point out the underlining in exercise 1. Ask students to listen again, this time to the stress in each month. It may help to focus students if they close their books and just listen.

3 Students work in pairs to complete the matching exercise. Check that students know the festivals.

Background note

These festivals are not celebrated in all countries, so students may not know them even if they recognise the English names. They are:

Christmas Day: the main celebration in the Christian calendar, celebrating the birth of Jesus.

New Year's Day: the first day of the new year. In the western world this is 1 January, but it varies in other parts of the world. In China, for example, it falls between late January and early February depending on the lunar calendar.

Valentine's Day: St Valentine is the patron saint of love. Valentine's Day is not a holiday but is a day for lovers to celebrate.

Australia Day: a national holiday in Australia. The date commemorates the arrival of the first convict ships from Britain in 1788.

Europe Day: the first proposal for a united Europe in 1950.

4 3.08–3.12 Students listen and check. After they have listened, ask about the prepositions and refer them to the *Language note*. If necessary, play the recording again.

1 c	2 d	3 a	4 e	5 b

on is the preposition used.

3.08–3.12

A: Is **Christmas Day** on the 24th of December?

B: No, it isn't. It's on **the 25th of December**.

A: In China **New Year's Day** is in January or February.

B: Oh really? For me it's always the **1st of January**.

A: Is **Valentine's Day** in March?

B: No, it's in February. It's on the **14th of February**.

A: **Australia Day**? When's that?

B: It's on the **26th of January**.

A: I think **Europe Day** is on the 8th of May.

B: No, it isn't. It's on the **9th of May**.

5 3.13 This exercise focuses students on ordinal numbers, including the spelling. Students work alone, then listen and repeat. For students who find the /θ/ sound difficult, help by showing the position of the tongue against the teeth, and drill as appropriate.

1st first	6th sixth
2nd second	7th seventh
3rd third	8th eighth
4th fourth	9th ninth
5th fifth	10th tenth

6 Monitor as students write out the numbers. Make it explicit to your students what the *th*, *st*, *nd* and *rd* stand for: they are the abbreviated ordinal.

1	thirty-first
2	twenty-second
3	eighteenth
4	twenty-third

7 If you can, before the lesson find out two or three important dates from a student in your class. Write them up on the board, or stick them up around the room. Students guess why these dates are important to him / her. Then students write down 3–4 important dates for themselves, before telling their partner.

Language note

When saying dates, learners might say: *My birthday is fourteen May*, forgetting the ordinal, the article *the* and the preposition *of*: *the fourteenth of May*. This is probably because in the written form, the article and the preposition are not necessary, eg *Brazil launched its first rocket on 23rd October*. Nowadays, even the abbreviated ordinal can actually be omitted in writing: *23 October*.

In fact, in American English, it is natural to omit the article and preposition even in spoken English, saying simply: *My birthday is May fourteenth*. At this level, however, teach your students the full forms.

When writing the dates in short form, in British English, the order is day, month, year. Thus, *1st December 2001* is: *01/12/2001* or *01.12.01*. In American English, the order is month, day, year: *12/01/2001*.

Reading (SB page 68)

1 First of all tell students what happened to you in 2004. The events could be relatively small, eg where you went on holiday, a course you did, etc. Refer students to the questions and give them two minutes to think about what happened to them. Then students discuss the three points in pairs. Pick up on any points of interest.

2 Ask students if they can remember anything that happened in the world in 2004. Refer students to the pictures. Ask students to cover the text at the top. In pairs, students tell each other what they know about the pictures.

3 Students silently read and match the sentences to the pictures. They compare answers with their partner.

a 2	b 3	c 4	d 5	e 6	f 1

4 Ask students to look at the first sentence: *Ten new countries, including Poland and Hungary, joined the _____ on 1 May*. Elicit the missing words *European Union* from the box. Students then complete the task alone. Monitor to assess how much time they need.

5 📀 **3.14** Students listen and check their answers.

a	Over 180,000 people died after an earthquake in the **Indian Ocean** made tsunami waves in Asia and Africa. (picture a)
b	Palestinian president Yasser Arafat died at the **age of 75**. (picture b)
c	The United Arab Emirates won its first medal at the **Olympic Games** in Greece. (picture c)
d	Wangari Maathai was the first African woman to win the **Nobel Peace** Prize. (picture d)
e	John Kerry didn't win the US Election. George W Bush won and stayed in the **White House**. (picture e)
f	Ten new countries, including Poland and Hungary, joined the **European Union** on 1 May. (picture f)

Grammar (SB page 69)

Refer students to the sentence under *Grammar*. Ask students what *didn't* is (*did* + *not*). Write the sentence on the board. Elicit the form and write it under the sentence:

Kerry   didn't   win the US election.
subject + didn't + infinitive

Read out the two points under the *Grammar* heading. Give two interesting or slightly bizarre examples about 2004 about yourself, eg *I didn't meet a rich man / woman. I didn't give up smoking!*

1 Focus students on the first sentence in the exercise and elicit the correct answer. Students continue individually before comparing answers in pairs. More confident students could try to do the task without re-reading the text, at least initially.

1 F	2 F	3 T	4 F	5 F

2 Students work alone to correct the false sentences. Monitor as they are doing this and assist as appropriate.

1	Wangari Maathai won the Nobel Peace Prize.
2	Poland joined the European Union.
4	Yassar Arafat died at the age of 75.
5	The tsunami started in the Indian Ocean.

Ⓖ Grammar focus

Show students the icon. Write *page 114* on the board and ask them to find it. Show students the second part of the language summary, the table on the negative form of the past simple.

You can use exercise 6 on page 115 for:

a) extra practice now

b) homework

c) review a couple of lessons from now.

The answers are on page 117 of the Teacher's Book.

Grammar extra

Do a mini general knowledge quiz. Prepare ten *True / False* statements, eg *Man first walked on the moon in 1967.* (F: 1969) *Shakespeare was born in the 1600s.* (F: 1500s) *Christopher Columbus discovered America in 1492.* (T) Prepare statements with your own students in mind. You could make some of them more local, eg local history, architecture. Put students in groups of three. Dictate the statements (or use a slide / hand-out), clarifying any key lexis as you do so. Give time for teams to decide if the statements are true or false. Take feedback, awarding points on the board per team: one point for judging correctness appropriately; another two points for giving the correct answer (if false). Encourage students to formulate full answers in feedback, eg *Man didn't walk on the moon in 1967. It was in 1969.*

Speaking (SB page 69)

1 Students should write at least three things that they did last year, and two things they didn't do (try to encourage students to write things they didn't do but wanted to, so that it is more natural use of the language), eg *I didn't buy the car I wanted.*

2 Put students in pairs and refer them to the *Language note*. Ask them to find out if their last years were at all similar. Students should listen only, not read or take notes. Warn students that they should try and remember what their partner tells them.

3 Tell students that they are going to see how good their memories are. Choose two confident students who worked together in exercise 2. Ask them to read the sample conversation aloud for the class, making it true for themselves. Then students do the same in their pairs.

Extra activity

Focus students on the *Language note* on page 69. Draw three columns on the board, with the headings: *in, on, at*. Ask students to copy this down. Say about ten sentences including different times, but instead of the preposition, say *beep*, eg *I teach on Mondays and Thursdays; My birthday is in July; I got married in 2004; I have an eye-test on Tuesday.* Students should write down the time-word in each case, eg *Mondays, July, 2004,* in the correct column. At the end, ask individuals to come up to the board and write up their answers.

Global voices

These lessons in *Global* are designed to provide students with exposure to authentic speakers of English from both native and non-native English backgrounds. In this unit we extend the theme of significant years for individuals.

Warm up (SB page 70)

1 Bring in some pictures to represent an event which was important to you, eg a graduation, a wedding, new baby, new house. Tell students the year, and then explain what happened, referring to the pictures. Then students think of their own important year, completing the sentence in their books.

Listening (SB page 70)

1 🔊 **3.15–3.19** Tell students that they are going to hear others discussing the same question. Students listen and match the year to the speaker.

> Bea: 1998
>
> Pilar: this year
>
> Carmen: 2001
>
> Mireille: 2002
>
> Maria: 2007
>
> (Note that Carmen uses the US form to say the year, ie *two thousand one*. See the *Language note* on page 81.)

🔊 **3.15–3.19**

Bea, England

A memorable year is 1998 because I went travelling round the world.

Pilar, Spain

My important year is this year because I am living in London and I think that is very difficult for me because I am from Spain and the weather and the food is very different.

Carmen, Spain

I think probably the most important year of my life was er… 2001 because it was the year before I started the university and it was a very hard year for me.

Mireille, US

I think probably 2002 because that's the year I moved to the United Kingdom.

Maria, Spain

I think a memorable year would be 2007 and that's because my son was born and so, life is very different now … since then.

2 Students listen again to complete the matching task. Give students time to read a–e first. If necessary, re-play the recording.

> 1 d   2 a   3 b   4 e   5 c

Language focus (SB page 70)

Write up the sentence in the *Language note* on the board, jumbled: *because my was born important me for 2007 was son*. Students order the words, with assistance from you as appropriate. Help them by giving the first (two) word(s). Highlight the use of *because*, then read the *Language note*.

Elicit the correct answer to the first sentence in the exercise, then students complete the exercise. After checking, ask students to go back to their sentence from the *Warm Up*. See if they can add *because* to their sentence. Monitor and help as appropriate.

> 1 A memorable year was 1998 **because** I went travelling round the world.
> 2 I think that is very difficult for me **because** I am from Spain and the weather and food is very different.
> 3 The most important year of my life was 2001 **because** it was the year before I started university.
> 4 I think probably 2002 **because** that's the year I moved to the United Kingdom.
> 5 I think a memorable year would be 2007 and that's **because** my son was born.

Speaking (SB page 70)

Let students read the conversation. Select two strong students across the class to model the task to the others. Put students in pairs to do the same. Particularly for early finishers, encourage them to think of at least one more important year each. Take whole class feedback on any points of interest.

Global review

These activities can be used at home but are designed to be used in class with students working together in pairs.

Aim: to review the language of the unit.

Tips:

- Encourage students to work together.
- Allow them to look back through the unit or consult their notes.
- In feedback, elicit more examples or the reason why an answer is correct.

Vocabulary (SB page 71)

1 1 start work
   2 have children
   3 go to university
   4 retire
   5 get married
   6 buy a house

2 Students' own answers.

3 J: June or July

5 1 1902
   2 1918
   3 1972
   4 1964
   5 1992
   6 2010
   7 2006
   8 2014

6 3 and 6

Grammar (SB page 71)

1 knew; met; read; spoke; went; wrote

2 know; meet; read; speak; go; write

3, 4 Students' own answers.

Listen again (SB page 71)

The *Listen again* text in this unit comes from the biography about Francis Crick on page 67. Here students listen again to consolidate earlier work on prepositions *in*, *at*, *on* and *to*.

1 🔊 **3.20**

Francis Crick was born **on** the 8th June 1916 **in** Northampton, England. He went to school **in** London and then studied physics **at** London University. He continued his research **in** Cambridge. He got married **in** 1940 and had a son, but he and his wife later got divorced. He got married again **in** 1949 and had 2 daughters. **In** 1951 he met another scientist, James Watson and they started working together. Crick finished his PhD **in** 1954. **In** 1962, Crick, Watson and Wilkins won the Nobel Prize in Physiology for their research into DNA. In 1976, Crick went **to** California to begin studies on the brain. He died **in** 2004, aged 88.

2
   1 b
   2 d
   3 a
   4 c

UNIT 12 Question & Answer

Coursebook

Unit 12	Language	Texts	Communicative skills
Part 1 SB page 72	Vocabulary Animals Grammar and Speaking Past simple questions	Reading *The Southern Day Frog*	Writing The Bali Tiger Speaking Animals that disappeared
Part 2 SB page 74	Pronunciation Stress and rhythm Extend your vocabulary *time*	Reading *Tribes* Listening The TV series *Tribe*	Speaking Visting another country Speaking Asking about a trip (2)
Global reading SB page 76	Biography of Mark Twain		
Global review SB page 77	Past simple verbs Animal vocabulary Redundant words		

Additional resources

eWorkbook	Interactive and printable grammar, vocabulary, listening and pronunciation practice Extra reading and writing practice Additional downloadable listening and audio material
TB resource CD	Communication activity worksheets to print and photocopy
Go global Ideas for further research	**Question** Ask students to research an animal from their country which is now extinct, write a paragraph about it and bring it to class for other students to read, ideally with a map and a photo. **Answer** Ask students to find out some information about another tribe, and to come to the next lesson ready to tell the class about their tribe, with visuals if possible.

Part 1

Lead-in

To link to previous classes and input some more past verbs do a quick sentence chain.

First write some common verbs on the board, eg *get*, *see*, *go*, *have*, *eat*, *watch*, *do*. Ask students to write the past form of the verbs, checking with the *Irregular verbs* list on page 126 to see if they are irregular, or writing the regular form.

Then say the first line, eg *Yesterday I got up at 7.00*. If you like you can do a mime of the action as you say the sentence. The first student repeats your sentence and adds one (and his / her own mime), using one of the verbs, eg *Yesterday I got up at 7.00 and I had eggs for breakfast.*

Students continue round the class, recapping previous sentences (and mimes) and adding one of their own.

Vocabulary (SB page 72)

1 Ask students to look at the pictures and repeat the animals' names. Ask if these animals live in their country. Read the descriptions a–e of each habitat and then ask students to work in pairs to match the animal with its home.

2 **3.21** Students listen and check.

1 d	2 c	3 a	4 e	5 b

> **3.21**
> 1 A fox lives in a hole underground.
> 2 A whale lives in the sea.
> 3 A bear lives in the forest.
> 4 A camel lives in the desert.
> 5 A rat lives near buildings.

3 Students discuss the questions in pairs. In feedback, ask some individual students to report back on their partner's answers to the questions.

Reading and Listening (SB page 72)

The text is about an extinct animal which used to live in Australia.

1 Before they read the text, ask students to look at the picture and tell you three things about this type of animal based on their existing knowledge, eg *It's brown. It lives in water and on land. Its babies look very different.* Then they read the text and answer the question. (Tell them not to worry about the missing words for now.)

> No, they disappeared in 1979.

You could input the word *extinct* at this point and ask if they know any animals in danger of extinction in their country.

Extra activity

If you think your students will need a quick reminder of question words before doing the next activity, write the following on the board: *7.00, the cinema, my mother, $4.50, because I like sport.* Ask students to work in pairs and invent possible questions in the present for each answer, eg *What time do you get up? (7.00)*.

2 Students work individually to fill in the missing question words. Look at the example and then do the next one together to get them started.

3 🔲 **3.22** Students listen and check. The recording includes discourse markers *Right*, *So*, *Well* and *And*. See the *Language note* on page 49 on discourse markers.

> **3.22**
> A: **Which** country did it come from?
> B: It came from Australia.
> A: **How** big was it?
> B: Well, it was very small. It was 3 cm long.
> A: **Where** did it live?
> B: It lived in the mountains, next to small rivers.
> A: Right, and **what** did it eat?
> B: It ate insects.
> A: **How** did it live?
> B: The frog was very busy in the day. It looked for food and went into the water a lot. It also sat in the sun. At night it went under rocks to sleep.
> A: So **why** did it disappear?
> B: Well, we don't know. Some people think there was a problem with the frog's habitat.
> A: And **when** did it disappear?
> B: There were a lot of frogs in the early 1970s but it disappeared in 1979.

4 With books closed, students try to recall three facts. Feed back on their ideas for the class to decide which are correct.

Grammar and Speaking (SB page 73)

Read the notes and examples.

Alternative procedure

If you prefer to work on grammar with students focusing on you at the board, you can build up past simple questions by analogy to present simple. Write *7.00* and elicit an appropriate present tense question, eg *What time do you get up?* Then write *Yesterday*, circle the auxiliary verb *do* and elicit the past question. Then write the question *Do you eat pasta?* And elicit *Yes / No* past questions and short answers in the same way.

12 Question & Answer

1 Students look at the information in the text and answer the questions, correcting where appropriate.

1 No, it didn't. It ate insects.
2 Yes, it did.
3 Yes, it did.
4 No, it didn't. It disappeared in 1979.

2 In the AB communication activity, students ask and answer questions about two more extinct animals. Note: initially A students need to work together and B students together in order to prepare questions, before forming AB pairs to find the answers. Divide the class in two halves, A and B; instruct those in group A to turn to page 98 and those in group B to turn to page 102. Make sure the students realise that the exercise continues over the page.

When the two groups have worked together to prepare the questions, ask the students to form AB pairs for the next stage.

3 **3.23** Ask students to look at the picture and check the word *donkey*. Students read to find four mistakes.

🔊 **3.23**
A: When I was little our family had a donkey.
B: Did it **have** a name?
A: Yes, it was Ronaldo.
B: What did it **eat**?
A: It ate carrots and grass.
B: **Where** did it live?
A: It lived in the garden.
B: Did you like it?
A: Yes, I **did**.

4 Give students a few minutes to think (and ask you vocabulary questions). Then put students into pairs to interview each other. If pets do not form a part of your students' culture, move on to the *Speaking extra* activity below.

Speaking extra

In some countries (eg the UK) having pets is very common and pets are considered an integral part of the family. In other cultures, animals are not viewed in this way. It could therefore be interesting to do some speaking on this subject, eg getting them to discuss the following questions in pairs or small groups before conducting class feedback:

1 Do people in your country usually have pets?

2 Which animals are pets in your country?

3 Do you normally see animals where you live?

G Grammar focus

Show students the icon. Write *page 116* on the board and ask them to find it. Show students the language summary on past simple questions.

You can use exercises 1–3 on page 117 for:

a) extra practice now

b) homework

c) review a couple of lessons from now.

The answers are on page 117 of the Teacher's Book.

Writing (SB page 73)

The sequence of activities helps students prepare to produce a text of their own about another extinct animal. A world map would be helpful for exercise 1.

1 Look at the picture and see if students are familiar with this bird. If possible take in a map and show students the location of Mauritius. Ask students to complete the text using the correct form of the verbs. If need be they can check with the *Irregular verbs* list on page 126.

Background note

The Dodo was a large, flightless bird, notable because it was one of the first species to become extinct during recorded history and as a result of man's introduction of new predatory animals into its habitat. It forms part of the English language culture for two reasons: firstly the Dodo was a character in Lewis Carroll's popular children's book *Alice's Adventures in Wonderland*. Additionally, the dodo forms part of two common expressions: the simile *As dead as a dodo* (unequivocally dead), and *Go the way of the dodo* (to become extinct or obsolete).

2 🔊 **3.24** Students listen and check.

1 came
2 was
3 lived
4 ate
5 disappeared

3 Working from the notes, students write a similar paragraph about the Bali Tiger. As this is a highly structured piece of writing, students' texts are likely to be similar, but it's still a good idea to take them in to correct.

Part 2

Speaking (SB page 74)

Take in some visuals or things you typically take on holiday (eg passport, camera) to establish the theme.

1 Ask students to look at the examples (in italics) and then complete the sentences about themselves. Monitor and help with vocabulary if needed.

2 Students compare their answers. Ask some individuals to feedback on what their partner said.

> **TEACH GLOBAL THINK LOCAL** **Alternative procedure**
>
> A good way to engage students in this activity is to do it as a live listening. With books closed, copy the sentence stems onto the board. Then talk students through your own answers, giving as much detail as they will understand. When you finish, put them in pairs to check what they understood and to think of two additional questions to ask you. This serves as a model for students doing the same in pairs or small groups.

Reading (SB page 74)

The text, and theme for the rest of this part of the unit, is about tribes. Here, students read some facts about tribes from different parts of the world.

1 Ask students to look at the pictures and the title. Check understanding with some concept questions, eg *Do tribes live in big cities? Are there any tribes in this country?* Ask them to work individually and read the facts about tribes, using the glossary to help them.

When they've finished, look at the *Useful phrases* together and drill the phrases. Ask students to tell their partner a fact they think is interesting from the list.

> **TEACH GLOBAL THINK LOCAL** **Mixed ability**
>
> If some students need more time for reading, you could ask students to read only four of the facts; any students who finish early could continue. Alternatively, take in a world map and ask early finishers to find the different countries referred to in the text.

2 Students read individually to find the answers before checking in pairs.

1	in New Zealand (a Maori station)
2	the Maasai (blood)
3	in the US
4	the Nenet (over 1,000 km per year)
5	the Layap (because of the weather)

Listening (SB page 75)

The listening is a conversation between two people about the BBC TV series *Tribe*.

> **Background note**
>
> British TV presenter Bruce Parry was a physical training instructor in the Royal Marines before he started working in film and television. Having made some children's programmes, in 2005 he started making the *Tribe* series in which he spent a month or more living as one of the tribe. He did this with many groups of indigenous people all over the world.

1 Students look at the picture of Bruce Parry to guess the answers. Write the following phrases on the board: *I think he's ... Me too. / Really! I don't, I think ...*

2 **3.25** Students listen to the first part of the conversation to check their ideas. Note: at this point don't tell students what the conversation is about – they have to listen for this.

1 c	2 b

> **3.25**
>
> A: Did you see that TV series about that man ... oh what's his name ... Bruce Parry?
>
> B: Bruce Parry? Who's he?
>
> A: He's a TV presenter. He made this incredible series called *Tribe*.

3 Students match the two parts of the question. Look at the example and elicit the answer to question 2. Note: two questions start *Where did*, so it's a good idea to ensure you establish that question 2 is *Where did he go?* to avoid alternative answers later on and to ensure questions are in the correct order for the listening.

1	c	What did he do?
2	g	Where did he go?
3	d	Who did he go with?
4	a / f	Where did he stay?
5	f / a	How long did he stay?
6	e	What food did he eat?
7	b	Did he have a good time?

4 **3.26** This is a more challenging listening. To prepare students, first elicit possible answers to the questions. As a guide, tell them the answer to question 1 is *He lived with tribes.* Look at question 2 *Where did he go?* and elicit names of countries, etc.

Students then listen to note the answers to the questions. This is the first time a note-taking approach is used. Explain that you're practising listening not grammar so they shouldn't worry about writing correct sentences. Encourage students to use note form (as in the example). Listen once, check answers in pairs and if necessary do the second listening with students following the audioscript. In feedback ensure that you praise the correct information without worrying about linguistic form.

1 He lived with tribes.
2 To lots of different countries (Malaysia, Brazil, Russia, Tanzania ...).
3 A TV production team.
4 With a family in the tribe.
5 A month.
6 Strange food – insects and rats.
7 Yes, it was difficult but the people were very friendly.

3.26

A: Did you see that TV series about that man ... oh what's his name ... Bruce Parry?

B: Bruce Parry? Who's he?

A: He's a TV presenter. He made this incredible series called *Tribe*.

B: What did he do?

A: He lived with tribes ...

B: Tribes? Where? Where did he go?

A: He went to lots of different countries – Malaysia, Brazil, Russia, Tanzania ...

B: Are there tribes in all those places?

A: Yeah, it was fascinating.

B: Who did he go with?

A: Obviously he went with a TV production team.

B: Yeah OK. Where did he stay?

A: This is the interesting thing. He stayed with a family in the tribe.

B: All the time?

A: Yes, day and night – and he did everything they did.

B: Wow. How long did he stay? Two or three days?

A: No, he stayed for a month.

B: A month? Wow. What food did he eat?

A: That was incredible. He had exactly the same food as the tribe – you saw him eat lots of strange food – insects, rats ...

B: Rats? That's horrible. But did he like it, did he have a good time?

A: I think so – the people were really friendly to him, but I think it was also quite difficult for him. Life in the tribe was quite hard.

B: It sounds really interesting ...

TEACH GLOBAL THINK LOCAL **Alternative procedure**

If you think this approach is too challenging for your students you could try this alternative.

Put the answers to exercise 4 in a jumbled order on the board, eg:

A month.

A TV production team.

To lots of different countries.

With a family in the tribe.

He lived with tribes.

Yes, it was difficult but the people were very friendly.

Strange food – insects and rats.

Before listening, students decide the correct answer for each of the questions in exercise 3. Then they listen and check.

5 Students work in pairs or small groups to answer the questions.

Pronunciation (SB page 75)

1 **3.27** The focus here is on rhythm and sentence stress. Initially, the students hear the questions in isolation. Play the first example, using your hand to indicate that the main stresses fall on *Where* and *go*. You could start by drilling just these two words and then adding in the unstressed words in between. Ask students to repeat as a whole class before calling on individuals. Continue in the same way with the other questions.

2 **3.28** Now the students hear the questions pronounced as a chant. After listening a couple of times, write prompts on the board, eg *Where / go* and ask students to repeat the full chant from memory.

Extend your vocabulary (SB page 75)

This section looks at three different meanings of the word *time*. Read the definitions and examples. If you have a monolingual class you could ask them to translate the three expressions to see if the same word is used for all three meanings in their own language.

Students categorise the examples.

1 B   2 A   3 B   4 C

TEACH GLOBAL THINK LOCAL **Speaking extra**

For some fluency practice, you could ask students to work in pairs and invent a conversation incorporating one of the phrases. After practising, they could perform the conversation for the class.

Speaking (SB page 75)

There are two alternatives.

If you wish to continue on the theme of tribes and have students who enjoy imaginative activities, choose option A, an interview roleplay.

If you wish to change the theme and your students prefer personalisation, choose option B, a conversation about a recent visit.

Weaker students can limit the conversation to the questions from *Pronunciation* exercise 1, but encourage stronger students to extend beyond this.

Monitor as they speak and give feedback afterwards, perhaps noting a few mistakes on the board and encouraging students to correct them, but also ensuring you praise their efforts.

Global reading

(SB page 76)

The *Global reading* pages encourage students to approach different text types and develop the ability to read for pleasure. Here the text gives some biographical information about American author, Mark Twain and also provides information about two of his most famous books.

1 Ask students to look at the pictures and describe what they can see. Write *Mark Twain* on the board and see if students are familiar with this author. Explain that the pictures are all connected with his life.

Background note

The son of a judge, Samuel Clemens started work at the age of 13 on his father's death. Initially he worked on the river, but later found a taste for writing and became a journalist. His pseudonym, Mark Twain, comes from his days on the river and is a term meaning a safe depth to navigate. He went on to write 28 books and numerous short stories.

He was married to Olivia Langdon and they had four children.

His two most famous books *The Adventures of Tom Sawyer* and *The Adventures of Huckleberry Finn* have been adapted as graded readers for Beginners by Macmillan.

2 Ask the students to read the biography and match the phrases in bold with the pictures.

a	*The Adventures of Tom Sawyer* (1876) and *The Adventures of Huckleberry Finn* (1884).
b	he was a soldier in the US civil war.
c	He worked on the boats on the Mississippi River.
d	he was a silver miner.
e	Mark Twain was an American writer.

3 Students match the two parts of the questions.

1 f	2 c	3 d	4 b	5 a	6 e

4 Students read to answer the questions. Explain that if they can't find the answer in the text, they should write *I don't know*.

1	30th November 1835.
2	In Hannibal, Missouri.
3	He was a river worker, soldier, journalist and silver miner.
4	In 1865.
5	The answer is not in the text.
6	21st April 1910.

Global review

These activities are designed to review the content of the unit. They can be used at home but are designed to be used in class with students working together in pairs.

Aim: to review the language of the unit.

Tips:

- Encourage students to work together.
- Allow them to look back through the unit or consult their notes.
- In feedback, elicit more examples or the reason why an answer is correct.

Grammar (SB page 77)

1

D	I	S	A	P	P	E	A	R	E	D
I	R	J	H	S	L	O	N	D	A	A
E	W	O	R	K	E	D	A	N	T	L
D	M	I	A	Y	F	M	A	D	E	I
W	E	N	T	R	T	C	L	A	Y	V
P	I	E	C	K	Z	X	E	R	I	E
N	G	D	S	A	W	A	G	O	T	D

2 1 Where did you go?

2 Who did you go with?

3 What did you see?

4 How long did you stay?

5 What did you eat?

6 When did you go?

3 Students' own answers.

Vocabulary (SB page 77)

1 1 forest

2 desert

3 sea

4 underground

2 1 rat

2 bear

3 camel

4 whale

Listen again (SB page 77)

3.29 The *Listen again* text in this unit is an extract from the *Listening* on page 75 about Bruce Parry's TV series. Here, students listen again to notice words that are not in the recorded conversation. Point out to your students that these are all common and expressions we use to gain 'thinking time' while speaking.

3.29

A: Did you see that TV series about that man … oh, what's his name … Bruce Parry?

B: <u>No, I didn't.</u> Bruce Parry? Who's he?

A: He's a TV presenter. He made this incredible series called *Tribe*.

B: <u>Oh. And</u> what did he do?

A: <u>Well, he lived er,</u> he lived with tribes …

B: Tribes? Where? Where did he go?

A: <u>Oh,</u> he went to lots of different countries – Malaysia, Brazil, Russia, Tanzania …

B: Are there tribes in all those places?

A: Yeah, it was fascinating.

B: <u>So,</u> who did he go with?

A: <u>Well,</u> obviously he went with a TV production team …

B: Yeah OK. <u>So,</u> where did he stay?

A: This is the interesting thing. He stayed with a family in the tribe.

B: <u>What,</u> all the time?

A: Yes, day and night – and he did everything they did.

Business & Pleasure

Coursebook

Unit 13	Language	Texts	Communicative skills
Part 1 SB page 78	Vocabulary Numbers over 100 Grammar Present continuous Functional language Buying a ticket	Reading *Eurostar in numbers* Listening A business trip	Speaking and Vocabulary Travelling for business
Part 2 SB page 80	Vocabulary Tourism Grammar Present continuous negative and questions Pronunciation Intonation in questions	Reading and Speaking *Moscow* Listening A bus tour of Moscow	Writing An email to a friend
Global game SB page 82	Forming sentences: affirmative, negative and questions *My turn. Your turn. That's right!*		
Global review SB page 83	Business and leisure travel Buying travel tickets Present continuous Completing a conversation		

Additional resources

eWorkbook	Interactive and printable grammar, vocabulary, listening and pronunciation practice Extra reading and writing practice Additional downloadable listening and audio material
TB resource CD	Communication activity worksheets to print and photocopy
Go global Ideas for further research	Business Ask students to find out which London station you travel from to go to the following places: Edinburgh, Dover, Liverpool, Heathrow Airport. Pleasure Ask students to find out flight times and prices to Moscow from their nearest airport, a hotel and price per night in Moscow, and the names of three more places to visit in Moscow.

Part 1

Speaking and Vocabulary (SB page 78)

The questions form a lead-in to the theme of business travel.

1 Ask students to form pairs and discuss the questions before conducting feedback with the whole class. This is a good opportunity for personalisation and a freer discussion, so encourage students to contribute. Here, communication is more important than linguistic accuracy.

2 Ask students to look at the picture of Anne Ross. Ask some questions about this type of person, eg *Where does she work? What time does she start and finish work? What things does she use at work?* etc. Then look at the pictures relating to her business trip and ask students to complete the sentence.

> Anne is travelling around Europe by train.

3 **3.30** Students listen and repeat the words used to label the pictures on page 78. To check meaning, ask students some concept questions, eg *Where do you buy your ticket? Where do you wait for the train?* Check that students understand *wait* by miming looking at your watch, pacing up and down, etc. You could also teach *suitcase* although students don't need to use this word in this exercise.

Vocabulary (SB page 78)

1 **3.31** Students listen and repeat the numbers.

> **3.31**
>
> two hundred
>
> five hundred
>
> two hundred and seventy-nine
>
> five hundred and sixty-four

2 In pairs, students try to work out the pronunciation of bigger numbers.

3 **3.32** Students listen to check their ideas.

> three hundred
>
> eight hundred
>
> four hundred and eighty-three
>
> six hundred and thirty-seven
>
> nine hundred and twenty-two
>
> three hundred and one

Refer students to the *Language note*. Highlight this at the board by writing numbers and using an omission mark to indicate the position, eg *7 ^ 32, 50 ^ 7* (note that the *0* is not pronounced).

Language note

In American English, the *and* is not always used, eg *seven hundred thirty-two*.

TEACH GLOBAL THINK LOCAL — Vocabulary extra

Your students may need consolidation of numbers before moving on. Two options for this are:

- numbers dictation: dictate three-digit numbers to students; then they dictate numbers to each other in pairs.
- sums: teach the word *plus* and then dictate some sums, the answers to which are three-digit numbers; students race to note the sum, do the addition and call out the answers.

Reading (SB page 78)

1 Students read the text on page 79 about Eurostar and work together to deduce the correct answers. Look at the *Language note* before they start.

Background note

The Eurostar is a high-speed train connecting London with Paris and Brussels via the Channel Tunnel. Services started in 1994 and are operated jointly by French, Belgian and British rail companies. It has had a considerable impact on travel between these cities, leading to a significant reduction in the number of flights taken.

2 **3.33** Students listen and check.

> **3.33**
>
> If you want to go from London St Pancras to Paris, the Eurostar takes just **135 minutes**. And if Brussels is your destination, then you can be there in **113 minutes**. The train has a top speed of **300 km per hour**. The **total number of passengers is 766** with **206 in first class** and **560 in standard class**. But what about tickets and prices? If you want to travel **first class**, your ticket will cost **£260** but if that's too expensive you can buy a **standard ticket** for just **£39**.

Listening (SB page 78)

The listening features three short phone conversations between business traveller Anne Ross and her husband, at various stages of her journey.

1 **3.34–3.36** Ask students to read the introduction to the listening and refer them to the pictures on page 78. Students listen and number the pictures in order.

> 1 timetable
>
> 2 ticket office
>
> 3 platform
>
> 4 seats

3.34–3.36

1

John: How was the meeting, Anne?

Anne: Fine, John, it went very well.

John: So, where are you now?

Anne: I'm at the train station and I'm just checking the timetable. I think the train leaves at 16.30 … Let me see, yes it does. OK, I'm at the ticket office now, speak later!

2

Anne: Hi John, I have the ticket.

John: No problems, then?

Anne: No, none at all. I'm on the platform just waiting for the train now.

John: What time does the train arrive in Brussels?

Anne: About 7.30 this evening. John – the train's arriving now …

3

Anne: Hi John. I'm just arriving in Belgium.

John: How's the Eurostar?

Anne: Great – the seats are very comfortable! I'm glad I took the train.

John: I hope you aren't working now.

Anne: Oh no, I'm reading a book.

John: OK, call me tonight from the hotel …

2 **3.37** Students now listen to a further conversation, this time between Anne and her colleague in Belgium and answer the questions.

1 b	2 c	3 b

3.37

Anne: Mr Peeters? Hello, this is Anne, Anne Ross.

Peeters: Good evening Anne. Welcome to Brussels!

Anne: Thank you, but I have a problem. I understand that someone from the office is meeting me at the station.

Peeters: Yes, that's right.

Anne: Well, I'm waiting but there's no-one here.

Peeters: Don't worry, I'm coming to meet you now.

Anne: Great, I'm waiting next to platform 6. See you soon.

Grammar (SB page 79)

Ask students to cover the grammar explanation, read the three sentences and ask who's speaking or who they refer to (Anne, Anne, Peeters).

Then ask them if the sentences are talking about habitual actions or specific actions now. Ask students to underline the verb form and ask them what verb the contractions come from. Then ask them to uncover the grammar explanation and read the rules.

TEACH GLOBAL THINK LOCAL **Extra activity**

If your students need some more controlled practice at this point to focus on correct production of form, write the following on the board:

read / he

work / they

write / I

speak / you

play / we

travel / she

shop / they

eat / she

sleep / you

Ask students to write the correct form: *he's working, they're writing,* and so on.

Alternatively, say the prompts and do this as an oral drill.

1 Before filling the gaps, ask students to read the text quickly to gain a general understanding and answer the questions.

Anne's in her hotel room. John's at home with the children, preparing dinner.

2 Check the following vocabulary: *snack* (use examples: *sandwich, hamburger, fruit*) and *rest*. Students work individually to complete the conversation with the correct verb form, before checking in pairs.

3 **3.38** Students listen and check.

1 'm having

2 'm watching

3 're resting

4 'm also reading

5 're always working

6 're playing

7 'm cooking

G Grammar focus

Show students the icon. Write *page 116* on the board and ask them to find it. Show students the language summary on present continuous (affirmative).

You can use exercise 4 on page 117 for:

a) extra practice now

b) homework

c) review a couple of lessons from now.

The answers are on page 117 of the Teacher's Book.

Functional language (SB page 79)

This section focuses on expressions for buying a ticket.

1 3.39 Refer back to the pictures on page 78 and re-elicit the expression *ticket office*. If you have a stronger class, you could try and elicit a typical conversation before reading the actual conversation.

Ask students to read the conversation. If you wish to provide an initial reading task you could give them the words *price*, *place*, *platform*, *time* and ask them to order the subjects of the conversation.

Draw students' attention to the *Language note* and point out that *16.30* means '4.30 in the afternoon'. *06.30* is usually pronounced *oh six thirty* when we are talking about timetables.

3.39

Anne:	Hello, can I buy a ticket to **Brussels**, please.
Ticket seller:	Are you travelling today?
Anne:	Yes. I think there's a train at **16.30**.
Ticket seller:	That's right. How do you want to pay?
Anne:	**Credit card**, please.
Ticket seller:	That's **£206**. Thank you. Here you are.
Anne:	Thanks. What time does the train arrive?
Ticket seller:	**19.44**, and it leaves from platform **2**.
Anne:	Thank you.

---

2 Read the first line of the conversation, stopping at *Bonn / Brussels*. Elicit some other words that could go in the gap. Ask students to continue like this in pairs, substituting the key information until they have built a new dialogue.

3 Practise the *Useful phrases* with students and then ask them to practise their own conversation, monitoring as they do so. After a few minutes, have a few pairs perform to the class.

Part 2

TEACH GLOBAL THINK LOCAL **Lead-in**

To continue with the theme of travel, draw a picture of a suitcase on the board and say *When I go away, I take a camera*. Ask the first student to repeat your sentence and add an item, eg *When I go away I take a camera and my passport*. If you like, you can draw the items in the suitcase, or invite one of the students to come up and do so. Continue round the class with each student repeating and adding to the chain.

Vocabulary (SB page 80)

1 Tell the students you are going to look at some pictures of things associated with travel. Look at the labelled pictures and then ask students to label the remaining pictures.

2 3.40 Students listen, check and repeat. Discuss the question.

The items are more likely to be associated with a holiday.

 3.40

a **a metro station**

b **a theatre**

c **a guidebook**

d **take a bus tour**

e a map

f a palace; take a boat trip

g visit a gallery

h a square

---

3 To reinforce the vocabulary, ask students to cover the pictures and then work in pairs to recall the words, using the questions. The follow-up questions are designed to encourage students to express personal opinions. Elicit some of these during feedback and ask some further questions about students' answers.

Places: metro station; theatre; square; palace; gallery

Three things to do: visit a gallery; take a bus tour; take a boat trip

Two things to take: a guidebook; a map

Reading and Speaking (SB page 80)

The text gives some information about visitors to Moscow, Russia.

Lead-in

To establish the theme you could play 'Where am I?' Ask students to close their books.

Give students three clues, eg *I'm travelling in a yellow taxi. I'm eating hamburgers. I'm walking in a famous park.* Then they can ask you three questions without directly asking where you are, eg *Do the people speak English? Are there some tall buildings? Is there a metro system?* Before guessing the location *Are you in New York?*

Play a few more rounds with students giving the clues. Then finish by giving clues for Moscow to lead in to the reading: *It's very cold. I'm standing in a famous square. The signs are in a different alphabet.*

1 Ask students to open books. Look at the graph of visitors to different cities, then explain that the title of the text is incomplete and that they have to choose one of the three phrases to complete it. Check students understand the phrases, then ask them to read individually before checking their answer in pairs.

2	a popular tourist destination.

2 Students read to answer more detailed questions.

1	Yes
2	$900
3	No

Background note

Note that the amount is given in US dollars as the text is aimed at western tourists. The currency of Russia is the rouble.

Speaking extra

Ask if any of your students have visited Moscow. If so, get the rest of the class to ask them questions about it. If you've been yourself, take in any pictures or souvenirs from your trip and tell students a little about it, encouraging them to ask you questions.

3 In this activity, students find out more statistics about Moscow for visitors. Divide the class in two halves, A and B. Explain that they are going to prepare some questions first, with all the student As working together (or in various groups of A students) and Bs together. Refer As to page 99 and Bs to page 103. Monitor as they work to check the questions. When they have finished preparing, put students into AB pairs. First A asks the questions and B answers using the information on the page.

Listening (SB page 81)

Here students return to Anne Ross's trip. Anne is now in Moscow and her husband John is visiting her there and spending time as a tourist while she works. Students listen to three extracts from John's day as he takes a sightseeing tour and finally his side of a phone conversation with his wife.

1 🔘 **3.41** Refer students to *Vocabulary* on page 80 and explain that as they listen, they have to tick the expressions they hear. It's not important to understand everything at this stage as they are listening for recognition only.

🔘 **3.41**

A: Hello. Is this the tour bus?

B: Yes, this is the Moscow City **Bus Tour**.

A: OK, great, one adult please.

B: That's 800 roubles please …

Good morning Ladies and Gentlemen and welcome to Moscow City Bus Tours. My name's Katya and I'm your guide this morning. This morning we're visiting the most important sights in Moscow including the Bolshoi **Theatre** and Red Square, so have your cameras ready! Please ask me …

OK Ladies and Gentlemen. The building you're looking at is the Tretyakov **Gallery**, one of the most important art museums in Moscow. If you only visit one museum in Moscow, visit this gallery …

A: Oh hi love … I'm fine. I'm seeing the city on one of those, er tourist buses. … Cold? No, it's not cold. I'm not wearing my coat anyway … How about you? What are you doing? … Yeah? Oh, OK, I have to go – we're arriving at the Kremlin **palace**. OK, see you later, bye.

---

2 Now students listen again for detail and choose the correct answer. For question 5, note that John actually says *It's not cold*, which is another way of saying *it isn't cold*.

1	800 roubles
2	Moscow City Bus Tours
3	art gallery
4	wife
5	isn't

Grammar (SB page 81)

On the board write *Cold? No, it's not cold.* Play the final part of the *Listening* and ask students to write the next sentence they hear (*I'm not wearing my coat.*). Ask students to tell you the parts of the negative present continuous (subject + *be* + *not* + present participle). Elicit the question form (*Are you wearing a coat?*). Then ask them to read the summary.

1 Students complete the sentences with the negative form of the present continuous.

1	isn't visiting	3	aren't taking
2	isn't wearing	4	isn't speaking

2 Read the example. Students work individually to form the questions. Then check them as a class. Don't ask the questions at this stage.

1 Are you feeling cold?	2 Who are you working with?
3 Is the teacher speaking now?	

TEACH GLOBAL THINK LOCAL **Extra activity**

For additional practice write further prompts on the board as follows:

How / you / feel?

The teacher / sit down?

What / you / do?

What / you / wear?

For the final question, ask students to go to page 104 and practise asking and answering questions about the items of clothing.

G Grammar focus

Show students the icon. Write *page 116* on the board and ask them to find it. Show students the language summary on present continuous (negative and question forms).

You can use exercises 5 and 6 on page 117 for:

a) extra practice now

b) homework

c) review a couple of lessons from now.

The answers are on pages 117–8 of the Teacher's Book.

Pronunciation (SB page 81)

1 🔘 **3.42** Students listen and repeat the questions. As you play the recording, use your hand to show how the intonation rises on *Yes / No* questions and falls on *Wh-* questions. Ask some individual students to repeat with correct pronunciation.

2 Students work in pairs to ask and answer the questions from *Grammar* exercise 2. Monitor for correct intonation and accurate formation of the present continuous.

Writing (SB page 81)

Students look at a personal email and then write their own.

1 Check students remember who John is. Ask *Who's John? Where is he? Is he working or on holiday?* Explain that the text is an email John writes to his friend Martin about his holiday. Students read and tick the subjects he writes about.

1	the bus tour
3	the metro
4	the food
6	the weather

2 Ask students to think about a place they have visited on holiday.

TEACH GLOBAL THINK LOCAL **Writing extra**

To help students prepare, put a chart on the board. First, elicit and complete the information about John's trip as follows:

	John	Me
the place	Moscow	
yesterday	went on a bus tour	
today	using the Metro	
adjectives	amazing, beautiful, cold, different, good, great, OK	

Ask students to make notes about their destination in the right hand column.

Working individually, students write their own email. Monitor as they work.

When they finish, ask students to work in groups. They exchange emails and decide which place sounds the most interesting.

Global game

(SB page 82)

The game gives students an opportunity to consolidate verb forms. Ask students to form groups of three or four students. Each group needs a dice and a counter or coin to represent each student. Drill the *Useful language*.

To play, the first student rolls the dice and moves forward the number of squares indicated. They have to say a sentence which can be in the present simple, past simple or present continuous as appropriate, eg:

Square 1: *He visited Spain in February.*

Square 2: *I don't live near the sea now.*

Square 13: *I usually go to a supermarket on Monday.*

Square 18: *Are you using a computer now?*

The others in the group have to decide if the sentence is grammatically correct and if not, help correct it. Then the next person takes a turn. Monitor to help with accuracy. Note any incorrect sentences you hear and when the students have finished playing the game, write these on the board for the class to correct.

If your students enjoy competitions, give each student five points at the start. They get an extra point for a correct sentence but lose a point for an incorrect sentence. At the end see who is the winner.

Global review

These activities can be used at home but are designed to be used in class with students working together in pairs.

Aim: to review the language of the unit.

Tips:

- Encourage students to work together.
- Allow them to look back through the unit or consult their notes.
- In feedback, elicit more examples or the reason why an answer is correct.

Vocabulary (SB page 83)

> **1** Travelling by train: ticket office; platform; seat; ticket; timetable
> Places in a city: gallery; museum; palace; theatre
> Things you take when you travel: guidebook; map; suitcase
> **2** 1 123
> 2 209
> 3 650
> **3** 1 three hundred and seventy-six
> 2 nine hundred and four
> 3 a / one hundred and eighty-six
> 4 two hundred and fifty-eight

Functional language (SB page 83)

> **1, 2** 🔘 **3.43**
> A: Good morning. What time's the next train to Cardiff?
> B: Six thirty.
> A: OK. Two tickets please.
> B: That's £48 please.
> A: Do you take credit cards?
> B: Yes, we do. Thank you. Here are your tickets.
> A: Thank you, goodbye. Oh, which platform is it?
> B: Platform 5, sir.

Grammar (SB page 83)

> **1**
>
> Are you enjoying yourself?
>
> I'm having
>
> Where are you staying?
>
> I'm staying
>
> I'm sitting
>
> some actors are telling
>
> I'm sitting
>
> What are you doing?
>
> I'm cooking
>
> **2, 3** Students' own answers.

Listen again (SB page 83)

The *Listen again* text in this unit comes from the conversation between Anne Ross and Mr Peeters in *Listening* on page 78. Here, students complete the conversation, then listen again to check.

> **1–4**
>
> 🎧 **3.44**
>
> Anne: Mr Peeters? Hello, this is Anne, Anne Ross.
>
> Peeters: Good **evening** Anne. **Welcome** to Brussels!
>
> Anne: Thank you, but I have a **problem**. I understand that someone from the **office** is meeting me at the station.
>
> Peeters: Yes, that's **right**.
>
> Anne: Well, I'm **waiting** but there's no-one here.
>
> Peeters: Don't worry, I'm coming to meet you now.
>
> Anne: Great, I'm waiting next to **platform** 6. **See** you soon.

TEACH GLOBAL THINK LOCAL **Speaking extra**

After listening, ask students to close their books. Write prompts for the conversation on the board, eg

A: *Mr P? / Hello / Anne R*

Mr P: *Good / Welcome* etc.

Elicit the full conversation but without writing it up. Then ask students to practise in pairs.

Arts & Technology

Coursebook

Unit 14	Language	Texts	Communicative skills
Part 1 SB page 84	Vocabulary Colours Grammar Describing nouns	Reading *Wall paintings* Listening and Speaking Two paintings	Functional language Agreeing and disagreeing
Part 2 SB page 86	Vocabulary Technology Grammar *Can / can't* Pronunciation *Can / can't*	Listening One laptop per child	Speaking What we have Writing Linking words
Global voices SB page 88	Listening to people from around the world talk about their favourite gadgets *My favourite … is …*		
Global review SB page 89	Colours Agreeing and disagreeing Adjectives and nouns *Can / Can't* Ordering sentence elements		

Additional resources

eWorkbook	Interactive and printable grammar, vocabulary, listening and pronunciation practice Extra reading and writing practice Additional downloadable listening and audio material
TB resource CD	Communication activity worksheets to print and photocopy
Go global Ideas for further research	**Arts** Ask students to find out information about their nearest art gallery (including opening times, costs, what kind of art, etc.) and to be prepared to compare notes next lesson. **Technology** Ask students to research a gadget that they would like to have, and to find out relevant details, eg what it can do, cost, to tell their partner(s) next lesson.

Part 1

TEACH GLOBAL
THINK LOCAL
Lead-in

Even beginners are likely to know some of the colours in English but just in case they don't, have ready a pencil or object in each colour, to clarify.

Ask students to think of the colour *yellow* and to write down one thing that comes into their head. They write just the association down, in English if they can, or they can draw it, eg *the sun*, *a dress they have*, *a flower*. Ask students to do the same for *red*, *blue*, *black*, *green* and *brown*. Then students work in threes to try to remember the colour from their objects, and compare their associations.

Vocabulary (SB page 84)

1 🔘 **3.45** This exercise extends students' knowledge of colours and assumes that they already know basic ones. Students work individually to look at the colours and complete the sentences, then listen and check.

> 1 Black and white make grey.
> 2 Red and yellow make orange.
> 3 Blue and yellow make green.
> 4 Red and blue make purple.
> 5 Blue and orange make brown.
> For 5, note that red and green also combine to make brown.

2 🔘 **3.46** Students listen and repeat the colours. Focus in on any problem words, eg orange /ˈɒrɪndʒ/, grey /greɪ/, purple /ˈpɜːp(ə)l/.

3 Ask a confident student to come and sit at the front of the class. Different students then ask him / her the three questions. Students then work in pairs to ask and answer.

Reading (SB page 84)

The texts are all descriptions of wall art from various places in the world and from different periods in history.

1 🔘 **3.47** The question given here is a gist question, which could probably be answered by just looking at the visuals. Let them look at the visuals first. Then, to confirm their guesses, students read and listen.

> True

2 Students read and match the pictures to the descriptions.

> 1 e
> 2 d
> 3 a
> 4 b
> 5 c

3 This is a scan reading exercise, where students just look for colours mentioned in the text.

> Purple, black and white are not in the text.

TEACH GLOBAL
THINK LOCAL
Reading extra

Bring in a map or allow students to use the internet, if appropriate. To get students to scan the text again for different information, ask them to order the paintings in terms of their distance from where they are now. They read to find out where each painting is located, then work in pairs to identify which one is nearer, writing them on a cline from nearest to furthest. Make sure you know the answers yourself!

4 Put students in different pairs to discuss these questions. For early finishers, add these questions to the board:

Do you ever paint?

What sort of things do you paint?

Do you have any paintings in your house?

Where are they?

What are they pictures of?

Grammar (SB page 85)

Write this sentence on the board:
I like the blue wall painting.

Ask students to identify the noun (*painting*; *I* is also a pronoun) and adjective (*blue*. *Wall* is a noun but acts as an adjective here. See *Language note* below). Then read aloud the rules, referring to the board as appropriate for each point.

Language note

The focus under *Grammar* highlights the use of nouns to describe nouns, eg *cave painting*; *train station*. These are often called 'compound nouns'.

Although words like *cave* and *train* are classified as nouns, in these examples they actually function adjectivally, describing the nouns they are with. Being part of a compound, these words have to go directly next to the noun they describe, even if there is another adjective, eg *an exciting football match*.

1 Students read and identify the word class of the underlined words. Let them check in pairs before feedback. Particularly for early finishers, you could ask them to check their answers in a monolingual dictionary. This will require them to look for the *noun* or *adjective* symbol. Alternatively, use a dictionary.

> nouns: wall; street; ball
> adjectives: favourite; British; young; red

2 First ask students to identify the word class of the word in brackets. Then they should apply the rule about position, placing the word in the correct gap. Students complete this task alone. Monitor to see how students are doing. If they are having problems, refer back to the relevant rule under *Grammar*.

3 **3.48** Students listen and check their answers.

---

1 I like the **blue** wall painting in Cuba.

2 He was a popular **wall** painter.

3 He's wearing a red **football** shirt.

4 Mattancherry is an **old** Indian palace.

5 I want to see the **African** cave paintings.

6 Cuba has lots of interesting **street** art.

Ⓖ Grammar focus

Show students the icon. Write *page 118* on the board and ask them to find it. Show students the first part of the language summary on describing nouns. You can use exercise 1 on page 119 for:

a) extra practice now

b) homework

c) review a couple of lessons from now.

The answers are on page 118 of the Teacher's Book.

Listening and Speaking (SB page 85)

1 **3.49** Give students a minute to look at the paintings. Ask the students as a class to put up their hand if they like the first; the second. Elicit why, if possible. Then students listen to find out which one is being talked about.

They are talking about the painting on the left.

3.49

A: I really like this painting.

B: Me too.

A: I like it because there's a lot of yellow in it.

B: Really? My favourite colour is blue.

A: The painting is of a street, er … in France.

B: Yes, I think so.

A: There's a café and there are some chairs and tables in the street. There are some people in the café. It's in the evening.

B: Really? I don't agree – I think it's at night.

Background note

The two paintings are Van Gogh's 'Café Terrace at Night' and 'Starry Night over the Rhône'.

2, 3 Students match the parts of the sentences from the conversation. Then they listen again to check.

---

1 b   2 d   3 a   4 c

---

4 Tell students that they are going to describe a picture for their partner to guess, as in exercise 1. Put students in AB pairs. The A students turn to page 99, Bs to page 103. Ask them to choose just one painting to describe. Point out the *Useful phrases* and give students two minutes to prepare what they will say. Write up on the board this outline:

1 Describe what you can see (at least three sentences).
2 Say why you (don't) like it (give reasons).

The A students start; B students listen without interrupting, saying which picture it is at the end. Students then swap roles.

Monitor and take notes on good or problematic language, for feedback later.

Functional language (SB page 85)

This section focuses on agreeing and disagreeing.

1 Let students read the phrases under *Agreeing* and *Disagreeing*. Students then listen and tick the phrases they hear. After feedback, focus on the phrases by saying, eg *I like this painting best* (point to one of the pictures in the unit), *and you?* Find someone who disagrees and agrees with you. Encourage them to use the target phrases. Ask about four students.

Agreeing: Me too. Yes, I think so.

Disagreeing: I don't agree. Really?

---

2 Put students in pairs. Ask students to look at all the paintings on pages 84 and 85 and pages 99 and 103 and choose just one. Alternatively, you could use pictures downloaded from the internet or art postcards and display these around the room, like a gallery.

Students see if their partner agrees or disagrees with them. Early finishers can discuss other paintings and their preferences. Monitor and give feedback on their language use, both good examples and problematic ones, as appropriate.

TEACH GLOBAL THINK LOCAL Extra activity

Write the following on the board or on a hand-out: *learning English, our classroom, English spelling, doing homework, getting up early, driving, strong coffee, chocolate*, etc. Try to localise the examples, adapting them for your particular students.

Put students in pairs and ask them to select one point each in turn. They then give their opinion about it, eg *I like our classroom, it's nice and light*. Their partner responds accordingly. Model with a confident student at the start.

Part 2

Speaking (SB page 86)

TEACH GLOBAL THINK LOCAL Lead-in

Put a gadget in your pocket, eg an mp3 player, a mobile phone, a watch. Tell students they can ask up to 12 questions to find out what it is. You can only answer *Yes* or *No*. They should use any language they can at this point. Tell them not to worry about the grammar, they just need to find out what it is! You could give one or two examples, eg *Is it expensive? Do you use it every day?*

1 Check that students understand the nouns in the sentences so that the context of each is clear. Students choose the best words for them to complete the sentences.

2 Students compare sentences with their partner. This exercise also revises the language of agreeing and disagreeing on page 85, so re-elicit this language at the start.

Vocabulary (SB page 86)

 3.50 Ask students if they have a computer. Students look at the pictures, then listen and repeat as they hear the different words.

> 💿 **3.50**
>
> a webcam
>
> a DVD drive
>
> a screen
>
> a keyboard
>
> a laptop

TEACH GLOBAL THINK LOCAL Speaking extra

To allow for some personalised oral fluency practice, put these questions up on the board:

What kind of laptop / computer do you have?
How often do you use it?
How many minutes every day?
What do you use it for, mostly?
Do you type quickly?
How did you learn to use it?

Listening (SB page 86)

1 Ask students to look at the picture of the child with the computer. Ask *Where do you think the child is from? Does this child look rich?* Focus students on the two questions in exercise 1, asking students to discuss these in pairs, referring them to the fact box. Take whole class feedback.

2 **3.51** Students listen to the start of the talk to see if they are right.

> 1   It helps children in developing countries.
>
> 2   It gives the children special computers to help their education.

> 💿 **3.51**
>
> The One Laptop Per Child organisation started in 2005. It helps children in developing countries. It gives the children special computers to help their education.

3 💿 **3.52** Let students read the five points before listening. Let students compare answers in pairs before feedback. Monitor to see if they need to listen again. Take whole class feedback.

> 1 b   2 a, b, e   3 b   4 a, b, c   5 a, c

> 💿 **3.52**
>
> The One Laptop Per Child organisation started in 2005. It helps children in developing countries. It gives the children special computers to help their education.
>
> Children in several countries, including Peru, Uruguay, Cambodia, Ethiopia and Afghanistan are using the special XO computers.
>
> The XO computer has a special design. It can operate with only 2 watts of electricity and you can read the screen in the sun. It only costs about $180.
>
> The children can read, write and play games. They can also connect to the internet. The computer has a camera and microphone so the children can take photos and have a video conference.
>
> Are there any problems? Well, the computers are slow to start and you can't use CDs or DVDs. But the main problem is politics; some governments don't want to spend money on the project and some computer companies aren't happy about the cheap price of the XO computer.

Background note

The OLPC organisation is a non-profit organisation, funded by several large US companies. Its objective is to help primary school children aged 6–12 in developing countries. The organisation has distributed thousands of laptops so far. For more information, go to the official website at www.laptop.org or type in the key words: *one laptop per child*. On the website is a selection of photos of the children with their laptops which could be exploited in class.

Grammar (SB page 87)

Ask *What can the students do on the computers?* Say this question naturally, without stressing *can*. Elicit some ideas, then ask students to follow as you read the notes and sentences in the *Grammar* box. As you read each rule, try to elicit an example for each one. If you think it would help, put an additional three examples on the board from the students' elicited examples: positive, negative and question form.

1 To make sure students understand the task, ask two or three random questions, eg *What do you have to do in question 6?* (write a question). Students work in pairs to transform the sentences.

In feedback, highlight visually the way the word *can* changes position in the question form. *They can play basketball → Can they ...?* A good way to do this is with objects such as Cuisenaire rods (or even board pens), to represent the subject, modal verb *can* and main verb.

```
1   You can't speak Chinese.
2   I can drive.
3   I can't swim.
4   Can her phone take photos?
5   He can play table tennis.
6   Can they play basketball?
```

2 Students look at the picture in the text about a pull-cord generator and give suggestions for its use. Then they read and find out.

```
It's used for making electricity.
```

3 Ask students to read the text again and complete it with the correct form of *can*. Do the first example together. Students should work individually, then check in pairs. In whole class feedback, ask students more questions to find out if they have understood the text itself, eg *Where can you use this generator? Why is it useful there? What can you use it for? What do you think of it?*

```
1   can't find
2   can make
3   can talk
4   can you use
```

Pronunciation (SB page 87)

1 ⚫ **3.53** Students in pairs say the sentences in exercise 1 to each other. Students then listen to the correct pronunciation of *can* and *can't*. Elicit how it is said in each case, replaying the recording if necessary. Write *can* /kæn/ and *can't* /kɑːnt/ on the board, with the examples from the book. Highlight the fact that the weak form of *can* /kən/ is used in positive sentences.

2 Students listen again and repeat. Really encourage natural pronunciation here. Ask students to repeat individually, if appropriate.

3 ⚫ **3.54** Students listen and respond. Highlight the fact that the weak form /kən/ is also used in question forms. Write this up in phonetics on the board with the example. Remind students that the full form of *can* /kæn/ is used in short answers. Drill the example sentences.

TEACH GLOBAL THINK LOCAL **Extra activity**

If your students enjoy and need further pronunciation work, ask them to go back to *Grammar* exercise 1 and to read sentences 1–6. In pairs they should read one sentence in turn, with their partner reading the transformed sentence in each case, eg:

A: *You can speak Chinese.*

B: *You can't speak Chinese.*

Remind them to pay special attention to their pronunciation. Early finishers can read the pull-cord generator text in *Grammar* exercise 2 again, one sentence each. As this is a challenging text, give them two minutes to read it silently first.

---

4 Ask a confident student to make a question with one of the prompts. Respond with a short answer. Give students four minutes to write at least four questions. This activity is a controlled drill of question forms and short answers. Stronger students should make up additional questions to ask other students at the end, around the class.

5 Students work in pairs to ask and answer. Monitor closely to correct pronunciation.

Language note

In American English the negative *can't* is pronounced /kænt/. Since the positive and negative forms sound very similar (often the 't' is barely audible), it can be harder to differentiate between positive and negative statements with *can / can't*.

Writing (SB page 87)

1 🔘 **3.55** Ask one of your students who owns an mp3 player to show it and talk about what it can do and why they like it, eg *You can listen to a sample of music*. Students then read and listen to the text, initially to see if any of the same ideas are mentioned.

Afterwards students match the linking words *because*, *and* and *but* with their use. Use the text to illustrate what the definition actually means. Use their first language if appropriate, as well as additional examples, eg *I like him, but he doesn't like me. I love French, but I can't speak it well.*

1 c	2 a	3 b

2 It is often useful to do mini writings like this in class time. With weaker writers, it may be appropriate to let them write in pairs. Monitor and assist, where appropriate, referring to the example text.

TEACH GLOBAL THINK LOCAL Alternative procedure

If all or most of your students need more support, first do a class composition on a different gadget, eg a TV. Elicit suggestions and write the text on the board, highlighting features of organisation as you do so. Then students do their own.

Alternatively or in addition to this, put some of the sentence beginnings on the board to stimulate ideas, eg: *I really like ... because ...*

I use it when ...

I can ...

It has ... but ...

I / It have / has ...

I / it can ...

G Grammar focus

Show students the icon. Write *page 118* on the board and ask them to find it. Show students the second part of the language summary about *can*: the information on forming affirmative, negative, question forms and short answers.

You can use exercises 2 and 3 on page 119 for:

a) extra practice now

b) homework

c) review a couple of lessons from now.

The answers are on page 118 of the Teacher's Book.

Global voices

These lessons in *Global* are designed to provide students with exposure to authentic speakers of English from both native and non-native English backgrounds. In this unit we extend the theme of gadgets and their uses.

Warm up (SB page 88)

1 Students write the missing letters of the gadgets in pairs. Tell them to refer to a dictionary to help. For stronger students, you could ask them to cover the pictures. Conduct this activity as a competition – the first pair to finish are the winners!

> a camera
> b mp3 player
> c watch
> d food processor
> e mobile phone

2 For fun, you could ask students to lie about one of these answers. Model the task first: students ask you the questions; you give the answers. At the end, say: *I lied about one of these answers. Which one, do you think?* Students do the same in pairs. Tell them to watch their partner's face carefully, and only at the end say which ones they think they lied about.

Listening (SB page 88)

1 **3.56–3.59** Tell students they are going to listen to four people answer the question *What's your favourite gadget?* Students listen and write the gadget next to each name.

> **3.56–3.59**
>
> **Nicole, Switzerland**
> So my favourite gadget is the **mobile phone**.
>
> **Dorothy, Scotland**
> My favourite gadget is a **food processor** because I enjoy cooking.
>
> **Abdul, Saudi Arabia**
> My favourite is my **mobile phone**.
>
> **Marc, France**
> One of my favourite gadgets erm ... my **watch** would be a gadget and it's my favourite one because it's useful to have a watch with you.

2 **3.60–3.63** Elicit one thing that you can do with a mobile phone. Then students listen to the same people talking about their own mobiles. Give them a moment to look at the grid before they listen.

> **3.60–3.63**
>
> **Nicole, Switzerland**
> I can **listen to music** with my mobile phone and I can also **take pictures** when I have forgotten my camera.
>
> **Dorothy, Scotland**
> I only have a very old mobile phone. I can **make telephone calls** and I can **send text messages**.
>
> **Abdul, Saudi Arabia**
> I can **send email** and **take photos**.
>
> **Marc, France**
> So what can I do with my mobile phone? Well, basically to **contact other people**. That's what I do with my mobile phone.

Language focus (SB page 88)

Read out the notes in the box. Write up the key phrases (those in bold) onto the board. Write the plural *s* in a different colour, to focus students: *One of my favourite gadgets is …* Then students complete the gap-fill exercise. Do the first one together. Students compare their answers before feedback.

> 1 gadget
> 2 sport**s**
> 3 citie**s**
> 4 drink

Speaking (SB page 88)

If your students need more support, ask them to first write out sentences 1–4 from the previous exercise, making them true for themselves. Then they work in pairs to ask and answer.

TEACH GLOBAL THINK LOCAL **Speaking extra**

To extend the above activity and provide further practice if your students need it, write out these prompts: *type of food, colour, local shop, day, word in English, place for a holiday, month, TV programme, part of the supermarket, car*, etc. Localise where possible.

Put these prompts either on the board or preferably on cut-up pieces of paper, one pile for each group of three. One person in turn then turns over one prompt and asks their two partners: *What's your favourite X?* The next person takes the next prompt, and so on. Encourage students to give reasons, as in the example activity under *Speaking*. Suggest they use either of the two answer forms: *My favourite ... One of my favourite ...*

Global review

These activities can be used at home but are designed to be used in class with students working together in pairs.

Aim: to review the language of the unit.

Tips:

- Encourage students to work together.
- Allow them to look back through the unit or consult their notes.
- In feedback, elicit more examples or the reason why an answer is correct.

Vocabulary (SB page 89)

> black
>
> blue
>
> brown
>
> green
>
> grey
>
> orange
>
> red
>
> white
>
> Pink and purple are also in the painting.

Speaking

Students' own answers.

Grammar 1 (SB page 89)

> **1**
>
> 1 flower: noun
>
> 2 mobile: adjective
>
> 3 living: adjective
>
> 4 DVD: noun
>
> 5 computer: noun
>
> 6 musical: adjective
>
> **2**
>
> 1 beautiful wall painting
>
> 2 new computer shop
>
> 3 modern art museum
>
> 4 expensive video camera
>
> 5 large kitchen table

> **3**
>
> 1 can't
>
> 2 can
>
> 3 can
>
> 4 can't
>
> **4**
>
> 1 and
>
> 2 because
>
> 3 but
>
> 4 and

Listen again (SB page 89)

The *Listen again* text in this unit comes from the description of the mp3 player in *Writing* on page 87. First, students use their knowledge of syntax to put the parts of the sentence in order, then they listen to check their answers.

> **1, 2** 🔘 **3.64**
>
> 1 I really like my mp3 player because it can do a lot of things.
>
> 2 I use it when I'm travelling to work.
>
> 3 I can listen to music and I can watch videos.
>
> 4 It has a microphone and it can record short conversations but I don't usually use this.
>
> 5 I have lots of photos on it and I can download language exercises to study on the train.

Coursebook

Unit 15	Language	Texts	Communicative skills
Part 1 SB page 90	Vocabulary Ways of saying numbers Extend your vocabulary *local* Grammar *Be going to* (future)	Listening Jersey	Speaking . Disappearing languages Writing A Papua New Guinea language
Part 2 SB page 92	Grammar Language review	Reading *The United Kingdom of language learners*	Speaking and Listening Language learning around the world Speaking Giving a presentation
Global reading SB page 94	Reading a dictionary extract and looking at different ways to record vocabulary *I like ... because ...*		
Global review SB page 95	Numbers *Be going to* Choosing the correct verb form		

Additional resources

eWorkbook	Interactive and printable grammar, vocabulary, listening and pronunciation practice Extra reading and writing practice Additional downloadable listening and audio material
TB resource CD	Communication activity worksheets to print and photocopy
Go global Ideas for further research	**Language** Ask students to find an online dictionary to check the meaning, pronunciation, word class and example sentence of two words they have recently heard or seen, to share next lesson. **Learning** Ask students to find four more facts about Scottish Gaelic, Irish Gaelic or Welsh, and to come prepared to tell their partner(s) next lesson.

15 Language & Learning

Part 1

Lead-in

Ask students to draw a 'Bingo' grid in their notebooks, with just six squares. Students fill in the squares with six different numbers between 210–222. Model this. Then read out random numbers between 210–222, eg 213, 217, 221, etc. You are the 'Bingo caller'. If you say one of the numbers in their grid, students should cross out the number. The first one to cross out all their numbers and so complete the grid shouts 'Bingo!'. They should read out their numbers to check.

Vocabulary (SB page 90)

1 Do the first one together. Then students match the words to the numbers.

1 e	2 f	3 a	4 c	5 b	6 d

2 🔘 **3.65** Students listen, check and repeat.

3 Ask students *Who likes maths?* Ask for a show of hands. Ask them to first read the sums and find out if the answer is correct. Then in pairs, they try to say the sums to each other. Monitor and listen for where any problems lie.

> Yes, they are all correct.

4 🔘 **3.66** Students listen and check.

> 1 A half plus a quarter is three quarters.
> 2 Fifty percent of ninety is forty-five.
> 3 Eighty-four is double forty-two.
> 4 Forty-seven is half of ninety-four.

Extra activity

In the same way, ask students to test their friends' maths skills! Students work in pairs to write four (or more) sums; one or two of their sums should be incorrect. They then sit with a different pair, in groups of four. Confident students could work in their new pairs. One person from each pair reads out their sums to the other two, who have to decide if they are correct or not. Allow the listeners to write the sums down if necessary. Monitor and give feedback.

Listening (SB page 90)

1 Write *Jersey* on the board. Ask *Do you know where this is?* Show students the map to help. Ask the two questions in exercise 1.

> 1 It's near France and the UK.
> 2 French and English

2 Students look at the two expressions and decide whether they are English. If they can't guess, draw their attention to the accents, which are not a feature of English words.

> They are not English. They are Jèrriais for *Hello* and *Goodbye*.

Background note

Jersey, together with Guernsey, forms part of the group of islands known as the Channel Islands. Jersey is part of the British Isles, but not part of the United Kingdom. It is independently governed and has its own laws on health, immigration and taxes. Its favourable tax laws make it well known as a tax haven. People from the island either consider themselves British, or prefer to see themselves as European / French.

3 🔘 **3.67** Look at the picture of Gemma. Students listen to find out more about Jèrriais.

> F (It's a local language that not many people speak now.)

> 🔘 **3.67**
>
> A: Gemma, you come from Jersey which is a small island. I know it's near France – do people speak both English and French?
>
> B: No, English is the main language, everyone speaks English. However, there are groups of Portuguese, Polish, French and Kenyans who speak their native languages.
>
> A: Right.
>
> B: There is another language called Jèrriais. It's a local language that people spoke in the past.
>
> A: So do many people speak that today?
>
> B: No, not really. There are about 90,000 people in Jersey and less than 4% speak Jèrriais – and it's mainly older people. Perhaps about 15% can understand some of it.
>
> A: Now I know many people are learning Jèrriais. Why is that?
>
> B: Well, for two reasons. The first is to keep the language and the culture of Jersey, and the second is for fun.
>
> A: What about the young people – are they interested?
>
> B: A little, there are classes at some schools now. The government is trying to make more young people learn it.
>
> A: A language disappears every two weeks – is Jèrriais going to disappear?
>
> B: I hope not. No, I think it's going to be here for some time.
>
> A: And what about you – do you speak Jèrriais?
>
> B: No, I don't. But I'm going to start classes next year.

4 Give students time to read the questions before they listen again. Tell students that you will play the recording twice if necessary and let students compare answers after the first listening.

1	all but German
2	90,000
3	15%
4	No

Extend your vocabulary (SB page 90)

Elicit the word *local*, asking: *What kind of language is Jèrriais?* Write the word up on the board and drill it. Then ask students to complete the exercise. Check answers.

1	language
2	time
3	radio
4	market
5	calls
6	currency

Ask students in pairs to try and use the words *local* + noun, eg *local currency*, *local radio station*, etc in their own contexts, changing the sentences accordingly. Give this example: *The local market is on X (day). They sell good fish there.* Encourage them to write down at least two sentences. Hear some examples as a whole class.

Language note

In some European languages, *local* is a false friend. It is used as a noun to mean 'a place', 'premises' or 'a bar'.

Grammar (SB page 91)

Ask *So, can Gemma speak the local language now?* (Emphasise the word 'now'.) *What did she say?* In this way try to elicit the target language: *I'm going to start classes next year.* Write this example on the board. Ask students *Why does she use 'going to' here?* (to talk about the future). Then highlight the structure, using the example:

subject + *be* + *going to* + infinitive

Finally, read out the general rules. With a monolingual class, you could use the students' first language at such points.

1 🔊 **3.68** Write up: *The teacher_____ because they didn't do their homework.* Try to elicit the missing words, guiding them to use *be going to* and using mime to show anger. Ask them to find the answer in exercise 1. Then students complete the exercise before listening to check their answers.

1 c	2 d	3 b	4 a			

2 Students work in pairs to complete the exercise. In feedback, first check they have the correct forms, then ask students to say the correct answers again, but naturally. At this point, highlight the contractions, drilling as appropriate. See *Pronunciation note* below.

1	am going to
2	are going to
3	are going to
4	is going to

Language note

Going to is used to talk about strong predictions that are based on clear evidence, eg a young child who is not walking steadily: *She's going to fall*. In the example *They didn't do their homework so the teacher is going to be angry*, the prediction is based on your knowledge of teachers' reactions, and perhaps your knowledge of this demanding teacher in particular!

Pronunciation note

In fast natural speech, the *be going to* structure is usually contracted, eg *I'm going to learn Jèrriais. She's going to have problems.* The words at the end of these examples are stressed, eg *learn Jèrriais; have problems. Going to* itself is contracted, and is likely to be pronounced as a weak form: /ˈɡəʊ(w)ɪntə/ or /ˈɡʌnə/ within the sentence. As a result, students often fail to hear (part of) the *going to* structure. It is important to raise students' awareness of this, primarily for receptive purposes at this level.

Ⓖ Grammar focus

Show students the icon. Write *page 118* on the board and ask them to find it. Show students the language summary, the information under *be going to*.

You can use exercise 5 on page 119 for:

a) extra practice now

b) homework

c) review a couple of lessons from now.

The answers are on page 118 of the Teacher's Book.

If you have a stronger group, and feel they can cope with question forms and negatives, show them the *Grammar focus* on page 118 and let them do exercise 4. This language will be revisited at *Global Elementary*.

UNIT 15 Language & Learning

Speaking (SB page 91)

Tell students they are going to read some interesting information about languages, but their information is not complete. They need to work in pairs to complete their texts. Put students in AB pairs. Students first read their unfinished texts, As on page 99 and Bs on page 103. Then write up the first part of the text to show how the two parts complement each other. Ask a strong pair to model the first sentence.

You could also put the following words and phrases on the board to help, clarifying as you do so:

full stop

new sentence

Can you repeat that please?

What's after …?

Can you start again?

Students do the task. Monitor and ensure students are listening, not reading their partner's text.

At the end, let students look at each other's texts and discuss the final question. Take feedback on points of interest.

Writing (SB page 91)

1 Students look at the picture. Ask students to read and answer the question.

> The national language is Tok Pisin. Wiarumus (one of the local languages) may die out.

2 Ask students *What language is spoken in Russia?* (Russian). Elicit any other languages students may know (Balkar is mentioned in the text). Then students read the notes. This is a parallel writing task, where they can very closely use the model (the Papua New Guinea text). Encourage students to work on their own, if possible, showing them how to use the model by focusing on the phrases in red.

Part 2

Lead-in

Put students in groups of three. Ask them to teach their partners a short phrase (or two to three separate words) in another language or dialect, besides English. Encourage students to drill their partners. Hear some examples aloud.

If you have a monolingual group and their combined knowledge of other languages is limited, ask those who do know one to teach the rest.

Speaking and Listening (SB page 92)

1 Students work in pairs to discuss and decide on the answers. If they work collaboratively, it also means that they will say the numbers aloud.

2 **3.69** Before listening, hear some of the students' answers to raise interest. Then students listen and check.

```
1 c
2 a
3 b
4 c
5 c
6 a
```

 3.69

There are about **7000** languages in the world and the language with the most native speakers is **Chinese**. Mandarin Chinese is also becoming a very popular foreign language with about **30 million** students round the world.

For many parents, English is a very important language and some children start learning it very young. In Japan, about **21%** of five-year-olds are already going to English conversation classes and **90%** of European schoolchildren study English.

English is very important in other countries but what about British people? Are they good language learners? No, they're not. Only **5%** of British adults can count to 20 in another language.

Extra activity

Ask students to work in pairs or groups of three. Write the following discussion questions on the board:

Which foreign languages do you study?

When do children start learning in your country?

Do you think it's important to learn languages?

Reading (SB page 92)

This reading text looks at the languages besides English which are spoken in the UK.

1 Students read the first paragraph and choose the correct sentence.

```
3
```

Write up the following on the board: *Croeso y Cymru.* Ask students if they know what language this is in, and what it might mean! It means *Welcome to Wales*, in Welsh (often learners do not realise that Welsh is a completely different language from English). Refer to the map of the UK on SB page 92 to highlight Wales.

Background note

There are three countries in Great Britain: England, Scotland and Wales. People from Scotland are not English, but Scottish; those from Wales are Welsh. (Scottish and Welsh people can also say they are British.)

The United Kingdom (UK) has four countries: the three countries of Great Britain and also Northern Ireland. The rest of Ireland (the south) is an independent republic called Éire.

The British Isles refers to both the UK and southern Ireland, although nowadays the terms 'Britain and Ireland' are often used.

2 **3.70** Pre-teach the words: *extinct* (adjective); *whisky* (noun). Students read and listen, then complete the table. Tell students to leave the 'Other information' column until the end. This can be done by faster and more confident readers as it demands greater understanding.

Language	How many speakers are there?	Where do they speak it?	Other information
Gaelic	60,000	north and west of Scotland	'whisky' is from Gaelic; BBC website
Manx	many	Isle of Man	The last Manx speaker died in 1974 but now many people are learning it
BSL	40,000	all over Britain	for the deaf; grammar and vocabulary is different from English
Welsh	750,000	Wales	numbers are increasing; all school children study it; adults too; Welsh radio and TV

3 Students match the questions to the answers.

```
1 c   2 d   3 a   4 b
```

Reading extra

There are some collocations in this text which your learners might find useful: *language learner, living language, official language, first / second language, national language* and also *native speaker*. These words may also be helpful for the presentation on page 93.

With a strong group, ask students to work in pairs and find the other five collocations with *language*, after giving the example *living language*. They will have to scan the text again to do this.

Put their answers on the board, and then students work in pairs to decide what the difference in meaning is between the collocations. They can refer to their own countries or to the text to do this. Check their understanding as a whole class.

Grammar (SB page 92)

1 This exercise reviews the present simple and continuous forms, as well as the past simple in context. The exercise is designed to raise linguistic awareness and to consolidate taught language.

Students find examples of the verbs in the text in brackets. Do the first example together, and make sure that students know what the names of the forms refer to, eliciting an example if necessary.

1	a	... **are** first language users
	b	BSL grammar and vocabulary **is** different ...
2	a	60,000 **speak** Gaelic
	b	The word 'whisky' **comes** from ...
		(or The BBC **has** a website ...)
3	a	The number of Welsh speakers **is increasing**.
	b	Lots of adults **are learning** Welsh ...
4	a	the last Manx speaker **died** ...
	b	some people **said** the language **was** extinct ...

2 Ask students to guess what Britain's second language is after English. Show students an example of Punjabi script (or simply point out the example on page 92). You can do this by doing an internet image search using the words *Punjabi script*. Ask *How many Punjabi speakers do you think there are in the UK?* Pre-teach *immigration* and be prepared to show a map of the Punjab region at this point. Then ask students to find out more about Punjabi, completing the text.

For stronger students you could make a separate hand-out or slide: delete the form, eg *past simple* and just keep the infinitive in all five cases, thus raising the challenge. Students then decide on the form themselves.

When students have finished reading, ask them what they think about the last point. Ask *Should British people learn Punjabi rather than French, for example? Why / Why not?*

1	started
2	came
3	speak
4	is
5	are starting

Background note

Besides the UK, there are also large populations of Punjabis in Canada, the US, the Middle East and Africa. Punjabis typically belong to one of three major religions: Islam, Sikhism or Hinduism. In the Punjab region itself, although their main language is Punjabi, the people typically also speak Urdu and Hindi, depending on whether they are from Pakistani or Indian Punjab.

Extra activity

Model this activity first yourself. Come prepared with two photos of two different friends.

Briefly describe who he / she is, then give the following details:

- job, eg *He works in a bank.*
- likes / dislikes, eg *He loves skiing.*
- how you met them, eg *I went to primary school with him.*
- at this moment, eg *He's probably sitting at his desk, having a coffee.*

Give students three minutes preparation. Monitor and assist as necessary. They then talk about at least one of their friends in groups of three. They could write this up for homework.

Speaking (SB page 93)

Giving a presentation should prove to be a motivating and confidence-building task for beginners, providing a rewarding culmination to their studies at this level.

Ask students to read the two tasks, A and B. Ask them as a class to choose either A or B for you to talk about (so come prepared with a short presentation on both). Give the presentation, incorporating some of the phrases from the *Useful phrases* expressions. Ensure that your talk is no longer than three minutes and that you choose a topic which will be different from the students'. This stage both serves as a model and raises the profile of the presentation.

1 Let students choose A or B for themselves. You decide if it would be beneficial to your students to prepare at home.

2 Students can either present to the class or to groups of three or four people. Presenting to smaller groups might be less daunting. It is advisable not to correct students or intervene in this fluency activity, unless there is a breakdown in communication. Bearing in mind the stage in the course and the nature of the task, it may be better to focus on positive feedback.

Global reading

The *Global reading* pages encourage students to approach different text types and develop the ability to read for pleasure. Here the text looks at how dictionary entries are made up.

1 Hold up a dictionary. Ask students who has one, and which one. Ask students if any of them have an English / English (monolingual) dictionary.

Elicit the word *deaf* and write it on the board. Let students read the entry. Ask them to complete the exercise. Do the first example together.

island
local
per cent
evening class
extinct
immigration
native speaker
population

2 It would be useful here to let students use English / English dictionaries to check the word class if possible. They should write *(n)* or *(adj)* on the line.

local and *extinct* are adjectives. The rest are nouns.

3 Ask students if they recorded any of the words in exercise 1 in their notebooks (they all came up in this unit). If students did, ask to see where and how they wrote them down. Show others in the class, but do so with sensitivity, talking through the strategies that students have used. Ask questions and make comments such as *Do you find this helpful? It's interesting that you ...* Then students complete the matching exercise.

1 C   2 A   3 B

4 Students discuss the question in pairs and give reasons. Take some whole class feedback, for interest and also to raise the profile of these strategies.

5 Ask students to select at least one word from exercise 1. Ask individuals randomly which word they have selected and which strategy (point to exercise 3) they are going to use to record it. Early finishers can choose an additional word and strategy. After a few minutes, let students compare what they have done in groups. Monitor and find some nice examples to show the class.

Global review

These activities are designed to review the content of the unit. They can be used at home but are designed to be used in class with students working together in pairs.

Aim: to review the language of the unit.

Tips:

- Encourage students to work together.
- Allow them to look back through the unit or consult their notes.
- In feedback, elicit more examples or the reason why an answer is correct.

Vocabulary (SB page 95)

1		
Across		**Down**
4	per cent	1 forty
7	thousand	2 hundred
8	eighty	3 quarter
10	million	5 double
		6 half
		9 twelve

2 Students read the poem aloud.

3 Number 6 is unhappy because number seven ate nine!

Grammar (SB page 95)

1 am / 'm going to
2 is / 's going to
3 are / 're going to
4 are / 're going to
5 are / 're going to

Listen again (SB page 95)

The *Listen again* text in this unit comes from the interview with Gemma about Jèrriais on page 90. Here, students practise manipulating different verb tense forms, before listening to check their answers.

1, 2 💿 **3.71**
come; speaks; speak; spoke; are; are learning; are; is trying; disappears; is going to be; am going to start

Grammar focus answer key

Units 1 & 2

1 1 passports
2 phones
3 addresses
4 coffees
5 buses
6 classes
7 cities
8 cameras

2 What's your name?
What's your phone number?
What's your address?
And what's your postcode?

3 1 d   I'm
2 a, e, g   we're
3 b, c, f   he's
4 a, e, g   they're
5 a, e, g   you're
6 b, c, f   she's
7 b, c, f   it's

4 1 Are you French?
2 They aren't doctors.
3 They're teachers.
4 She's a student.
5 I'm not from Russia.
6 Are you in a café?

5 Teacher: Hi. I am Lucy. I am the teacher. What's your name?
Student 1: I am Andrea.
Teacher: OK. This is your book. Sit there.
Student 2: Hi Andrea. My name's Oliver and this is Susanne. We are from Germany.
Student 3: Are you from Spain?
Student 1: No, I am from Venezuela.

6 Teacher: Hi. I'm Lucy. I'm the teacher. What's your name?
Student 1: I'm Andrea.
Teacher: OK. This is your book. Sit there.
Student 2: Hi Andrea. My name's Oliver and this is Susanne. We're from Germany.
Student 3: Are you from Spain?
Student 1: No, I'm from Venezuela.

Units 3 & 4

1 1 He is my brother.
2 They are from Mexico.
3 It's a photo of my family.
4 Her father's name is Jonas.
5 This is my aunt and uncle and this is their daughter.

6 My cousin is American. She is from Hawaii.
7 Is this his wife?

2 1 ✔
2 ✘ She's my mother's sister.
3 ✘ My daughters' names are Rhona and Maya.
4 ✘ My sister's husband is Australian.
5 ✔
6 ✘ This is a photo of my father's birthday party.
7 ✘ My brother's name is Lester.
8 ✘ My sisters' husbands are teachers.

3 1 Are they your sisters? / They are your sisters.
2 It is my car. / It isn't my car.
3 Is she your cousin? Yes, she is.
4 They aren't my brothers.
5 Are they your photos?
6 Is he your brother? No, he isn't.

4 1 There is a car park. / There's a car park.
2 There are 3 cinemas.
3 There is a big hotel. / There's a big hotel.
4 There is a shopping mall. / There's a shopping mall.
5 There are many cafés.
6 There are 8 restaurants.
7 There is a bank. / There's a bank.
8 There are many bookshops.

5 1 Is there a DVD player? Yes, there is. / No, there isn't.
2 Are there dictionaries? Yes, there are. / No, there aren't.
3 Are there lots of students? Yes, there are. / No, there aren't.
4 Is there a computer? Yes, there is. / No, there isn't.
5 Are there books? Yes, there are. / No, there aren't.
6 Is there a television? Yes, there is. / No, there isn't.
7 Is there a board? Yes, there is. / No, there isn't.
8 Are there windows? Yes, there are. / No, there aren't.

6 A: Hi. It's me. I'm at the hotel in London.
B: Is it a big hotel?
A: Yes, there are lots of rooms. There are two restaurants and a café and there's a big car park.
B: What about your room? Are there windows?
A: Yes, there are three windows.
B: Is there a telephone?
A: Yes. And there's a television too.

Units 5, 6 & 7

1 1 There aren't any students in the school.
2 There aren't any retired people in our class.
3 There isn't a computer in the office.
4 There aren't any students in the basketball team.
5 There isn't an important race in my city.
6 There isn't a football in the office.

2 1 My brother likes cricket.
2 A: Do you like running?
B: No, I don't.
3 I like table tennis.
4 A: Do you like swimming?
B: Yes, I do.
5 We like American football.
6 My mother and father like golf.
7 A: Do you like sport?
B: Yes, I do.
8 My cousin likes tennis very much.

3 1 In class we listen to the CD.
2 He has breakfast at 7.15.
3 They like football.
4 She watches television in the evening.
5 He goes to work at 8.30.
6 We start class at 9.00.
7 He does sport at the weekend.
8 I work in a school.

4 1 I don't have a shower in the evening.
2 We live in the capital city.
3 He likes basketball.
4 They don't go to school in the morning.
5 She has time to watch television.
6 I don't work in an office.
7 He studies at home.
8 You don't have lunch in a restaurant.

5 My brother has a shower at 7.00. He doesn't have breakfast. He starts work at 8.30. He stops for lunch at 12.30. He finishes work at 5.00 but he doesn't go straight home; he goes to the gym. After that he goes home. In the evening he watches television. He goes to bed at about 11.00.

6 1 What's the name of the lake?
2 How much is a ticket for the national park?
3 Where is the Sahara Desert?
4 When / What time does the park open?
5 Where is the park office?
6 What do people do in the mountains in summer?

7 1 Do you work?

2 When do you study English?

3 What's your neighbour's name?

4 Do you like your boss?

5 Do you like fishing?

6 What are the names of your colleagues?

7 Do you live near a park?

8 1 Where does he live?

2 What does he do?

3 When / What time does he start work?

4 Who does he live with?

5 Do they have any children?

6 What are their names?

Units 8 & 9

1 1 We always have breakfast at home.

2 My son is always late for breakfast.

3 We usually have fruit for breakfast.

4 I sometimes have a sandwich for lunch.

5 We never invite friends for dinner.

6 We always have a pizza on Friday night.

7 It is usually a four-cheese pizza.

8 My husband sometimes cooks dinner at the weekend.

2 1 We sometimes eat in a restaurant.

2 We never eat Japanese food.

3 We usually / sometimes eat at my mother's house.

4 We usually have pasta.

5 We never drink wine.

6 We sometimes invite friends to eat.

3 1 I always / usually / sometimes / never eat Indian food.

2 I always / usually / sometimes / never have fruit for breakfast.

3 I always / usually / sometimes / never drink coffee in the morning.

4 I always / usually / sometimes / never eat at my mother's house.

5 I always / usually / sometimes / never have a sandwich for lunch.

6 I always / usually / sometimes / never eat at a restaurant at the weekend.

7 I always / usually / sometimes / never cook dinner.

8 We always / usually / sometimes / never invite friends to eat at our house.

4 Most likely answers:

1 a

2 f

3 g

4 c

5 d

6 b

5 1 Don't buy things at the hotel shop. It's expensive.

2 Don't walk in the park at night.

3 Take photographs at the market. It's exciting.

4 Go in December. It's sunny.

5 Don't swim in the river. It's very cold.

6 Ask the police for help. They're friendly.

7 Go to the shopping malls. There are many interesting shops.

8 Don't have dinner at the hotel. The restaurant's terrible.

6 1 Don't go.

2 Don't walk.

3 Don't smoke.

4 Don't talk.

5 Don't drive fast.

6 Don't swim.

Units 10 & 11

1 1 My grandfather was a doctor.

2 Vegetables were very important for the Mayans.

3 The typical food for the Khmer was rice.

4 There were fantastic architects in Egypt.

5 We were at the Pyramids last week.

6 There was good weather.

7 My sister was on a horse.

8 I was on a camel.

2 1 Were the people friendly?

2 Was the traffic bad?

3 Were the restaurants cheap?

4 Was your sister with you?

5 Were you in a good hotel?

6 Were you happy to come home?

3 1 Yes, they were.

2 No, it wasn't.

3 No, they weren't.

4 Yes, she was.

5 Yes, we were.

6 No, I wasn't.

4 1 In March I started university.

2 I studied French and German.

3 There were many students and we worked very hard.

4 I met some interesting people.

5 One student was from Australia. She liked me very much.

6 I began to see her every day.

7 We went to restaurants and the cinema together.

8 We got married in November.

5 1 ✔

2 ✔

3 ✘ My grandparents died in 1998.

4 ✘ Well done! You won the election!

5 ✘ My father stopped work last month.

6 ✘ We became the first students to study in space.

7 ✔

8 ✔

6 1 My parents didn't get married in 1965.

2 I passed my exam.

3 He didn't want to be a politician.

4 They didn't go to a football match.

5 We had a good time.

6 My grandmother didn't speak French.

Units 12 & 13

1 1 f

2 a

3 e

4 c

5 b

2 1 When did he go?

2 Did you see the weather on TV?

3 Why did the animals disappear?

4 Where did the people live?

5 Did they like the TV programme?

6 How long did we stay?

7 What did she eat yesterday?

8 Did everyone have a good time?

3 1 Did you have a pet when you were little? Yes, I <u>had</u>.   *did*

2 What did you <u>had</u>? A cat.   *have*

3 <u>Why</u> name did you give it? Snowy.   *What*

4 What <u>had</u> it look like? It was white.   *did*

5 <u>Does</u> it eat fish? Yes, it did. It liked fish a lot.   *Did*

6 <u>What</u> did it sleep? On my bed.   *Where*

7 Did it die of old age? Yes, it <u>died</u>.   *did*

4 1 You're having breakfast.

2 They're visiting Jordan.

3 She's taking photographs.

4 We're buying a ticket.

5 I'm sitting on the train.

6 The train's leaving the platform.

7 She's talking on the phone.

8 They're writing a report .

5 1 You're studying Russian.

2 We're visiting the museum today.

3 She's wearing a coat.

4 They're staying in a hotel.

5 I'm feeling cold.

6 He's sitting on the bus.

7 We're taking a boat trip.

8 They're looking at the map.

6 1 f
  2 a
  3 b
  4 c
  5 g
  6 d

Units 14 & 15

1 1 He lives in a small country house.
  2 She has a blue mountain bike.
  3 That's a big kitchen table.
  4 This is a new bus station.
  5 What a boring football match.
  6 She works at the local flower farm.

2 1 We can swim.
  2 She can't ride a horse.
  3 You can generate electricity with this gadget.
  4 I can't speak Arabic.
  5 They can't drive.
  6 My computer can download music.

3 1 Can you cook Italian food? Yes, I can.
  2 Can they use a computer? No, they can't.
  3 Can your mp3 player record conversations? Yes, it can.
  4 Can your mobile phone take pictures? No, it can't.
  5 Can he understand science? No, he can't.
  6 Can she paint pictures? Yes, she can.

4 1 It's not going to be a nice day.
  2 They're going to be happy.
  3 We're not going to make a lot of money.
  4 Is she going to fail the exam?
  5 Liverpool are going to win this year.
  6 Is she going to marry Peter?

5 1 d
  2 a
  3 f
  4 b
  5 g
  6 c

Global Teacher's Resource disc

The Global Teacher's Resource disc includes a comprehensive range of resources

The Communication activities section contains a number of photocopiable worksheets for classroom use provided as printable PDFs. There are two worksheets directly linked with the content of each of the units in the Coursebook. In addition, there are generic worksheets appropriate for different points of the course (e.g. beginning of the year)

global

Teacher's Resources

Help

COMMUNICATION ACTIVITIES

TESTS

VIDEO

COMMON EUROPEAN FRAMEWORK

© Macmillan Publishers 2010

Also included are video clips for classroom use, with their corresponding worksheets and teacher's notes provided as printable PDFs.

Each level of Global is mapped against the corresponding level in the Common European Framework

global

Tests Menu

home

Help

PLACEMENT & DIAGNOSTIC TESTS

UNIT TESTS

PROGRESS TESTS

END-OF-YEAR TESTS

© Macmillan Publishers 2010

The Teacher's Resource disc also contains numerous Global-related tests for use in class.

Examples of Communication activities

Unit specific activity

UNIT 9 **The studio apartment** Worksheet

A

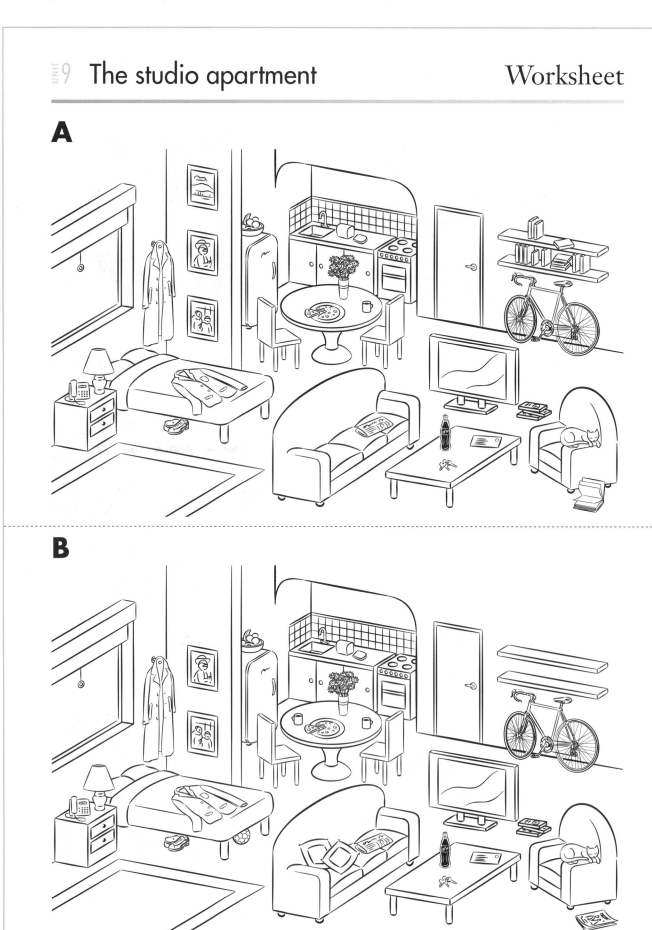

B

Examples of Communication activities

Generic activity for the beginning of the course

What English do you know?

COMPUTER

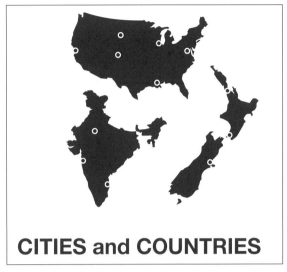

CITIES and COUNTRIES

FOOD and DRINKS

NUMBERS

TRAVEL

ANIMALS

Examples of Communication activities

Generic activity for the end of the course

DIY revision quiz   Worksheet

1 Answer the questions in the revision quiz.

REVISION QUIZ

Section 1: **Reordering sentences**
Put the words in order to make sentences.

1 What you do do free your in time?

2 Jill sister's My is name.   ____ / 2 points

Section 2: **Cloze exercise**
Fill the gap with a suitable word.

1 She _____ born in 1909.

2 It's a quarter past five. You are going _____ be late
   for class.   ____ / 2 points

Section 3: **Error correction**
Correct the mistake.

1 There are one cinema in the mall.

2 I bought a laptop from that shop computer new.   ____ / 2 points

Section 4: **Multiple choice**
Choose the correct option.

1 Their names *is / are / am* Ali and Ben.

2 Six plus nine is *fifteen / fifty / fourteen*.   ____ / 2 points

Section 5: **Matching**
Match categories 1–4 with words a–d.

1 *job*   a *parents*

2 *family*   b *bread*

3 *colour*   c *teacher*

4 *food*   d *yellow*   ____ / 2 points

Total ____ / 10 points

2 Work in pairs. Make a similar quiz of ten points. Use different question types and revise grammar and vocabulary from your coursebook.

3 Exchange your revision quiz with another pair of students. Do the quiz.

DEDICATED TO OUR GODCHILDREN:
JAMES ROBBINS, CARSON KEHOE, ZACHARY KEHOE, BENJAMIN KEHOE, JOSIE KEHOE, OLIVIA KUCHER, PHOEBE O'NEILL, CECILIA KUCHER, MARY KUCHER, CONNOR O'NEILL, AND ELIZABETH KUCHER

MANY THANKS, ESPECIALLY TO:

Chris and Millie Carney for bringing our vision to fruition through Don Carney and Phil Halpin at Storytel Press, whose mission is to restore the sacred.

Our dedicated team of editors: Annemarie Burton, Donna-Marie Frommeyer, Lisa Maxson, and Bridget Wedoff. As well as editorial assistance from Matt and Sarah Ann Doetsch, Paul and Jeanette Doetsch, Tom and Lena Hudson, Luke and Renee Kehoe, Cynthia Martinez, The Masterson Family, Mary Smith, and Marilyn Weadon.

Prayers and theological review and support from The Canons Regular of Saint John Cantius, especially Rev. Anthony Rice S.J.C. and Rev. Nathan Caswell S.J.C., as well as Rev. John McNamara.

Creative set inspirations by our team of builders, our children: Madelyn, Colin, Liam, Brigid, Molly, Moira, and Fulton O'Neill, as well as our guest builders: Zack Kendall, Gabriel Lugo, and Andrew Smith.

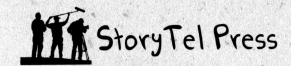

StoryTel Press

StoryTel Press
A division of StoryTel Foundation, a 501(c)(3) organization
10506 Burt Circle
Omaha, NE 68114
www.storytel.org

Nihil Obstat: Reverend Matthew J. Gutowski, STL

Imprimatur: Most Reverend George J. Lucas
Archbishop of Omaha
February 3, 2018, Omaha, NE

ISBN: 978-0-9995087-0-1

Printed in the United States

PUBLISHER Don Carney
MANAGING EDITOR Phil Halpin
ART DIRECTOR Chrissy Doremus
COPY EDITORS Annemarie Burton,
Donna-Marie Frommeyer, Lisa Maxson,
and Bridget Wedoff

CATECHISM
OF THE
SEVEN SACRAMENTS

Kevin and Mary O'Neill

TABLE OF CONTENTS

INTRODUCTION

I often say that, as Catholics, we read the Bible in 3-D. This is because our faith comes alive through Sacred Scripture, Sacred Tradition and the Magisterium of the Catholic Church. Never while saying this did it ever occur to me that someday I would combine those same 3-D biblical teachings with fun 3-D images to help teach the beauty of the faith in a simple way. Using these fun images alongside precise Catholic terminology, this book is a theological work aimed to both entertain and teach a broad audience. This book is for everyone – from 0 years old to 120 years old.

After falling in love with the beauty of the Bride of Christ, the Church, my wife Mary and I want to help others discover that same beauty. Where better to begin than the sacraments! Since the fall of mankind, sin has separated humanity from God. Christ instituted the sacraments to reunite humanity with God. We explain the sacraments by starting with the New and Everlasting Covenant, the Holy Eucharist. Every sacrament both stems from and points to the Holy Eucharist – the source and summit of our Catholic faith.

This book follows Pope Emeritus Benedict XVI's teaching on Theology of Covenant, which is a framework for interpreting Scripture centered on Christ, grounded in the unity of the entire Bible. Theology of Covenant is said to be the master key to unlock the biblical understanding of salvation history.

While telling this story of salvation history through scriptural teachings of the sacraments, we make use of typology, one of the best ways to teach the faith and a favorite tool of Venerable Archbishop Fulton J. Sheen. Typology is a method of biblical study in which elements found in the Old Testament are shown to prefigure those found in the New Testament. As you read, you will see biblical typology unlocked with memorable side-by-side building block illustrations that show how the Old is fulfilled in the New and the New is revealed in the Old.

We consider ourselves to be products of Pope St. John Paul II's New Evangelization, learning and building our faith through all types of media. Now, through the Building Blocks of Faith Series, we hope to contribute to the New Evangelization by helping to catechise and evangelize others. After spending nearly two years writing this book and building the illustrations as a family, we are excited and humbled to be able to share it with you and your family!

—Kevin O'Neill

THE EUCHARIST

WAIT A MINUTE. WHAT IS A PASSOVER?
TO EXPLAIN THE PASSOVER, WE HAVE TO GO BACK THOUSANDS OF YEARS BEFORE JESUS. THE **FIRST** PASSOVER HAPPENED DURING THE TIME OF MOSES AND PHARAOH ...
POOF!
983
1510
1820
1985

MOSES WAS AN ISRAELITE BY BIRTH, BUT HE WAS RAISED AS AN EGYPTIAN PRINCE.

AFTER MOSES DEFENDED AN ISRAELITE, HE FLED FROM EGYPT.

GOD LOVED THE ISRAELITES. HE APPEARED TO MOSES AND TOLD HIM TO DELIVER A MESSAGE TO PHARAOH: "LET MY PEOPLE GO TO WORSHIP ME!"

DURING THE FIRST PLAGUE, THE NILE RIVER TURNED TO BLOOD.

THE SECOND PLAGUE BROUGHT FROGS.

THE THIRD PLAGUE BROUGHT BUGS AND LICE.

AND THE FOURTH PLAGUE BROUGHT WILD ANIMALS AND FLIES.

EX 8:16-17, EX 8:24

THE FIFTH PLAGUE WAS DISEASED LIVESTOCK.

THE SIXTH PLAGUE WAS BOILS.

THE SEVENTH PLAGUE BROUGHT HAIL AND FIRE.

THE EIGATH PLAGUE WAS LOCUSTS.

EX 9:23, EX 10:14

THE NINTH PLAGUE WAS DARKNESS FOR THREE DAYS.

AND THEN CAME THE TENTH PLAGUE. MOSES TOLD PHARAOH THAT IF HE DID NOT LISTEN TO GOD, ALL OF EGYPT'S FIRSTBORN SONS WOULD DIE. BUT PHARAOH'S HEART WAS HARDENED, AND HE WOULD NOT LISTEN.

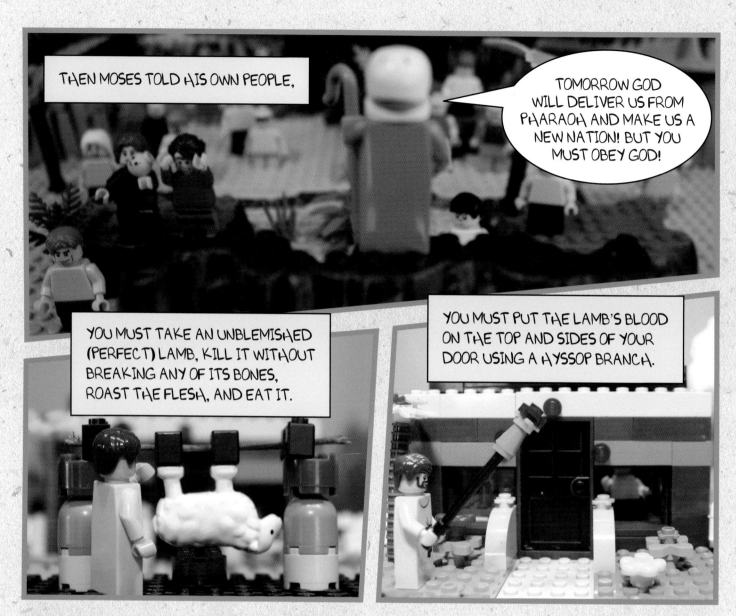

EX 12:3, EX 12:5, EX 12:22, EX 12:19, EX 12:11

THE ISRAELITES OBEYED GOD, SO THE ANGEL OF DEATH "PASSED OVER" THEIR HOUSES.

BUT THE EGYPTIANS DID NOT OBEY GOD. SO ALL OF THEIR FIRSTBORN SONS DIED, INCLUDING PHARAOH'S OWN SON.

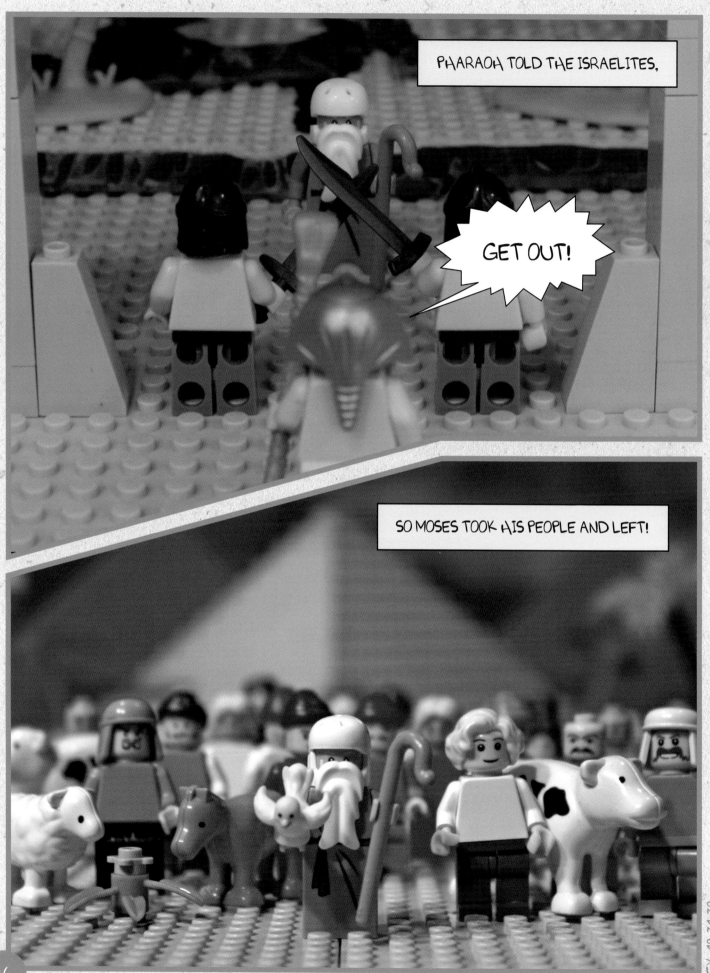

EX. 12.31-32

BUT PHARAOH WAS ANGRY! EVEN THOUGH HE TOLD THEM TO LEAVE, HE AND HIS ARMY CHASED AFTER THEM.

GOD DELIVERED HIS PEOPLE, THE ISRAELITES, THROUGH THE RED SEA.

BUT PHARAOH AND HIS ARMY WERE OVERTHROWN.

EX 14:5-6, EX 14:15-18, EX 14:27-28

SO THE ISRAELITES WERE BORN A NEW NATION, WITH MOSES LEADING THEM AND GOD DELIVERING THEM FROM SLAVERY AND BONDAGE THROUGH THEIR OBEDIENCE DURING THE FIRST PASSOVER.

EX 14:30-31

THE PASSOVER MEAL, ALTHOUGH IT IS ONE MEAL, IS DIVIDED INTO FOUR CUPS.

THE FIRST CUP IS THE CUP OF **SANCTIFICATION.** IT REPRESENTS THE ISRAELITES' BITTER TIME IN SLAVERY AND BONDAGE. DURING THIS CUP THEY EAT BITTER HERBS AND SPICES.

AFTER THE FIRST CUP, A HYMN IS SUNG.

THE SECOND CUP IS THE CUP OF **PROCLAMATION.** IT REPRESENTS THE ISRAELITES LEAVING EGYPT. DURING THIS CUP THEY TELL THE STORY OF THE ISRAELITES' EXIT FROM EGYPT.

THE THIRD CUP IS THE CUP OF **BLESSING.** IT REPRESENTS THE ISRAELITES BEING DELIVERED THROUGH THE RED SEA. DURING THIS CUP THEY EAT THE SACRIFICED LAMB AND THE UNLEAVENED BREAD.

AFTER THE THIRD CUP, A HYMN IS SUNG AGAIN.

THE FOURTH CUP IS THE CUP OF **PRAISE.** IT REPRESENTS THE ISRAELITES BECOMING A NEW NATION.

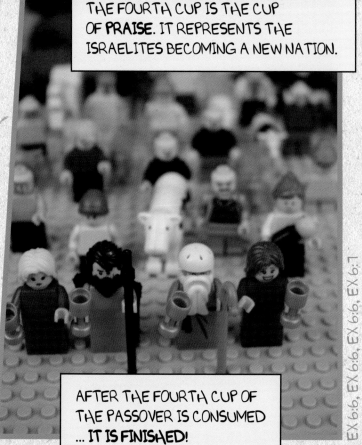

AFTER THE FOURTH CUP OF THE PASSOVER IS CONSUMED ... *IT IS FINISHED!*

THERE ARE MANY SIMILARITIES BETWEEN CHRIST AND MOSES.

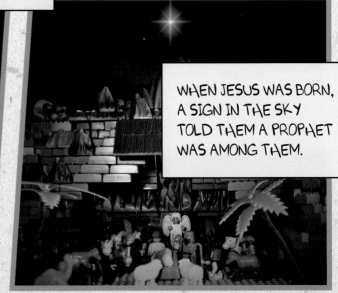

WHEN JESUS WAS BORN, A SIGN IN THE SKY TOLD THEM A PROPHET WAS AMONG THEM.

WHEN MOSES WAS BORN, A SIGN IN THE SKY TOLD THEM A PROPHET WAS AMONG THEM.

WHEN MOSES WAS BORN, PHARAOH SENT OUT AN EDICT (ORDER) TO HAVE ALL THE YOUNG BOYS KILLED SO HE COULD KILL THE PROPHET.

WHEN JESUS WAS BORN, HEROD SENT OUT AN EDICT TO HAVE ALL THE YOUNG BOYS KILLED SO HE COULD KILL THE PROPHET.

MOSES WAS SENT DOWN THE RIVER INTO THE HEART OF EGYPT TO ESCAPE PHARAOH'S WRATH.

JESUS, MARY, AND JOSEPH FLED INTO THE HEART OF EGYPT TO ESCAPE HEROD'S WRATH.

MAT 2:2, EX 1:22, MAT 2:16, EX 2:3, MAT 2:13

MOSES WAS THE PRINCE OF EGYPT, WHO STEPPED OUT OF HIS KINGDOM TO BE WITH HIS PEOPLE AND LEAD THEM OUT OF SLAVERY THROUGH A PASSOVER MEAL.

JESUS IS THE PRINCE OF PEACE, WHO STEPPED OUT OF HIS KINGDOM TO BE WITH HIS PEOPLE AND LEAD THEM OUT OF THE SLAVERY OF SIN THROUGH FULFILLING THE PASSOVER MEAL.

MOSES' FIRST PUBLIC MIRACLE WAS TURNING THE RIVER TO BLOOD.

CHRIST'S FIRST PUBLIC MIRACLE WAS TURNING THE WATER INTO WINE AT THE WEDDING FEAST AT CANA. LATER HE CHANGED WINE INTO HIS BLOOD AT THE PASSOVER HE CELEBRATED THE NIGHT BEFORE HE DIED.

THIS BRINGS US BACK TO THE LAST SUPPER WITH CHRIST AND HIS DISCIPLES – MY FAVORITE SACRAMENT!

EX 2:10, ISA 9:6, EX 7:19, JN 2:9, MAT 26:18

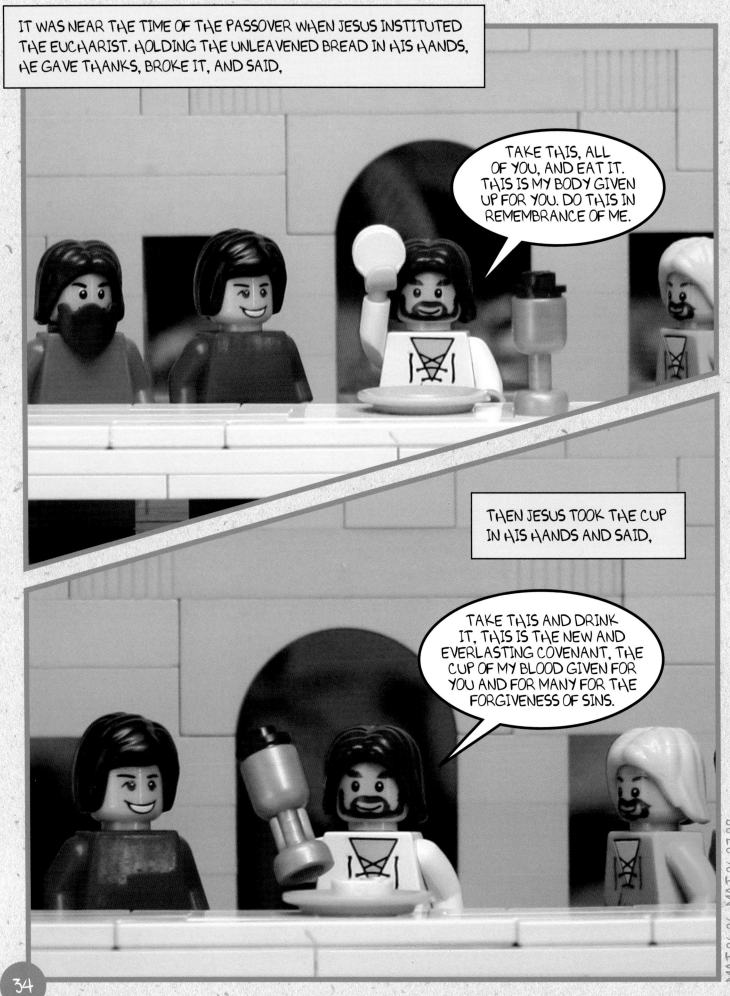

AFTER JESUS DID THIS, HE SAID,

I WILL NOT DRINK OF THE FRUIT OF THE VINE AGAIN UNTIL I ENTER MY FATHER'S KINGDOM.

THEN THEY SANG A HYMN, AND, NOT FINISHING THE FOURTH CUP OF THE PASSOVER, WENT INTO THE GARDEN OF GETHSEMANE.

IN THE GARDEN JESUS SAID,

FATHER, IF IT IS POSSIBLE, LET THIS CUP PASS, BUT LET NOT MY WILL, BUT YOUR WILL, BE DONE.

WHILE JESUS WAS PRAYING IN THE GARDEN, HE KNEW HE WOULD HAVE TO FINISH THE PASSOVER ON THE CROSS.

MAT 26:29, MAT 26:30, MAT 26:39, MAT 26:40

EX 12:5, JN 19:4

HE WAS, HOWEVER, PUNISHED ANYWAY.

HE WAS BEATEN, LED TO THE CROSS, AND EVEN NAILED TO THE CROSS. YET NO BONES WERE BROKEN, JUST LIKE THE PASSOVER LAMB.

INRI

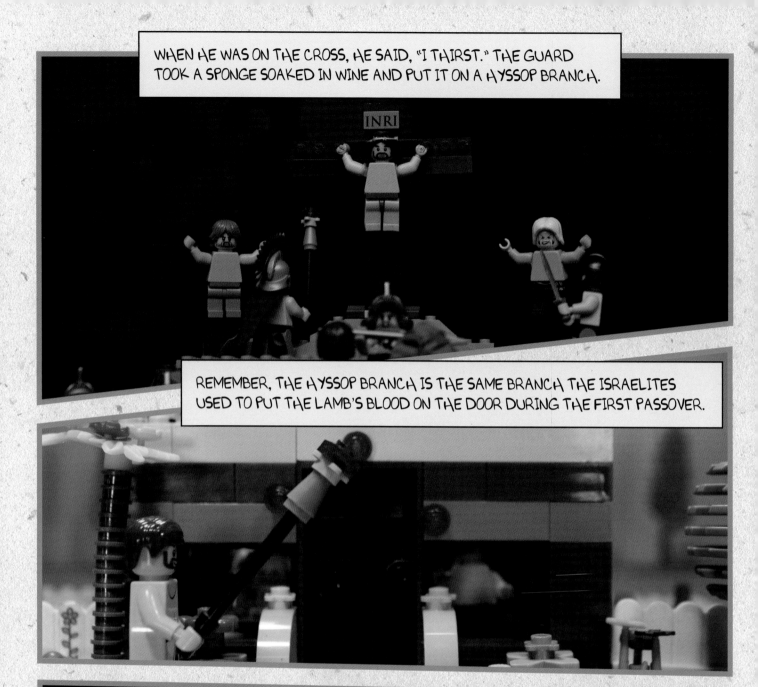

WHEN HE WAS ON THE CROSS, HE SAID, "I THIRST." THE GUARD TOOK A SPONGE SOAKED IN WINE AND PUT IT ON A HYSSOP BRANCH.

REMEMBER, THE HYSSOP BRANCH IS THE SAME BRANCH THE ISRAELITES USED TO PUT THE LAMB'S BLOOD ON THE DOOR DURING THE FIRST PASSOVER.

THEN CHRIST DRANK IT AND SAID,

IT IS FINISHED.

JN 19:28-29, EX 12:22, JN 19:30

MAT 26:11-30, 1 COR 5:7, 1 COR 5:7-8, LK 22:20, CCC 1150, EPH 2:12

IN THE **FIRST COVENANT**, ADAM AND EVE WERE MADE FOR EACH OTHER AND GIVEN TO EACH OTHER IN MARRIAGE. GOD COMMANDED THEM TO BE FRUITFUL AND MULTIPLY.

GEN 1:28.

IN THE **SECOND COVENANT**, NOAH AND HIS FAMILY (EIGHT IN ALL), PLUS SEVEN PAIRS OF THE CLEAN ANIMALS AND ONE PAIR OF THE UNCLEAN ANIMALS, WERE SAVED FROM THE FLOOD THAT COVERED THE WHOLE EARTH. AFTER THE FLOOD, GOD COMMANDED THEM TO BE FRUITFUL AND MULTIPLY.

GEN 9:1

IN THE **THIRD COVENANT**, GOD CALLED ABRAM AND GAVE HIM THE NAME ABRAHAM, WHICH MEANS, "THE FATHER OF A MULTITUDE OF NATIONS." GOD PROMISED TO MAKE HIM THE FATHER OF A GREAT NATION WITH DESCENDANTS AS NUMEROUS AS THE STARS.

GEN 22:17

43

THE **FOURTH COVENANT** IS WHEN GOD CHOSE MOSES TO LEAD HIS PEOPLE OUT OF SLAVERY TO THE PROMISED LAND. HE GAVE THEM THE TEN COMMANDMENTS. ALSO, THE LEVITICAL PRIESTHOOD WAS ESTABLISHED.

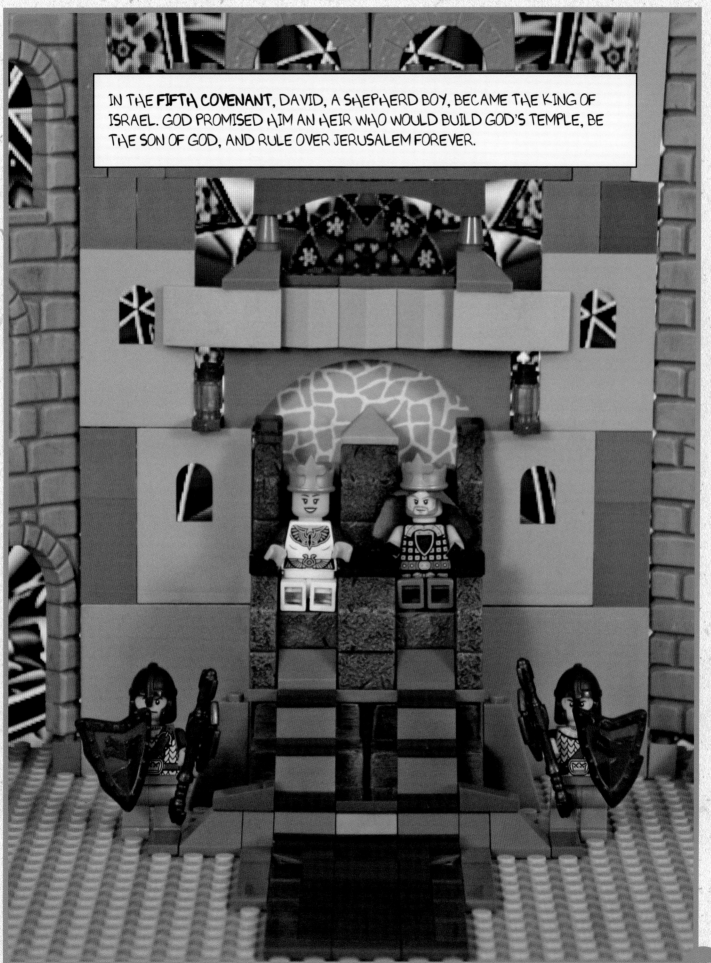

IN THE **FIFTH COVENANT**, DAVID, A SHEPHERD BOY, BECAME THE KING OF ISRAEL. GOD PROMISED HIM AN HEIR WHO WOULD BUILD GOD'S TEMPLE, BE THE SON OF GOD, AND RULE OVER JERUSALEM FOREVER.

AND FINALLY, **THE NEW AND EVERLASTING COVENANT** IS THE EUCHARIST! JESUS CAME TO FULFILL ALL OF THE OLD COVENANTS AND ESTABLISHED THE NEW AND EVERLASTING COVENANT, THE EUCHARIST! HIS BODY AND BLOOD WERE SACRIFICED ON THE CROSS FOR THE SINS OF ALL AND ARE MADE PRESENT IN THE HOLY EUCHARIST!

LK 22:20

JN 6:53-56

JESUS SAID TO THEM,

AMEN, AMEN, I SAY TO YOU, UNLESS YOU EAT THE FLESH OF THE SON OF MAN AND DRINK HIS BLOOD, YOU DO NOT HAVE LIFE WITHIN YOU. WHOEVER EATS MY FLESH AND DRINKS MY BLOOD HAS ETERNAL LIFE, AND I WILL RAISE HIM ON THE LAST DAY. FOR MY FLESH IS TRUE FOOD, AND MY BLOOD IS TRUE DRINK. WHOEVER EATS MY FLESH AND DRINKS MY BLOOD REMAINS IN ME AND I IN HIM.

ST. IGNATIUS OF ANTIOCH, A FOLLOWER OF ST. JOHN, ALSO TEACHES US ABOUT THE EUCHARIST.

ST. IGNATIUS SAID,

THE EUCHARIST IS THE MEDICINE OF IMMORTALITY AND THE ANTIDOTE AGAINST DEATH, ENABLING US TO LIVE FOREVER IN JESUS CHRIST.

ST. IGNATIUS OF ANTIOCH, PRAY FOR US!

WE WERE BITTEN BY THE VENOM OF SIN IN THE GARDEN OF EDEN, SO WE NEED AN ANTI-VENOM.

ANTI-VENOM IS MADE FROM THE SAME POISON OF THE SNAKE THAT BIT YOU,

BUT IT IS TRANSFORMED AND GIVEN TO YOU AS MEDICINE.

THAT'S WHAT JESUS DID FOR US!

HE TOOK THE VENOM, WHICH IS OUR SIN, UPON HIMSELF.

HE DIED ON THE CROSS TO DESTROY SIN!

INRI

THEN HE RESURRECTED FROM THE DEAD TO GIVE US HIS FLESH TO CURE US FROM THE ETERNAL DEATH OF SIN.

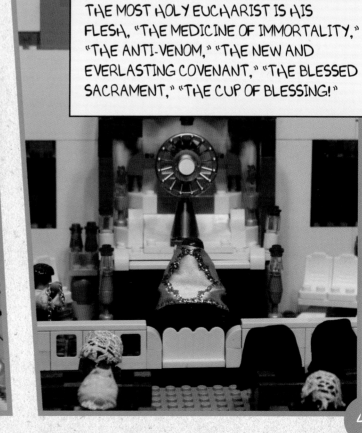

THE MOST HOLY EUCHARIST IS HIS FLESH, "THE MEDICINE OF IMMORTALITY," "THE ANTI-VENOM," "THE NEW AND EVERLASTING COVENANT," "THE BLESSED SACRAMENT," "THE CUP OF BLESSING!"

REMEMBER, THE CUP OF BLESSING IS THE THIRD CUP OF THE PASSOVER MEAL, WHEN YOU EAT THE LAMB AND THE UNLEAVENED BREAD.

ST. PAUL SAID,

THIS CUP OF BLESSING IS A PARTICIPATION IN THE BODY AND BLOOD OF OUR LORD JESUS CHRIST.

JESUS IS "THE LAMB OF GOD," "THE BREAD OF LIFE," AND "THE CUP OF BLESSING," WHICH WE RECEIVE IN THE EUCHARIST.

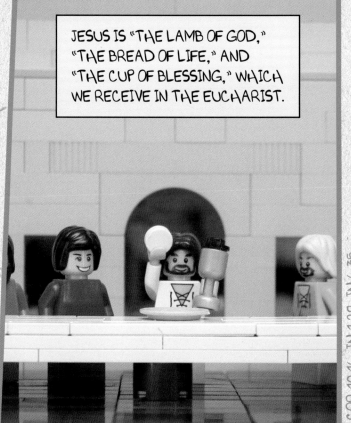

IN THE GOSPEL OF JOHN, CHAPTER 6, JESUS PERFORMS ANOTHER MIRACLE: THE MULTIPLICATION OF THE LOAVES AND FISH.

THE GOSPEL SAYS THAT IT WAS NEARING THE FEAST OF THE JEWISH PASSOVER.

AMAZING, IT ALWAYS SEEMS TO REFERENCE BACK TO THE PASSOVER!

JESUS TOOK FIVE LOAVES AND TWO FISH, GAVE THANKS, AND DISTRIBUTED THEM TO THE CROWD.

THERE WAS ENOUGH FOR THE CROWD OF 5000 MEN, NOT INCLUDING WOMEN AND CHILDREN, PLUS 12 BASKETS FILLED WITH LEFTOVERS!

MOSES AND HIS PEOPLE ATE MANNA IN THE WILDERNESS. MANNA IS THE BREAD COME DOWN FROM HEAVEN.

GOD GAVE THEM THIS BREAD FROM HEAVEN TO SUSTAIN THEM ON THEIR JOURNEY IN THE DESERT.

JN 6:1-33

JESUS NOW TELLS US THAT HE IS THE MANNA AND WE MUST EAT OF HIM!

HE IS THE "BREAD OF LIFE."

JESUS SAID, "YOUR ANCESTORS ATE THE MANNA, BUT THEY DIED."

"I AM THE LIVING BREAD. WHOEVER EATS OF ME WILL LIVE FOREVER. I WILL GIVE MY FLESH FOR THE LIFE OF THE WORLD."

JN 6:34-59

JESUS WAS BORN IN BETHLEHEM, A TOWN WHOSE NAME MEANS "HOUSE OF BREAD" AND "HOUSE OF FLESH."

HE WAS WRAPPED IN SWADDLING CLOTHES, WHICH IS WHAT A LAMB BEING SACRIFICED WOULD WEAR.

HE WAS LAID IN A MANGER, WHICH IS WHERE THE SHEEP COME TO EAT.

IMAGINE THAT! JESUS IS THE "BREAD OF LIFE" BORN IN THE "HOUSE OF BREAD." HE IS THE "WORD BECOME FLESH" BORN IN THE "HOUSE OF FLESH." HE IS THE "GOOD SHEPHERD" LAID IN A MANGER WHERE THE SHEEP COME TO EAT! AND HE TELLS US (HIS SHEEP) TO EAT HIS FLESH AND DRINK HIS BLOOD TO HAVE ETERNAL LIFE!

AFTER JESUS RESURRECTED FROM THE DEAD, HE WALKED SEVEN MILES TO EMMAUS WITH TWO OF HIS FOLLOWERS. BUT THEY DID NOT RECOGNIZE HIM UNTIL ...

HE REVEALED HIMSELF IN THE EUCHARIST, WHEN HE BROKE THE BREAD.

THE FOLLOWERS OF JESUS FELT THEIR HEARTS WERE ON FIRE WHEN JESUS TOLD THEM ABOUT THE PROPHETS AND THE SCRIPTURE.

IN THE BOOK OF REVELATION, JESUS SAYS,

I STAND AT THE DOOR AND KNOCK TO EAT WITH YOU.

54

THE BOOK OF REVELATION TEACHES US THAT JESUS WILL GIVE THE HIDDEN MANNA TO THE ONE WHO OVERCOMES (THE ONE WHO TURNS AWAY FROM SIN AND CHOOSES TO DO GOD'S WILL).

JESUS TOLD US THAT HE IS "THE MANNA COME DOWN FROM HEAVEN." HE IS HIDDEN IN THE EUCHARIST.

INRI

THE EUCHARIST IS THE TRUE FLESH OF JESUS, AND HE WANTS TO BE UNITED WITH US WHEN WE RECEIVE HIM IN HOLY COMMUNION.

THE CATHOLIC CHURCH IS "THE BRIDE OF CHRIST" BECAUSE SHE SHARES THE ONE-FLESH, LIFE-GIVING UNION WITH CHRIST.

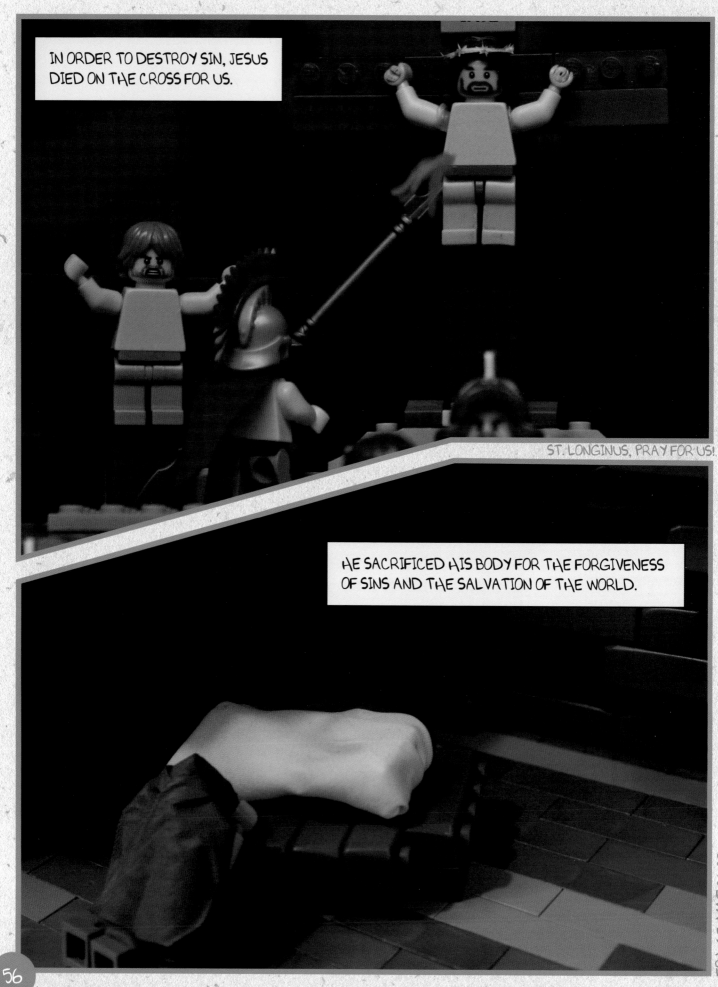

WHEN THE PRIEST SAYS THE WORDS OF CONSECRATION, THE BREAD AND WINE TRANSUBSTANTIATE (CHANGE SUBSTANCE). BECAUSE GOD IS OUTSIDE OF TIME, THE SACRIFICE ON THE CROSS IS MADE PRESENT ON THE ALTAR. THE BREAD AND WINE ARE NO LONGER BREAD AND WINE, BUT INSTEAD THEY TRULY BECOME JESUS CHRIST'S BODY, BLOOD, SOUL, AND DIVINITY!

LK 22:19, MAT 26:26, 1 COR 11:24

THEREFORE, WE ARE TRULY PRESENT AT THE CRUCIFIXION OF CHRIST WHEN WE ARE AT HOLY MASS, AND WE SHOULD DRESS APPROPRIATELY AND BEHAVE ACCORDINGLY.

WE SHOULD ALWAYS WEAR OUR BEST CLOTHES FOR GOD!

WE SHOULD ALWAYS BEHAVE REVERENTLY (WITH RESPECT).

PS 96:9, LEV 19:30

WE SHOULD ALWAYS BE IN CONSTANT PRAYER DURING THE HOLY MASS AND NOT ALLOW OURSELVES TO BE DISTRACTED.

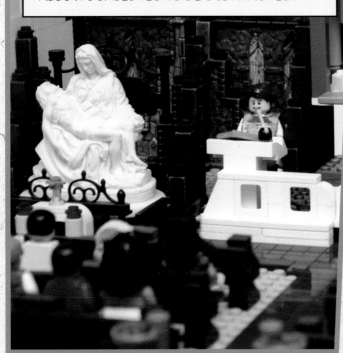

MOST IMPORTANTLY, WE SHOULD ALWAYS BE IN THE STATE OF GRACE (FREE FROM MORTAL SIN) BEFORE RECEIVING JESUS IN THE HOLY EUCHARIST!

ST. JOHN BOSCO SAID, "YOU CAN FLY TO HEAVEN ON THE WINGS OF CONFESSION AND COMMUNION."

SIMILAR TO THE PASSOVER, THE MASS HAS FOUR TYPES OF PRAYER. FIRST, WE **PRAISE** GOD. THEN, WE OFFER HIM OUR **PETITIONS**. NEXT, WE ASK FOR THE **INTERCESSION** OF THE ANGELS AND SAINTS. FINALLY, WE GIVE **THANKSGIVING** TO GOD FOR HIS SACRIFICE AND HIS MERCY.

1 TIM 2:1-4

AFTER MASS, JESUS IS RESERVED IN THE TABERNACLE (DWELLING PLACE). WHEN WE RECEIVE COMMUNION, WE ALSO BECOME A TABERNACLE OF THE LORD. A SANCTUARY LAMP (RED CANDLE) IS LIT WHEN JESUS IS PRESENT. WE ALL GENUFLECT WHEN WE ENTER OR LEAVE THE CHURCH. IN DOING ALL OF THESE THINGS, WE ARE PROFESSING THAT THE KING OF HEAVEN AND EARTH IS PRESENT!

ROMANS 14:11

WE CAN ALSO ADORE THE LORD WHEN HE IS EXPOSED IN THE MONSTRANCE. THIS IS CALLED ADORATION. DURING THIS TIME, JESUS IS FULLY PRESENT IN THE CONSECRATED HOST INSIDE THE MONSTRANCE. YOU CAN KNEEL OR SIT AND PRAY OR TALK TO GOD IN SILENCE. REMEMBER IN THE GARDEN OF GETHSEMANE WHEN JESUS ASKS HIS APOSTLES, "COULD YOU NOT WAIT ONE HOUR WITH ME?" WELL, THE INVITATION IS THE SAME FOR US NOW. JESUS WANTS US TO WAIT AND PRAY BEFORE HIM IN ADORATION.

MK 14:37

THE ARK (MARY) AND THE COVENANT (JESUS) ARE INSEPARABLE, AS JESUS TOOK ON HIS FLESH THROUGH HIS MOTHER, MARY.

IT ALL GOES BACK TO THE GARDEN OF EDEN.

REMEMBER WHEN ADAM AND EVE SINNED? WELL, THE DEVIL THOUGHT HE HAD OUTSMARTED GOD.

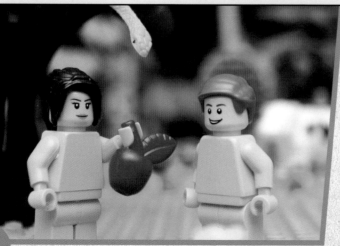

HE THOUGHT ALL OF HUMANITY, WHICH WAS MADE IN GOD'S IMAGE AND LIKENESS, WOULD NOW BE SEPARATED FROM GOD FOREVER!

REV 11:19-12:1, LK 1:31, JN 1:14, GEN 3:1-24

BUT GOD ALREADY HAD A PLAN TO SAVE HIS PEOPLE!

INRI

GOD TOLD THE DEVIL HIS PLAN TO DESTROY SIN.

GOD SAID,

I WILL PUT HATRED BETWEEN YOU (DEVIL) AND THE WOMAN (MARY),

BETWEEN HER OFFSPRING (MARY'S) AND YOURS (DEVIL'S).

"SHE (MARY) WILL CRUSH YOUR (DEVIL'S) HEAD."

GN 3:15

AND SO IT BEGAN. A NEW PLAN FOR SALVATION, BROUGHT FORTH THROUGH MARY AND JESUS.

IN THE OLD TESTAMENT, THE OLD ARK WAS MADE TO CARRY THE COVENANT OF GOD. IT WAS MADE SPECIAL AND PURE.

ALTHOUGH IT WAS MADE BY HUMAN HANDS, GOD GAVE THEM SPECIFIC BUILDING INSTRUCTIONS SO THE ARK WOULD BE PERFECT.

EX 25:10-22

THE NEW ARK, MARY, ALSO WAS MADE PERFECTLY PURE (FULL OF GRACE AND SINLESS). SHE CARRIED THE NEW COVENANT (JESUS). YET, UNLIKE THE OLD ARK, WHICH WAS MADE BY HUMAN HANDS, MARY WAS MADE PERFECT BY GOD!

ST. BERNADETTE OF LOURDES, PRAY FOR US!

THE SIMILARITIES BETWEEN THE OLD ARK AND THE NEW ARK ARE NUMEROUS.

JUST LISTEN TO THIS!

THE OLD ARK WAS OVERSHADOWED BY GOD.

MARY WAS OVERSHADOWED BY GOD.

LK 1:35

69

THE ARK WAS THE DWELLING PLACE FOR THE LORD.

JESUS DWELLED WITHIN MARY'S WOMB, AND THE HOLY SPIRIT DWELLED WITHIN HER SOUL.

EX 40:34, LK 1:46-47

THE OLD ARK CONTAINED THE TEN COMMANDMENTS (THE WORD OF GOD), THE ROD OF AARON (THE HIGH PRIESTHOOD), AND THE MANNA (BREAD FROM HEAVEN).

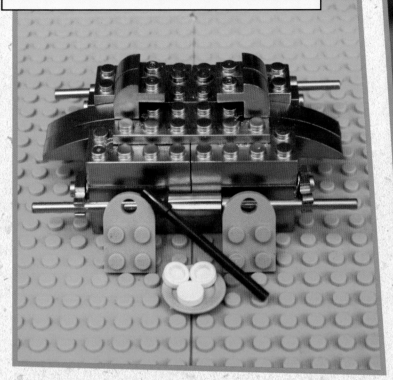

MARY, THE NEW ARK, CONTAINED JESUS! JESUS IS THE WORD BECOME FLESH, THE HIGH PRIEST, AND THE BREAD FROM HEAVEN.

THE OLD ARK TRAVELED TO THE HILL COUNTRY OF JUDEA.

MARY TRAVELED TO THE HILL COUNTRY OF JUDEA.

DAVID LEAPT FOR JOY IN THE PRESENCE OF THE ARK.

JOHN THE BAPTIST (INSIDE ELIZABETH'S WOMB) LEAPT FOR JOY IN THE PRESENCE OF THE NEW ARK (MARY).

DAVID SAID, "WHO AM I THAT THE ARK OF MY LORD SHOULD COME TO ME?"

ELIZABETH SAID, "WHO AM I THAT THE MOTHER OF MY LORD SHOULD COME TO ME?"

2 SAM 6:14, LK 1:41, 2 SAM 6:9, LK 1:43

THE OLD ARK STAYED WITH DAVID FOR ABOUT THREE MONTHS.

MARY STAYED WITH HER COUSIN, ELIZABETH, FOR ABOUT THREE MONTHS.

THE OLD ARK RETURNED TO JERUSALEM FOR GOD'S GLORY TO BE REVEALED.

MARY AND JESUS RETURNED TO JERUSALEM FOR GOD'S GLORY TO BE REVEALED.

WHEN THE GOLDEN ARK LEFT THE TENT OF WORSHIP, IT WAS COVERED WITH A BLUE VEIL.

WHEN MARY APPEARS, SHE IS OFTEN COVERED WITH GOLD AND BLUE.

THE ARK WAS HONORED AND LOVED AMONG JEWS.

MARY IS HONORED AND LOVED AMONG CATHOLICS.

NUM 4:5-6, CCC 839-840, 1 KINGS 3:15, LK 1:48

EXACTLY! IN THE BOOK OF REVELATION, IT SAYS THAT THE WOMAN (MARY) WILL PROTECT HER OFFSPRING FROM THE DRAGON (THE DEVIL).

JUST AS THE ISRAELITES WERE PROTECTED WHEN THEY WERE LED INTO BATTLE WITH THE ARK AND THE COVENANT,

TODAY, CATHOLICS ARE PROTECTED WHEN WE ENGAGE IN SPIRITUAL WARFARE. WE ARE LED INTO BATTLE WITH THE ARK (MARY) AND THE COVENANT (JESUS) WHO IS PRESENT IN THE EUCHARIST.

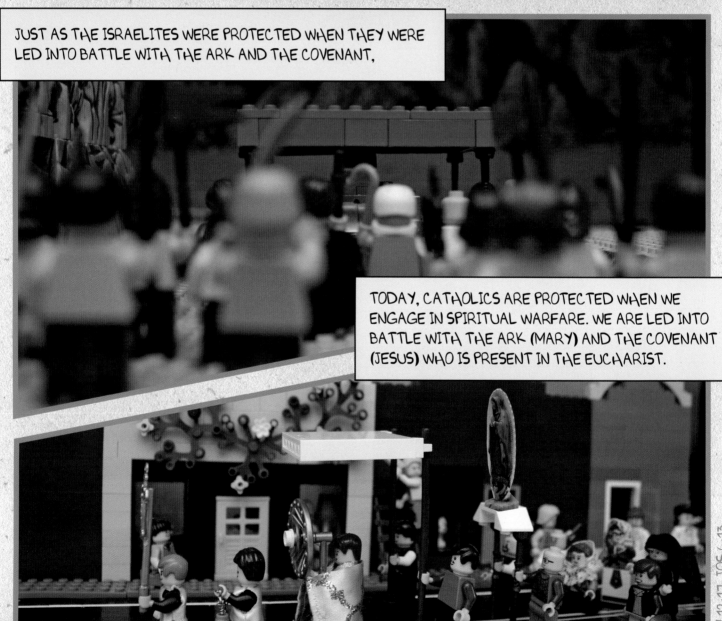

REV 12:11, JOS 6:13

WOW! MARY REALLY IS THE NEW ARK. THAT'S AMAZING!

SHE IS ALSO THE NEW EVE.

THE NEW EVE? AS IN ADAM AND EVE?

THAT'S RIGHT! EVE TIED THE KNOT OF SIN WHEN THE DEVIL TRICKED HER INTO TAKING THE FRUIT FROM THE FORBIDDEN TREE AND DISOBEYING GOD!

MARY LOOSENED THE KNOT OF SIN WITH HER "FIAT" (YES) TO GOD. SHE OBEYED GOD'S WILL WHEN THE ANGEL GABRIEL TOLD HER GOD'S DIVINE PLAN. MARY SAID,

LET IT BE DONE UNTO ME ACCORDING TO GOD'S WILL.

EVE, WHICH MEANS "MOTHER OF THE LIVING," WAS THE FIRST MOTHER OF ALL MANKIND.

MARY, WHO IS JESUS' MOTHER, BECAME THE NEW MOTHER OF ALL MANKIND. JUST BEFORE CHRIST DIED ON THE CROSS, HE GAVE HER TO US THROUGH HIS COMMAND, "BEHOLD YOUR MOTHER."

CCC 975, GEN 3:6, LK 1:38, GEN 3:20, JN 19:26-27

YOU SEE, SIN CAME INTO THE WORLD THE SAME WAY IT LEAVES: GOD WALKS WITH MAN.

THEY ARE IN A GARDEN (THE GARDEN OF EDEN).

A MAN (ADAM) AND A WOMAN (EVE) ARE AT A TREE.

THEY TAKE THE FRUIT FROM THE TREE.

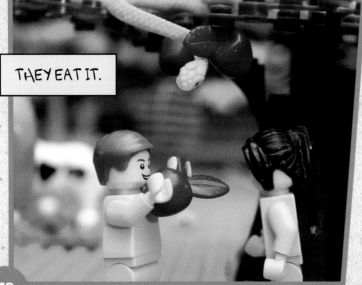

THEY EAT IT.

SIN AND DEATH COME INTO THE WORLD.

GEN 3:8, GEN 3:6, GEN 2:17

AND SIN LEAVES THE WORLD THE SAME WAY IT CAME IN: JESUS (WHO IS GOD) WALKS WITH MAN.

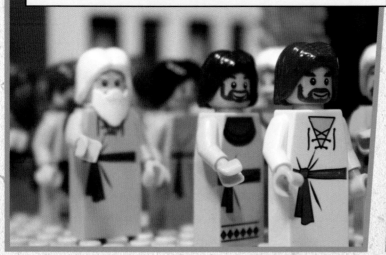

HE IS IN A GARDEN (THE GARDEN OF GETHSEMANE).

A MAN (JESUS) AND A WOMAN (MARY) ARE AT A TREE (THE CROSS).

BUT THIS TIME THE FRUIT (JESUS) IS PUT BACK ON THE TREE (THE CROSS). THIS IS SCRIPTURAL. REMEMBER WHEN ELIZABETH SAID,

BLESSED IS THE **FRUIT** OF YOUR WOMB!

WE MUST EAT OF THE FRUIT OF THAT TREE (THE TREE OF LIFE).

UNLESS YOU EAT MY FLESH AND DRINK MY BLOOD, YOU HAVE NO LIFE IN YOU.

THROUGH THE SACRAMENTS, SIN LEAVES THE WORLD, GOD'S GRACE IS RESTORED IN US, AND WE ARE GIVEN NEW LIFE!

JN 1:14, MAT 26:36, JN 19:25, LK 1:42, JN 6:53, CCC 1129

GEN 3:23

ADAM AND EVE ATE THE FRUIT AND DIED. NOW WE MUST EAT THE FRUIT IN ORDER TO LIVE. THAT "FRUIT" IS JESUS!

HE IS THE FRUIT OF THE TREE OF LIFE MENTIONED IN THE BOOK OF REVELATION. HE IS THE NEW COVENANT. HE IS THE EUCHARIST!

BY EATING THE FRUIT OF THIS TREE, WE CAN CONQUER DEATH AND HAVE ETERNAL LIFE IN HEAVEN!

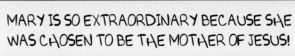

MARY IS SO EXTRAORDINARY BECAUSE SHE WAS CHOSEN TO BE THE MOTHER OF JESUS!

SHE IS THE NEW ARK, THE NEW EVE, THE MOTHER OF GOD, THE MOTHER OF THE EUCHARIST, AND THE MOTHER OF THE LIVING.

WOW, FULTON! MARY TRULY IS EXTRAORDINARY!

SHE SURE IS! SHE INTERCEDES FOR US, TOO!

WHAT DO YOU MEAN "INTERCEDES?"

82

INTERCEDES MEANS THAT MOTHER MARY CAN ASK GOD FOR US ON OUR BEHALF.

DO YOU REMEMBER JESUS' FIRST MIRACLE?

YES, HE TURNED THE WATER INTO WINE AT THE WEDDING FEAST AT CANA.

YES, AND GUESS WHAT TIME OF THE YEAR IT WAS.

BINGO!

PASSOVER?

WELL, MARY INTERCEDED FOR THE WEDDING PARTY. SHE ASKED JESUS TO HELP THEM.

JESUS PROVIDED FOR THEM AND BLESSED THEM BECAUSE MARY INTERCEDED ON THEIR BEHALF. THAT WEDDING PARTY SYMBOLIZES US, THE CHURCH. WE CAN ASK MOTHER MARY TO INTERCEDE FOR US WHEN WE PRAY.

CCC 969, JN 2:1-11, JN 2:12, JN 2:3, JN 2:1-11

WE KNOW THAT JESUS KEPT THE TEN COMMANDMENTS PERFECTLY. ONE OF THE COMMANDMENTS IS TO HONOR YOUR FATHER AND MOTHER.

WE, TOO, HONOR MARY BECAUSE WE ARE TO BE LIKE JESUS.

IN THE GOSPEL OF LUKE, MARY TELLS US ALL GENERATIONS WILL CALL HER BLESSED.

WE FULFILL THESE WORDS EVERY TIME WE PRAY THE "HAIL MARY."

HAIL MARY, FULL OF GRACE,
THE LORD IS WITH THEE;
BLESSED ART THOU AMONGST WOMEN,
AND BLESSED IS THE FRUIT OF THY WOMB, JESUS.
HOLY MARY, MOTHER OF GOD, PRAY FOR US SINNERS,
NOW AND AT THE HOUR OF OUR DEATH.
AMEN.

PHIL 2:8, CCC 971, LK 1:48, JN 1:14

THE GREETING OF THE ANGEL GABRIEL:

HAIL MARY, FULL OF GRACE. THE LORD IS WITH YOU.

THE GREETING OF ELIZABETH:

BLESSED ARE YOU AMONG WOMEN AND BLESSED IS THE FRUIT OF YOUR WOMB, JESUS.

AND THE INTERCESSION FOR US, LIKE THAT AT THE WEDDING AT CANA: "HOLY MARY, MOTHER OF GOD, PRAY FOR US SINNERS, NOW AND AT THE HOUR OF OUR DEATH."

WOW, THAT PRAYER IS LOADED!

MARY IS ALSO THE "QUEEN MOTHER."

QUEEN MOTHER?

WHAT IS THAT?

WELL, IN THE OLD TESTAMENT, THE QUEEN MOTHER WAS ALWAYS THE MOTHER OF THE KING JUST AS MARY IS THE MOTHER OF JESUS.

LK 1:28, LK 1:42, JN 2:3, CCC 966, 1 KGS 2:19

MARY WAS ASSUMED INTO HEAVEN AND CROWNED QUEEN OF HEAVEN AND EARTH BY HER SON, JESUS, WHO IS THE KING OF HEAVEN AND EARTH. THAT'S WHY WE CALL HER OUR HEAVENLY MOTHER.

WOW, I NEVER KNEW HOW EXTRAORDINARY MOTHER MARY IS!

I'M GOING TO START ASKING FOR HER INTERCESSION EVERY DAY!

A GREAT WAY TO DO THIS IS TO PRAY THE ROSARY EVERY DAY.

THE ROSARY?

THE ROSARY IS A PRAYER WE PRAY THAT HELPS US MEDITATE ON THE MYSTERIES OF THE LIFE OF JESUS AND PRAY FOR MARY'S INTERCESSION IN OUR LIFE.

The Holy Rosary

THE ROSARY HAS FIVE **DECADES**, AND WE MEDITATE ON A DIFFERENT MYSTERY OF CHRIST'S LIFE FOR EACH DECADE. WHILE PRAYING A ROSARY, WE CHOOSE ONE OF FOUR SETS OF **MYSTERIES** TO FOCUS ON: THE JOYFUL, SORROWFUL, LUMINOUS, OR GLORIOUS MYSTERIES.

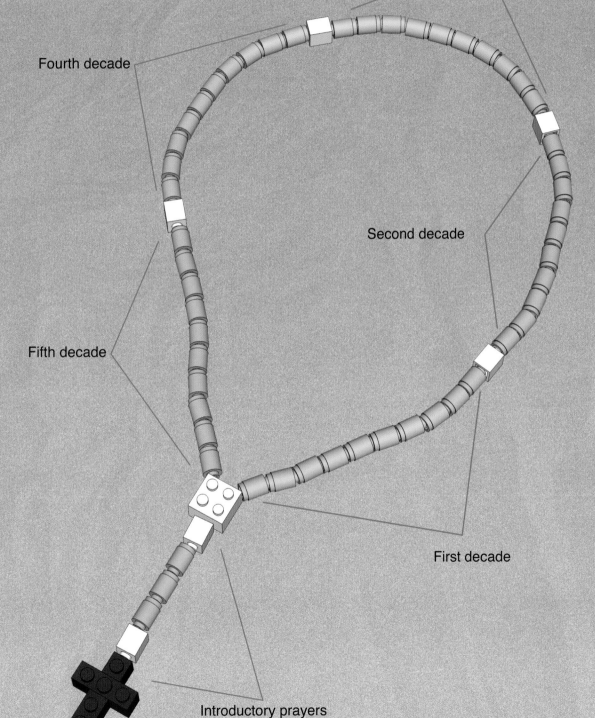

Third decade

Fourth decade

Second decade

Fifth decade

First decade

Introductory prayers

THE **JOYFUL MYSTERIES** CONTEMPLATE THE JOYFUL TIMES IN JESUS' LIFE.

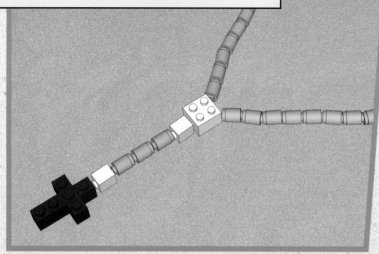

MONDAY AND SATURDAY

THE FIRST JOYFUL MYSTERY IS THE ANNUNCIATION.

THE SECOND JOYFUL MYSTERY IS THE VISITATION.

THE THIRD JOYFUL MYSTERY IS THE NATIVITY.

THE FOURTH JOYFUL MYSTERY IS THE PRESENTATION.

THE FIFTH JOYFUL MYSTERY IS THE FINDING OF JESUS IN THE TEMPLE.

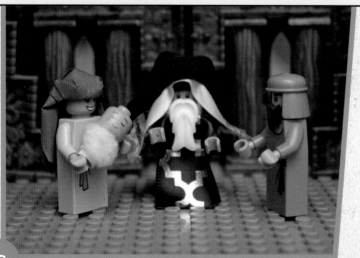

LK 1:26-38, LK 1:39-40, LK 2:1-20, LK 2:22-40, LK 2:49

THE **LUMINOUS MYSTERIES** CONTEMPLATE JESUS' PUBLIC LIFE AND MIRACLES.

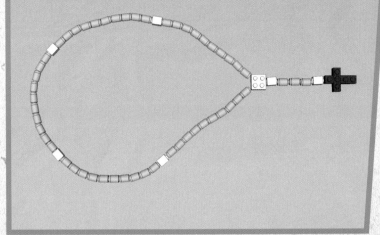

THURSDAY

THE FIRST LUMINOUS MYSTERY IS THE BAPTISM OF THE LORD.

THE SECOND LUMINOUS MYSTERY IS THE WEDDING AT CANA.

THE THIRD LUMINOUS MYSTERY IS THE PROCLAMATION OF THE KINGDOM.

THE FOURTH LUMINOUS MYSTERY IS THE TRANSFIGURATION.

THE FIFTH LUMINOUS MYSTERY IS THE INSTITUTION OF THE EUCHARIST.

MAT 3:13-17, JN 2:1-11, MK 1:14-15, MAT 17:1-3, MK 14:22-24

89

THE **SORROWFUL MYSTERIES** CONTEMPLATE THE SAD TIMES IN JESUS' LIFE.

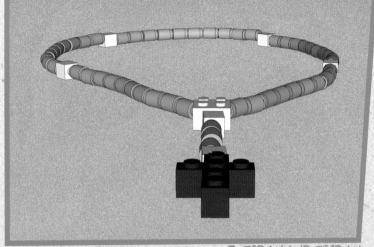

TUESDAY AND FRIDAY

THE FIRST SORROWFUL MYSTERY IS THE AGONY IN THE GARDEN.

THE SECOND SORROWFUL MYSTERY IS THE SCOURGING AT THE PILLAR.

THE THIRD SORROWFUL MYSTERY IS THE CROWNING WITH THORNS.

THE FOURTH SORROWFUL MYSTERY IS THE CARRYING OF THE CROSS.

THE FIFTH SORROWFUL MYSTERY IS THE CRUCIFIXION.

MAT 26:36-46, JN 19:1, JN 19:2, JN 19:17, JN 19:18

THE **GLORIOUS MYSTERIES** CONTEMPLATE THE PLAN OF SALVATION.

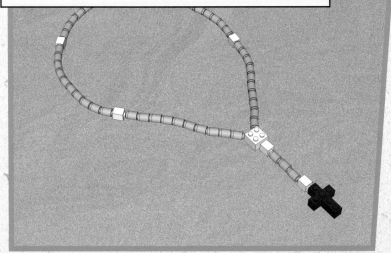

WEDNESDAY AND SUNDAY

THE FIRST GLORIOUS MYSTERY IS THE RESURRECTION.

THE SECOND GLORIOUS MYSTERY IS THE ASCENSION.

THE THIRD GLORIOUS MYSTERY IS THE DESCENT OF THE HOLY SPIRIT.

THE FOURTH GLORIOUS MYSTERY IS THE ASSUMPTION.

THE FIFTH GLORIOUS MYSTERY IS THE CORONATION.

MAT 28:5-6, ACTS 1:9, ACTS 2:1-4, CCC 966, REV 12:1

1

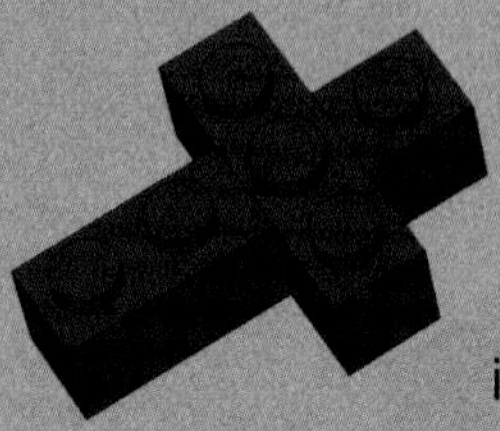

In the name of the Father, and of the Son, and of the Holy Spirit. Amen.

I believe in God, the Father Almighty, creator of heaven and earth. I believe in Jesus Christ, His only Son, our Lord. He was conceived by the power of the Holy Spirit and born of the Virgin Mary. He suffered under Pontius Pilate, was crucified, died, and was buried. He descended into Hell. On the third day He rose again. He ascended into heaven and is seated at the right hand of the Father. He will come again to judge the living and the dead. I believe in the Holy Spirit, the holy catholic Church, the communion of saints, the forgiveness of sins, the resurrection of the body, and the life everlasting. Amen.

2

Our Father Who art in Heaven, hallowed be Thy Name; Thy kingdom come; Thy will be done on earth as it is in heaven. Give us this day our daily bread, and forgive us our trespasses, as we forgive those who trespass against us, and lead us not into temptation, but deliver us from evil. Amen.

3

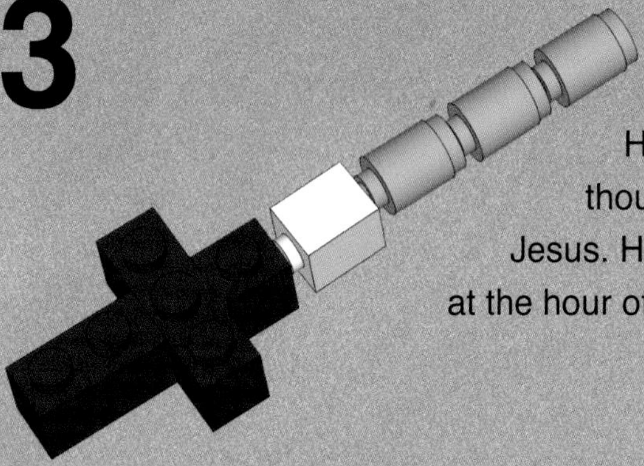

Hail Mary, full of grace, the Lord is with thee. Blessed art thou amongst women, and blessed is the fruit of thy womb, Jesus. Holy Mary, Mother of God, pray for us sinners, now and at the hour of our death. Amen.

4

Glory be to the Father, and to the Son, and to the Holy Spirit, as it was in the beginning, is now, and ever shall be, world without end. Amen.

5

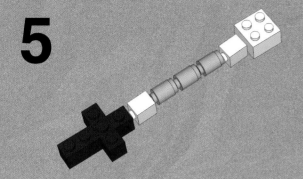

6

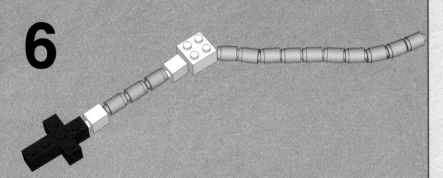

7

O my Jesus, forgive us our sins, save us from the fires of hell, and lead all souls to Heaven, especially those in most need of Thy mercy.

8

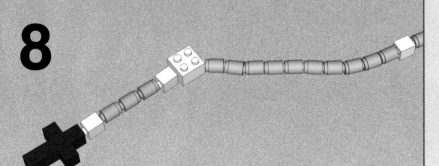

Rosary Instructions

Choose which set of mysteries you will meditate on. (Suggestions: Joyful on Monday & Saturday, Luminous on Thursday, Sorrowful on Tuesday & Friday, Glorious on Wednesday & Sunday.)

1. Begin with the Sign of the Cross, followed by the Apostles' Creed prayer.

2. Pray one Our Father prayer, also called The Lord's Prayer.

3. Pray three Hail Mary prayers for the virtues of faith, hope, and charity.

4. Pray one Glory Be prayer.

5. State the first mystery, and pray one Our Father prayer.

6. Pray 10 Hail Mary prayers while contemplating the stated mystery.

7. Conclude the decade by praying the Glory Be prayer and the Fatima Prayer.

8. Continue saying four more decades, meditating on each of the five mysteries in order.

9. Conclude the decades by praying the Hail Holy Queen prayer.

10. Some people also recite the Rosary Prayer, the Memorare, and the Prayer to St. Michael the Archangel. Some also recite one Our Father prayer, one Hail Mary prayer, and one Glory Be prayer for the intentions of the pope.

11. Finally, conclude with the Sign of the Cross.

9 Hail, Holy Queen, mother of mercy, our life, our sweetness, and our hope. To thee do we cry, poor banished children of Eve. To thee do we send up our sighs, mourning and weeping in this valley of tears. Turn then, most gracious advocate, thine eyes of mercy toward us, and after this our exile show us the blessed fruit of thy womb, Jesus. O clement, O loving, O sweet Virgin Mary. Pray for us, O Holy Mother of God. That we may be made worthy of the promises of Christ.

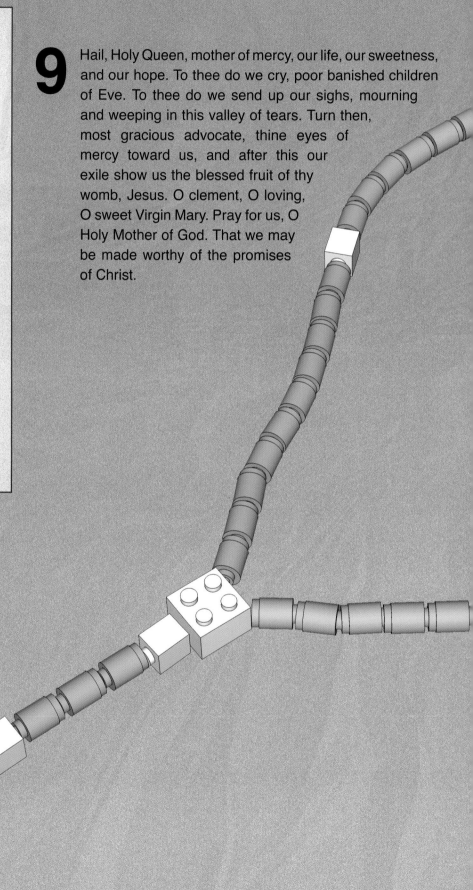

10 Let us pray: O God, whose Only Begotten Son, by his life, death, and resurrection, has purchased for us the rewards of eternal life, grant, we beseech thee, that while meditating on these mysteries of the most holy rosary of the Blessed Virgin Mary, we may imitate what they contain and obtain what they promise, through the same Christ our Lord. Amen.

Remember, O most gracious Virgin Mary, that never was it known that anyone who fled to thy protection, implored thy help, or sought thine intercession was left unaided. Inspired by this confidence, I fly unto thee, O Virgin of virgins, my mother; to thee do I come, before thee I stand, sinful and sorrowful. O Mother of the Word Incarnate, despise not my petitions, but in thy mercy hear and answer me. Amen.

For the Pope's intentions: Our Father ..., Hail Mary ..., Glory Be ...

St. Michael the Archangel, defend us in battle. Be our protection against the wickedness and snares of the devil. May God rebuke him, we humbly pray, and do thou, O Prince of the heavenly host, by the power of God, cast into hell Satan, and all the evil spirits, who prowl about the world seeking the ruin of souls. Amen.

11 In the name of the Father, and of the Son, and of the Holy Spirit. Amen.

BAPTISM

JN 6:53, CCC 1215, TI 3:5, JN 3:5

"AFTER THIS, JESUS AND HIS DISCIPLES WENT INTO THE REGION OF JUDEA, WHERE HE SPENT SOME TIME WITH THEM BAPTIZING."

JN 3:22

GEN 3:24, CCC 1262-1263, CCC 1218

EXACTLY! IN THE BIBLE, THE WATER AND THE SPIRIT MAKE THINGS NEW.

IN THE BEGINNING WHEN THE WORLD WAS CREATED, IT WAS ALL WATER, AND THE SPIRIT HOVERED ABOVE IT.

THEN GOD CALLED THE GROUND OUT OF THE WATER. IT WAS A NEW CREATION THROUGH THE WATER AND THE SPIRIT.

MANY YEARS LATER DURING THE TIME OF NOAH, THE WORLD TURNED WICKED, AND GOD, IN HIS MERCY, DECIDED TO MAKE IT NEW.

IT RAINED FOR 40 DAYS AND 40 NIGHTS. GOD USED THE WATER OF THE FLOOD TO CLEANSE HIS CREATION OF EVIL (SIN).

AFTER THE FLOOD, NOAH RELEASED THE DOVE, A SYMBOL OF THE HOLY SPIRIT.

GEN 6: 5-13, GEN 7:12, GEN 8:8-12

MAT 3:16

EX 14:23-24

EX 16:4-5, JN 6:49-51

THE ISRAELITES WERE LED INTO BATTLE WITH THE ARK AND THE COVENANT.

WE ARE LED INTO SPIRITUAL BATTLE WITH THE ARK (MARY) AND THE COVENANT (JESUS IN THE EUCHARIST).

JOS 6:13

THE ISRAELITES' JOURNEY WAS TO GET TO THE PROMISED LAND.

OUR JOURNEY IS TO GET TO THE ETERNAL PROMISED LAND (HEAVEN)!

NUM 27:12, RV 21:2

THAT'S WHY WE NEED TO BE BAPTIZED! IT'S HOW WE BECOME BORN AGAIN,

NOT INTO THE ORIGINAL SIN OF ADAM AND EVE, BUT AS A NEW CREATION IN CHRIST AND A CHILD OF GOD.

ST. PAUL TELLS US,

WE ARE BAPTIZED INTO THE RESURRECTION OF CHRIST.

ST. PAUL, PRAY FOR US!

CHRIST'S PASSION, DEATH, AND RESURRECTION DEFEATED SIN AND DEATH AND OPENED HEAVEN'S GATES.

THE RESURRECTION IS THE DAY OF NEW CREATION, THE EIGHTH DAY.

WHAT IS THE EIGHTH DAY?

GOD ORIGINALLY CREATED THE WORLD IN SIX DAYS, AND ON THE SEVENTH DAY, SATURDAY, HE RESTED. THAT WAS THE SABBATH DAY (DAY RESERVED TO WORSHIP GOD AND REST).

JN 3:5, RM 6:4-5, REV 1:18, CCC 2174, GEN 1:1-2:4

EX 20:8, ACTS 20:7, CCC 2174, ACTS 20:7

LEV 12:3, COL 2:11-12

THE EIGHTH DAY, THE DAY OF NEW CREATION, IT'S WHEN WE'RE TRULY BORN AGAIN!

IS THIS WHY CHURCHES USUALLY HAVE EIGHT-SIDED BAPTISMAL FONTS?

EXACTLY! THE EIGHT SIDES POINT TO THE RESURRECTION!

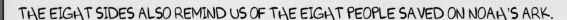

THE EIGHT SIDES ALSO REMIND US OF THE EIGHT PEOPLE SAVED ON NOAH'S ARK.

THOSE EIGHT PEOPLE WHO WERE SAVED PREFIGURE (REPRESENT) THE EIGHTH DAY, THE DAY OF NEW CREATION AND BAPTISM.

ST. PETER SAYS,

IN THE DAYS OF NOAH, EIGHT IN ALL WERE SAVED THROUGH WATER. THIS PREFIGURED BAPTISM, WHICH SAVES YOU NOW! IT IS NOT FOR THE WASHING OF THE BODY, BUT AN APPEAL TO GOD FOR A CLEAR CONSCIENCE, THROUGH THE RESURRECTION OF JESUS CHRIST.

JN 3:3, CCC 628, MAT 22:37-40, CCC 2174, MAT 28:1, 1 PT 3:20, 1 PT 3:21

ACTS 2:38, 1 PT 2:5, CCC 901-913

JESUS SAYS,

GO MAKE DISCIPLES OF ALL NATIONS,

BAPTIZING THEM IN THE NAME OF THE FATHER, AND OF THE SON, AND OF THE HOLY SPIRIT.

THROUGH BAPTISM, WE BECOME CHILDREN OF GOD AND RECEIVE SANCTIFYING GRACE, FORGIVENESS OF ALL OUR SINS, AND THE GIFT OF THE HOLY SPIRIT!

THESE PROMISES ARE FOR OUR ENTIRE FAMILY.

MAT 28:19, CCC 1279, ACTS 2:38, ACTS 2:39

THE ULTIMATE RESPONSIBILITY OF PARENTS IS TO BRING THEIR CHILD INTO THE FAMILY OF GOD THROUGH BAPTISM. THEY MAKE A DECLARATION OF FAITH ON BEHALF OF THE CHILD AND PROMISE TO TEACH THE CHILD TO REJECT SIN AND EMBRACE THE TRUTHS OF THE CATHOLIC FAITH.

IT'S ALSO THEIR RESPONSIBILITY TO RAISE THE CHILD IN THE PRACTICES OF THE CHURCH.

IN THE NAME OF THE FATHER ...

THEY SHOULD TEACH THE CHILD TO OBEY THE TEN COMMANDMENTS BY LOVING GOD AND LOVING NEIGABORS.

THESE PRACTICES WILL HELP THE CHILD LIVE A LIFE THAT LEADS TO ETERNAL SALVATION!

CCC 1255, CCC 2225-2226, CCC 2083

MAT 28:19, CCC 1279, CCC 1212

Rite of Baptism

1 **Proclamation of the Gospel**. Hear the Word of God, choose to reject sin, and make promises to live for Christ.

2 **Oleum Sanctorum (Oil of Catechumens)**. Anointed by the Holy Spirit, join Christ's mission of priest, prophet, and king.

3 **White Garment**. Put on Christ and rise with Him.

4 **Prayer of Epiclesis.** Invoke the Holy Spirit upon the water to be baptized by water and the Spirit.

5 **Water**. Be cleansed with water, die to sin, and be born into the Trinity.

6 **Godparents**. Present the child and take co-responsibility for the child's religious education.

7 **Candle**. Enlightened by Christ, be the light of Christ to the world.

8 **Easter Candle**. Remember the Paschal Mystery: the Passion, Death, and Resurrection of Jesus.

9 **Sign of the cross.** Be claimed for Christ through the grace of His cross.

10 **Essential Rite**. "I baptize you in the name of the Father, and of the Son, and of the Holy Spirit." Pour water three times.

RECONCILIATION

RM 3:23-24, CCC 1486, CCC 1487-1489.

NM 21:6, NM 21:8

131

CCC 1854-1855, 1 JN 5:16-17

SCRIPTURE SAYS THERE ARE SINS THAT ARE NOT UNTO DEATH (VENIAL)

AND SINS THAT ARE UNTO DEATH (MORTAL).

BANK

1 JN 5:16-17

CCC 1861, CCC 1451-1454, MT 5-7, RM 12-15

A MORTAL SIN HAS THREE CONDITIONS:
1. IT MUST BE A GRAVE ACT: IT MUST BE INTRINSICALLY EVIL AND IMMORAL.
2. YOU MUST HAVE FULL KNOWLEDGE: YOU MUST KNOW THAT IT IS WRONG.
3. YOU MUST HAVE DELIBERATE CONSENT: YOU MUST FREELY CHOOSE TO DO IT.

C.C.C. 1858-1859, MK 10:19, LK 16:19-31

HOWEVER SCARY THIS MAY SOUND, THERE IS GOOD NEWS. WE CAN RECEIVE COMPLETE FORGIVENESS OF OUR SINS BY CONFESSING THEM IN THE SACRAMENT OF RECONCILIATION!

THAT IS WHY WE MUST SPREAD THE GOOD NEWS OF CHRIST'S GRACE AND FORGIVENESS TO EVERYONE WE MEET!

JN 20:23, MK 16:15

HOME
SWEET HOM
THAT IS GOOD NEWS! I WANT TO SHARE IT. CAN YOU TELL ME MORE ABOUT RECONCILIATION?
OF COURSE!
DID YOU KNOW, IN THE BIBLE, GOD BREATHED ON HIS PEOPLE TWO TIMES?

THE FIRST TIME WAS WHEN GOD BREATHED LIFE INTO THE NOSTRILS OF ADAM.

GN 2:7

IT WASN'T LONG AFTER THIS THAT ADAM SINNED AND DEATH CAME INTO THE WORLD.

AFTER ADAM SINNED, GOD ASKED HIM,

WHAT HAVE YOU DONE?

EVEN GOD, WHO KNOWS EVERYTHING, WANTED ADAM TO CONFESS HIS SINS.

THE SECOND TIME GOD BREATHED ON HIS PEOPLE WAS AFTER THE RESURRECTION. JESUS, WHO IS GOD, APPEARED TO HIS APOSTLES IN THE UPPER ROOM, AND HE BREATHED ON THEM.

JN 20:22

AFTER JESUS BREATHED ON HIS APOSTLES, HE SAID,

WHOSE SINS YOU FORGIVE ARE FORGIVEN THEM, AND WHOSE SINS YOU RETAIN ARE RETAINED.

THE CHURCH AND THE APOSTLES, WHO WERE THE FIRST PRIESTS, WERE GIVEN AUTHORITY FROM AND THROUGH GOD TO FORGIVE SINS.

THIS AUTHORITY TO FORGIVE SINS HAS BEEN PASSED DOWN THROUGH THE CHURCH SUCCESSIVELY WITHIN THE HOLY PRIESTHOOD.

JN 20:23, CCC 1461, 2 COR 5:18, CCC 1120, LK 24:47, MT 28:18-20

GEN 3:11, CCC 1456, MT 18:18

WE NEED FORGIVENESS OF SINS THROUGH RECONCILIATION BECAUSE IT BREATHES GOD'S LIFE BACK INTO US

AND FILLS US WITH GOD'S GRACE SO WE CAN RECEIVE THE HOLY EUCHARIST!

CCC 1997, CCC 1468, LK 15:32

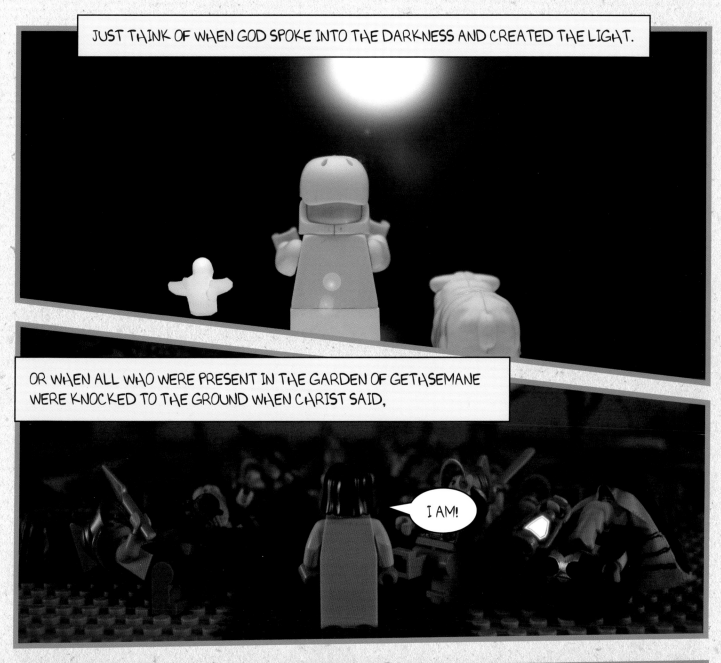

OR WHEN ALL WHO WERE PRESENT IN THE GARDEN OF GETHSEMANE WERE KNOCKED TO THE GROUND WHEN CHRIST SAID,

I AM!

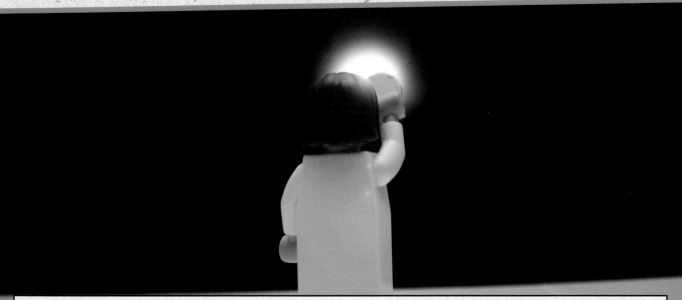

THE EUCHARIST (WHICH IS GOD) IS THE SAME POWER SOURCE THAT CREATED THE UNIVERSE!

145

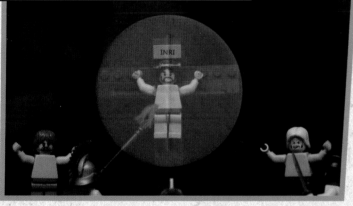

ST. JOHN VIANNEY, PRAY FOR US!

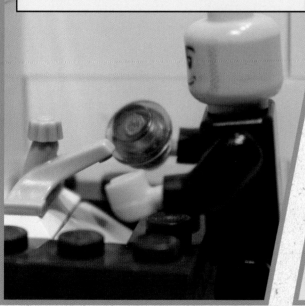

CCC 1333, CCC 1376, MT 26:26, MK 14:22, LK 22:19, 1 COR 11:24, 1 COR 11:27

THE SAME IS TRUE ABOUT THE EUCHARIST, WHICH IS A FAMILY MEAL.

WE HAVE A LOVING FATHER WHO WAITS AT THE TABLE FOR US,

THE SON WHO PREPARED THE MEAL,

THE HOLY SPIRIT WHO UNITES US,

AND A MOTHER WHO CALLS US TO THE SUPPER.

BUT REMEMBER, YOU MUST FIRST "WASH UP" IN THE SACRAMENT OF RECONCILIATION.

1 COR 10:16-17, 1 THES 1:10, CCC 1359, CCC 690, JN 16:14, CCC 964, 1 COR 11:28

CCC 1457, CCC 1455-1456

I I AM THE LORD YOUR GOD. YOU SHALL WORSHIP THE LORD YOUR GOD AND HIM ONLY SHALL YOU SERVE.

II YOU SHALL NOT TAKE THE NAME OF THE LORD YOUR GOD IN VAIN.

III REMEMBER TO KEEP HOLY THE SABBATH DAY.

CCC 2067, EX 20:1-17.

AND THE OTHER SEVEN CONCERN LOVE OF NEIGHBOR.

IV HONOR YOUR FATHER AND YOUR MOTHER.

V YOU SHALL NOT KILL.

VI YOU SHALL NOT COMMIT ADULTERY.

VII YOU SHALL NOT STEAL

VIII YOU SHALL NOT BEAR FALSE WITNESS AGAINST YOUR NEIGHBOR.

IX YOU SHALL NOT COVET YOUR NEIGHBOR'S WIFE.

X YOU SHALL NOT COVET YOUR NEIGHBOR'S GOODS.

THEN YOU SAY,

BLESS ME FATHER FOR I HAVE SINNED. IT HAS BEEN (HOW LONG) SINCE MY LAST CONFESSION.

THEN TELL HIM ALL OF YOUR SINS AND HOW MANY TIMES YOU COMMITTED EACH ONE. COMPLETE YOUR LIST BY SAYING,

FOR THESE AND ALL MY PAST SINS, I AM TRULY SORRY.

HE WILL GIVE YOU A PENANCE, WHICH IS A WAY FOR YOU TO MAKE AMENDS FOR YOUR SINS. IT'S USUALLY A TASK SUCH AS A FEW PRAYERS TO RECITE OR AN ACT OF KINDNESS TOWARD OTHERS.

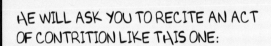

HE WILL ASK YOU TO RECITE AN ACT OF CONTRITION LIKE THIS ONE:

Act of Contrition

O my God, I am heartily sorry for having offended Thee, and I detest all my sins, because I dread the loss of heaven, and the pains of hell; but most of all because they offend Thee, my God, Who are all good and deserving of all my love. I firmly resolve, with the help of Thy grace, to confess my sins, to do penance, and to amend my life. Amen.

CCC 1548, CCC 1461, JN 20:23, 2 COR 5:18

AND YOU NEVER HAVE TO WORRY BECAUSE A PRIEST IS NOT PERMITTED TO TELL ANY OF YOUR SINS TO ANYONE, NO MATTER WHAT! NOT THE POLICE, NOT YOUR PARENTS, NO ONE!

THE BEST PART OF RECEIVING A SACRAMENTAL CONFESSION IS THAT YOU ARE PERFECTLY CLEAN AND FULL OF GRACE AGAIN.

THIS MEANS YOU CAN RECEIVE THE EUCHARIST!

JUST IMAGINE SIN AS A SIMPLE MATH PROBLEM.

IF SIN EQUALS DEATH, THEN WHAT EQUALS THE DEATH OF SIN?

WELL, THE BIBLE SAYS BAPTISM REMOVES SIN.

MAT 18:22, ACTS 2:38

THE BIBLE SAYS CONFESSION REMOVES SIN.

THE BIBLE SAYS THE EUCHARIST REMOVES SIN.

SO, WE CAN CONCLUDE:

SIN = DEATH

BAPTISM +
CONFESSION + = NO SIN
EUCHARIST

NO SIN = LIFE

CCC 1127, CCC 1113

CCC 2003, CCC 1114-1116

CONFIRMATION

CCC 2003, CCC 1212, CCC 1285, CCC 1254-1255, CCC 1308

HEB 6:1, CCC 2041-2043

IT IS A LOT OF RESPONSIBILITY, BUT WE CAN CHOOSE A SPONSOR (A CONFIRMED ADULT ROLE MODEL) TO HELP GUIDE US IN OUR CHRISTIAN LIFE.

WE ALSO CHOOSE A SAINT (A PERSON WHO IS IN HEAVEN UNITED WITH GOD) WHO IS A ROLE MODEL FOR HOLINESS AND SOMEONE WE CAN TURN TO FOR INTERCESSION.

ST. GIANNA BERETTA-MOLLA, PRAY FOR US!

THROUGH THE SACRAMENT OF CONFIRMATION, WE RECEIVE GIFTS FROM GOD TO HELP US LIVE AN AUTHENTICALLY CHRISTIAN LIFE. CHRIST PROMISED TO GIVE US HIS GIFTS THROUGH THE HOLY SPIRIT.

CCC 1311, CCC 956, MK 12:27, JN 14:26

AT PENTECOST, WHEN THE HOLY SPIRIT DESCENDED LIKE TONGUES OF FIRE, ALL PRESENT WERE FILLED WITH THE HOLY SPIRIT, WHICH ENABLED THEM TO PROCLAIM THE GOSPEL.

DURING THE RITE OF CONFIRMATION, THE BISHOP LAYS HANDS ON THE CONFIRMANDS AND ANOINTS THEM WITH SACRUM CHARISMA (HOLY CHARISM OIL). THE CONFIRMANDS ARE SEALED WITH THE GIFT OF THE THE HOLY SPIRIT, WHICH GIVES THEM THE GRACES NECESSARY TO PROCLAIM AND LIVE THE GOSPEL.

BE SEALED WITH THE GIFT OF THE HOLY SPIRIT.

ACTS 2:1-11, CCC 1289

173

WE RECEIVE AN INCREASE IN THE SEVEN GIFTS OF THE HOLY SPIRIT.

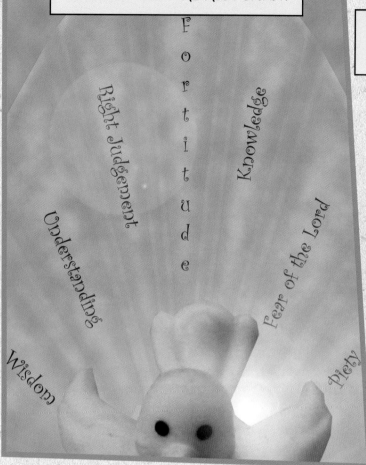

Fortitude

Right Judgement

Knowledge

Understanding

Fear of the Lord

Wisdom

Piety

WISDOM ALLOWS US TO SEE THINGS AS GOD DOES AND TO DESIRE GOD AND NOT THE WORLD.

J.M.J.

If the new crime be, to believe in God, let us all be criminals.

UNTIL NEXT TIME, GOD LOVE YOU!

VEN. ARCHBISHOP FULTON J. SHEEN, PRAY FOR US!

UNDERSTANDING HELPS US TO UNDERSTAND THE FAITH. IT GIVES US INSIGHT THROUGH PRAYER, SCRIPTURE, AND THE SACRAMENTS.

RIGHT JUDGMENT OR COUNSEL HELPS US TO AVOID SIN THROUGH KNOWLEDGE OF RIGHT AND WRONG.

174

ST. PATRICK, PRAY FOR US!

ST. PADRE PIO, PRAY FOR US!

CCC 1303, IS 11:1-2, CCC 1831, CCC 1845

FORTITUDE OR COURAGE ALLOWS US TO ENDURE EVIL, DEFEND OUR FAITH, AND PERSEVERE IN THE LIFE OF CHRIST.

ST. JOAN OF ARC, PRAY FOR US!

KNOWLEDGE IS THE ACTUAL ABILITY TO JUDGE ALL THINGS ACCORDING TO THE TRUTHS OF THE CATHOLIC FAITH AND TO SEE THE CIRCUMSTANCES OF OUR LIFE THE WAY THAT GOD SEES THEM.

ST. THOMAS AQUINAS, PRAY FOR US!

PIETY IS THE WILLINGNESS TO WORSHIP AND OBEY GOD.

ST. TERESA OF CALCUTTA, PRAY FOR US!

FEAR OF THE LORD GIVES US THE DESIRE NOT TO OFFEND GOD OUT OF LOVE FOR HIM.

ST. AUGUSTINE, PRAY FOR US!

CCC 1831, CCC 1845

CCC 1832, GAL 5:22-23

IN ADDITION TO RECEIVING THE GIFTS OF THE HOLY SPIRIT IN CONFIRMATION, WE ARE ALSO SEALED WITH AN INDELIBLE MARK WHEN WE ARE ANOINTED WITH THE SACRED OIL.

I REMEMBER THAT IN BAPTISM WE ARE SEALED WITH AN INDELIBLE MARK THAT CLAIMS US AS CHILDREN OF GOD.

YES! AND JUST AS SOLDIERS OF OLD WERE ANOINTED AND CLAIMED FOR THEIR KING, OUR ANOINTING IN CONFIRMATION CLAIMS US AS SOLDIERS FOR CHRIST THE KING OF KINGS!

CCC 1304, 1317, 2 COR 1:21-22

BECAUSE OUR ANOINTING MARKS US AS SOLDIERS FOR CHRIST, WE MUST NOW STAND UP AND FIGHT FOR OUR FAITH.

THINK ABOUT A SOLDIER'S JOB. IT'S AN INTENSE DUTY!

BUT CHRIST ARMS US WITH HIS GRACE, THE GIFTS OF THE HOLY SPIRIT, AND OUR CHRISTIAN TRAINING. SO, FIGHTING FOR CHRIST IS A SOURCE OF GREAT JOY!

CCC 1297, CCC 1295

CCC 1294, MAT 14:27

ASHES ON OUR FOREHEADS REMIND US AND SHOW OTHERS THAT OUR VERY EXISTENCE IS A GIFT FROM GOD.

THE SIGN OF THE CROSS REMINDS US AND SHOWS OTHERS THAT EVERYTHING WE RECEIVE IS FROM GOD, INCLUDING SALVATION.

IN THE NAME OF THE FATHER ...

CRUCIFIXES, HOLY MEDALS, AND SCAPULARS KEEP US ALL AWARE OF CHRIST'S PRESENCE IN OUR DAILY LIVES.

CCC 1667, CCC 1668, CCC 1672

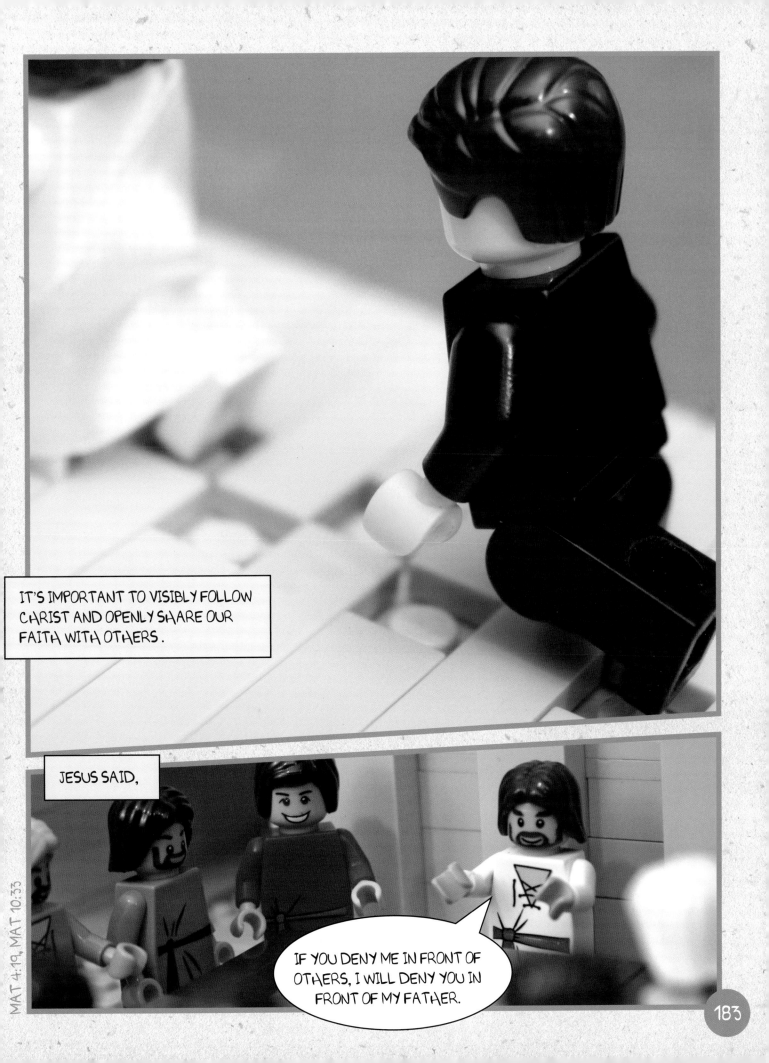

SUFFERING IS HOLY TO GOD.

OUR SUFFERING IS A PARTICIPATION IN THE SAME CURRENCY THAT PURCHASED OUR SALVATION.

WE ALSO ARE ASKED TO WORK. THERE ARE TWO TYPES OF WORK WE CAN DO: CORPORAL WORKS (FOR THE BODY) AND SPIRITUAL WORKS (FOR THE SOUL).

MAT 25:34-40, CCC 2447

MAT 25:34-40, CCC 2447

CCC 2447, JN 8:7, JN 20:24-29, MAT 21:12-13

JN 21:15-17, JN 4:4-26, LK 23:28, JN 11:1-44

ST. VERONICA, PRAY FOR US!

Speech bubble: YOU SEE, IT'S OUR CHRISTIAN DUTY, AS DISCIPLES OF CHRIST, TO BE DISCIPLINED AND DO THESE WORKS.

DISCIPLE (N.) BIBLICAL BORROWING FROM LATIN *DISCIPULUS*, MEANING PUPIL, STUDENT, FOLLOWER, SPECIFICALLY, A FOLLOWER OF CHRIST.

DISCIPLINE (N.) PUNISHMENT, INSTRUCTION, TRAINING, A FIELD OF STUDY. THE WORD DISCIPLINE COMES FROM *DISCIPULUS*, THE LATIN WORD FOR DISCIPLE.

EVEN THE VERY WORD "DISCIPLINE" COMES FROM THE WORD "DISCIPLE."

WE NEED A DISCIPLINED PRAYER LIFE BECAUSE PRAYING IS TALKING WITH GOD.

CCC 1816, MAT 6:5, CCC 2564-2565

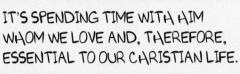

IT'S SPENDING TIME WITH HIM WHOM WE LOVE AND, THEREFORE, ESSENTIAL TO OUR CHRISTIAN LIFE.

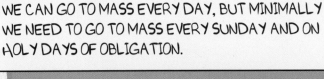

WE CAN GO TO MASS EVERY DAY, BUT MINIMALLY WE NEED TO GO TO MASS EVERY SUNDAY AND ON HOLY DAYS OF OBLIGATION.

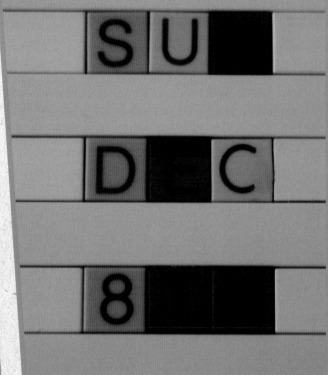

WE NEED TO UNDERSTAND THAT MASS IS NOT ABOUT BEING ENTERTAINED.

MASS IS A SACRED ENCOUNTER WITH GOD. WE ARE THERE TO WORSHIP AND PRAISE HIM, HEAR HIS WORD, AND BE UNITED WITH HIM AND RECEIVE HIS SACRAMENTAL GRACE IN HOLY COMMUNION.

LK 18:9-14, CCC 2559, MK 2:27-28, CCC 2176, CCC 1156-1158, CCC 1359-1361

CCC 2003, CCC 2017, 1 COR 12, CCC 1212, CCC 1534, CCC 1601, EPH 5:31-32

MARRIAGE

IT BEGINS WITH A WEDDING (ADAM AND EVE).

JESUS' FIRST PUBLIC MIRACLE WAS AT A WEDDING (THE WEDDING FEAST AT CANA).

THE BIBLE ALSO ENDS WITH A WEDDING IN THE BOOK OF REVELATION (THE WEDDING FEAST OF THE LAMB, WHICH IS THE HOLY EUCHARIST).

ULTIMATELY, WE ARE CALLED TO AN "ETERNAL MARRIAGE." WE WILL HAVE PERFECT UNION WITH GOD FOREVER IN HEAVEN.

GEN 2:21-23, JN 2:1-8, REV 19:6-9, CCC 1021, CCC 1602, CCCC 2550

197

CCC 772-773, EPA 1:1-14

IN THE BIBLE, A COMMON PLACE TO MEET YOUR SPOUSE WAS AT THE WELL.

WE ARE NO DIFFERENT. WE BECOME PART OF THE CHURCH (THE BRIDE OF CHRIST) AT THE WELL OF OUR BAPTISM.

THE BIBLE TELLS US THAT THE BRIDE AND GROOM BECOME ONE FLESH AFTER THEIR WEDDING.

AND WE BECOME ONE FLESH WITH GOD IN THE NUPTIAL UNION OF THE EUCHARIST AT OUR FIRST HOLY COMMUNION.

AFTER THE WEDDING, LIFE CONTINUES IN THIS WORLD THROUGH THE ONE-FLESH MARRIAGE UNION OF A HUSBAND AND WIFE.

GEN 24:12-14, GEN 29:1-6, EX 2:11-21, CCC 1277, MK 10:6-8, CCC 1617, CCC 1652, GEN 1:28

CCC 1612-1614, - CCC 1639-1640, CCC 221,CCC 1652-1654, GEN 1:28, GEN 9:7

JUST AS THERE IS NO LIMIT TO GOD'S LIFE-GIVING LOVE, WE PROMISE UNLIMITED LIFE-GIVING LOVE WHEN WE GET MARRIED.

IF WE PUT LIMITS ON BEING FRUITFUL IN MARRIAGE, THEN WE CHANGE THE REFLECTION OF GOD.

AND CHANGING GOD'S IMAGE IS A FORM OF IDOLATRY.

CCC 2366-2367, CCC 2354-2355, EX 20:3, CCC 1643-1666

JP II TOTB, ECC 3:14, 1 COR 1:9, JN 15:4-5, CCC 1644, 1 SAM 2:6

GEN 1:28, CCC 2366-2367, LK 1:38

EPA 5:25-27, CCC 1146

DID YOU KNOW THE FRONT OF THE CHURCH, THE SANCTUARY, RESEMBLES THE GROOM? CHRIST, THE GROOM, WAITS HERE FOR US TO APPROACH HIM.

AND THE PEWS, WHERE THE LAITY SIT, RESEMBLE THE BRIDE, THE CHURCH. WE PROCESS FORWARD JUST AS A BRIDE WOULD TO RECEIVE CHRIST, THE BRIDEGROOM, IN COMMUNION.

THE HIGH POINT OF THE MASS IS A WEDDING FEAST, WHERE HEAVEN CALLS US FORWARD TO RECEIVE THE BRIDEGROOM IN THE EUCHARIST.

CCC 1383, CCC 1153, CCC 777

JUST THINK ABOUT IT: WE WALK UP THE AISLE TOWARD THE ALTAR TO RECEIVE CHRIST. THE PRIEST SAYS, "BODY OF CHRIST," AND WE EACH RESPOND WITH OUR VOW, "AMEN!"

THIS IS ONE REASON WHY SOME WOMEN WEAR VEILS IN CHURCH.

THEY ARE VEILED LIKE A BRIDE AT A WEDDING.

THIS POINTS TOWARD OUR UNION WITH GOD IN HEAVEN,

OUR UNION WITH GOD, WHICH BEGAN AT BAPTISM WHEN WE MET OUR SPOUSE JESUS AT THE WELL.

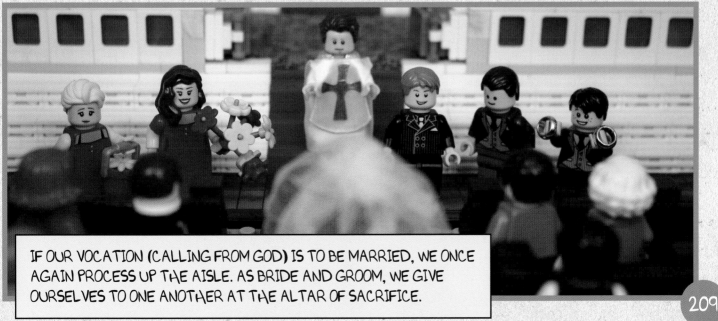

IF OUR VOCATION (CALLING FROM GOD) IS TO BE MARRIED, WE ONCE AGAIN PROCESS UP THE AISLE. AS BRIDE AND GROOM, WE GIVE OURSELVES TO ONE ANOTHER AT THE ALTAR OF SACRIFICE.

1 COR 11:4-10, REV 19:7-9, EZ 16:8-14, CCC 1383

For the unbelieving husband is made holy because of his wife, and the unbelieving wife is made holy because of her husband. Otherwise your children would be unclean, but as it is, they are holy.

1 Corinthians 7:14

I'M SANCTIFYING HER!

I'M SANCTIFYING HIM!

MARRIAGE IS A SACRAMENT OF SERVICE. ITS AIM IS THE SALVATION OF OTHERS. SPOUSES ARE TO HELP EACH OTHER GET TO HEAVEN.

1 COR 7:14, CCC 1535

MARRIAGE FULLY POINTS TO ETERNITY IN HEAVEN WITH GOD WHERE WE WILL BE "ETERNALLY MARRIED TO GOD" (IN PERFECT UNION WITH GOD FOREVER).

EVEN A FUNERAL RESEMBLES MARRIAGE.

THE DECEASED PERSON IS BROUGHT UP THE AISLE ONE FINAL TIME AND VEILED BEFORE THE ALTAR OF THE LORD TO BE GIVEN IN MARRIAGE TO GOD.

MARRIAGE IS TRULY A GIFT FROM GOD THAT AIDS IN THE SALVATION OF SOULS! SPOUSES STRIVE TO HELP EACH OTHER AND THEIR CHILDREN GET TO HEAVEN.

IN A SIMILAR WAY, PRIESTS TAKE VOWS AND ARE MARRIED TO THE CHURCH, WHICH THEY SERVE FOR THE SALVATION OF OTHERS.

AND THE CHURCH IS THE BRIDE OF CHRIST.

INRI

JUST AS EVE WAS BORN FROM THE SIDE OF ADAM, CHRIST'S BRIDE, THE CHURCH, WAS BORN FROM CHRIST'S SIDE!

BECAUSE THE PRIEST IS THE GROOM AND THE CHURCH IS THE BRIDE, HE LIVES HIS LIFE IN DEDICATION AND SUBMISSION TO HER.

CCC 1547, CCC 766, 1 COR 7:32-35, CCC 1577, CCCC 1579

CCC 1577, MK 3:14-19, LK 6:12-16, 1 TIM 3:1-13, 2 TIM 1:6, TIT 1:5-9, CCC 1591-1592

HOLY ORDERS

CCC 874, CCC 1536, CCC 1544

MELCHIZEDEK WAS A HIGH PRIEST IN THE OLD TESTAMENT. HE OFFERED A SACRIFICE OF BREAD AND WINE. HE WAS THE KING OF SALEM (PEACE).

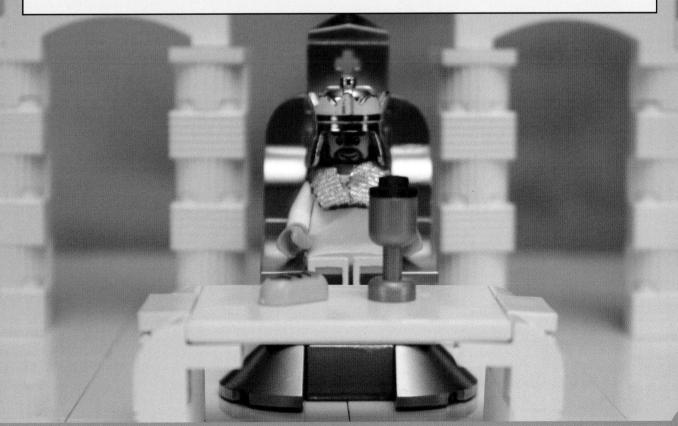

CHRIST IS THE HIGH PRIEST OF HEAVEN AND EARTH WHO OFFERED HIS BODY AND BLOOD IN THE FORM OF BREAD AND WINE. HE IS THE KING OF KINGS AND THE PRINCE OF PEACE.

HEB 7:1, 1 TIM 6:15, CCC 1545

217

NICENE CREED

I BELIEVE IN ONE GOD,
THE FATHER ALMIGHTY,
MAKER OF HEAVEN AND EARTH,
OF ALL THINGS VISIBLE AND INVISIBLE.

I BELIEVE IN ONE LORD JESUS CHRIST,
THE ONLY BEGOTTEN SON OF GOD,
BORN OF THE FATHER BEFORE ALL AGES.
GOD FROM GOD, LIGHT FROM LIGHT,
TRUE GOD FROM TRUE GOD,
BEGOTTEN, NOT MADE, CONSUBSTANTIAL WITH THE FATHER;
THROUGH HIM ALL THINGS WERE MADE.
FOR US MEN AND FOR OUR SALVATION
HE CAME DOWN FROM HEAVEN,

AND BY THE HOLY SPIRIT WAS INCARNATE OF THE VIRGIN MARY,
AND BECAME MAN.

FOR OUR SAKE HE WAS CRUCIFIED UNDER PONTIUS PILATE,
HE SUFFERED DEATH AND WAS BURIED,
AND ROSE AGAIN ON THE THIRD DAY
IN ACCORDANCE WITH THE SCRIPTURES.
HE ASCENDED INTO HEAVEN
AND IS SEATED AT THE RIGHT HAND OF THE FATHER.
HE WILL COME AGAIN IN GLORY
TO JUDGE THE LIVING AND THE DEAD
AND HIS KINGDOM WILL HAVE NO END.

I BELIEVE IN THE HOLY SPIRIT, THE LORD, THE GIVER OF LIFE,
WHO PROCEEDS FROM THE FATHER AND THE SON,
WHO WITH THE FATHER AND THE SON IS ADORED AND GLORIFIED,
WHO HAS SPOKEN THROUGH THE PROPHETS.

I BELIEVE IN ONE, HOLY, CATHOLIC AND APOSTOLIC CHURCH.
I CONFESS ONE BAPTISM FOR THE FORGIVENESS OF SINS
AND I LOOK FORWARD TO THE RESURRECTION OF THE DEAD
AND THE LIFE OF THE WORLD TO COME.

AMEN.

IN THIS CREED, WE PROFESS ONE, HOLY, CATHOLIC, AND APOSTOLIC CHURCH.

THE WORD "APOSTOLIC" MEANS FROM THE APOSTLES.

THE APOSTLES WERE THE FIRST BISHOPS. THEY WERE ORDAINED BY CHRIST HIMSELF!

WE, AS CATHOLICS, KNOW THAT PETER WAS OUR FIRST POPE. THE POPE IS THE HEAD BISHOP OF THE CHURCH AND THE BISHOP OF ROME.

HOW DO WE KNOW THAT PETER WAS THE FIRST POPE?

THE BIBLE TELLS US.

CCC 811-810, CCC 869, REV 21:14, CCC 880, MAT 16:18-19

PETER, WHO WAS ORIGINALLY NAMED SIMON, WAS AMONG THE FIRST APOSTLES CALLED BY JESUS.

MAT 4:18-22

SIMON PETER WAS AMONG THE FIRST CALLED BY JESUS FOR A REASON.

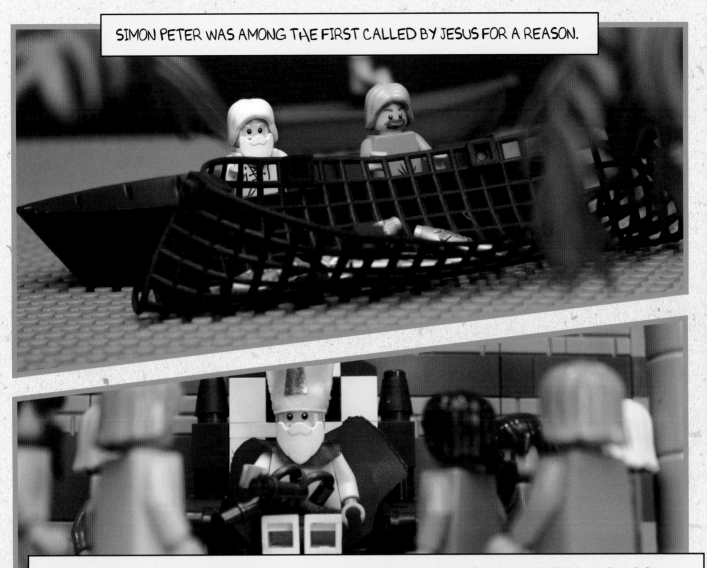

JESUS KNEW THAT HE WOULD FULFILL THE OLD TESTAMENT PROPHECY AND SIT IN A SEAT OF HONOR AMONG HIS PEOPLE AS THE HEAD OF HIS CHURCH, AS THE FIRST POPE.

WHAT PROPHESY FROM THE OLD TESTAMENT?

THE PROPHECY WAS FORETOLD BY THE PROPHET ISAIAH. HE DESCRIBES A KEY THAT HELD THE AUTHORITY TO RULE OVER ISRAEL, THE KINGDOM OF DAVID.

THE BIBLE TELLS US WHATEVER DOOR THIS KEY OPENS WILL REMAIN OPEN,

AND WHATEVER DOOR IT SHUTS WILL REMAIN SHUT.

THE BIBLE DESCRIBES THE AUTHORITY OF THE DAVIDIC KINGDOM AS AN IMMOVABLE PEG. IN GOD'S COVENANT WITH DAVID, HE PROMISED THAT AN ETERNAL ROYAL KINGDOM WOULD BE ESTABLISHED THROUGH HIS DESCENDANTS.

YOU SEE, FROM THE BEGINNING, GOD ALWAYS HAD A COVENANT WITH HIS PEOPLE. DO YOU REMEMBER THE OLD COVENANTS WE DISCUSSED?

YES, GOD CREATED COVENANTS WITH ADAM, NOAH, ABRAHAM, MOSES, AND DAVID.

IS 22:22-25, GEN 2:15-16, GEN 9:1-17, GEN 15:18-21, EX 19:24, 2 SAM 7:8-11

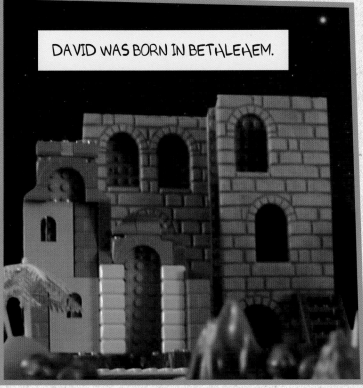

DAVID WAS BORN IN BETHLEHEM.

JESUS WAS BORN IN BETHLEHEM.

DAVID WAS A SHEPHERD. HE WAS ANOINTED BY THE PROPHET SAMUEL, AND THE SPIRIT OF THE LORD DESCENDED UPON HIM.

JESUS IS THE GOOD SHEPHERD. HE IS THE MESSIAH, WHICH MEANS "ANOINTED ONE." THE HOLY SPIRIT DESCENDED UPON HIM AT HIS BAPTISM IN THE JORDAN.

DAVID BECAME KING AT AGE 30.

JESUS BEGAN HIS PUBLIC MINISTRY AT AGE 30.

DAVID CAST OUT DEMONS.

JESUS CAST OUT DEMONS.

1 SAM 16:11-13, JN 10:11, JN 20:31, LK 3:22, 2 SM 5:4, JN 2:1-2?, 1 SM 16:23, MAT 8:31-32

DAVID WAS BETRAYED BY HIS TRUSTED ADVISOR.

JESUS WAS BETRAYED BY HIS OWN APOSTLE, JUDAS.

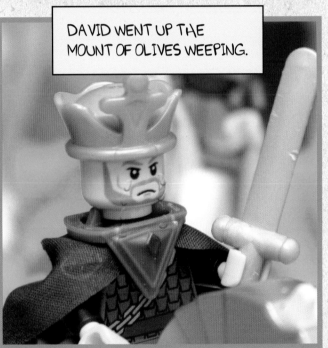

DAVID WENT UP THE MOUNT OF OLIVES WEEPING.

JESUS WEPT AT THE MOUNT OF OLIVES.

DAVID WROTE THE PSALMS.

...They have pierced my hands and my feet. I can count all my bones. They stare at me and gloat; they divide my garments among them; for my clothing they cast lots....

MY GOD, MY GOD, WHY HAVE YOU ABANDONED ME?

FROM THE CROSS, JESUS QUOTED THE PSALMS THAT SHOWED HE CAME TO FULFILL THE PROPHECIES!

PS 41:9, LK 22:1-5, 2 SM 15:30, LK 22:39-46, PS 22, MAT 27:46

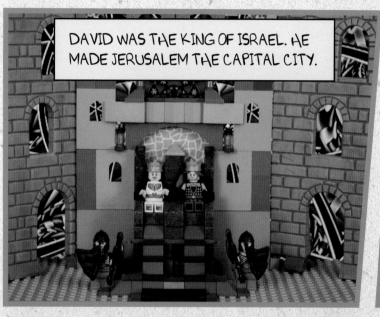

DAVID WAS THE KING OF ISRAEL. HE MADE JERUSALEM THE CAPITAL CITY.

JESUS IS THE KING OF KINGS FROM THE LINE OF DAVID. HE SITS UPON THE THRONE IN THE HEAVENLY JERUSALEM.

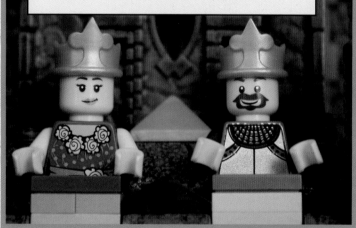

DAVID HAD A SON, SOLOMON, WHO ALSO RULED AS KING OF JERUSALEM. SCRIPTURE CALLS HIM "A SON OF GOD," TASKED TO BUILD GOD'S TEMPLE AND RULE ON A PERPETUAL THRONE.

LIKEWISE, JESUS IS KING OF THE "HEAVENLY JERUSALEM." HE IS THE SON OF GOD AND BUILT THE TEMPLE, HIS CHURCH. THEREFORE, JESUS IS THE FULFILLMENT OF SOLOMON!

SOLOMON RODE INTO JERUSALEM ON A DONKEY.

JESUS ENTERED JERUSALEM ON A DONKEY.

2 SM 5:1-3, 1 TIM 6:16, 1 KGS 2:4, HEB 12:22, ZEC 9:9, JN 12:14-15

THE MOTHER OF SOLOMON WAS HIS QUEEN, AND HE COULD NOT REFUSE HER REQUEST.

MARY IS THE MOTHER OF JESUS AND THE QUEEN OF HEAVEN AND EARTH. JESUS DID NOT REFUSE HER REQUEST.

SOLOMON BUILT THE TEMPLE ON A HUGE ROCK FOUNDATION IN JERUSALEM.

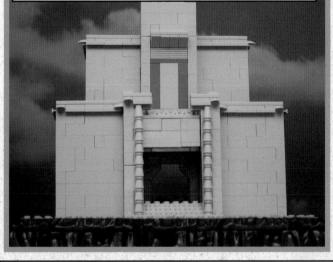

JESUS CALLED SIMON "PETER," WHICH MEANS "ROCK." HE BUILT THE CATHOLIC CHURCH, THE NEW JERUSALEM, UPON THIS ROCK.

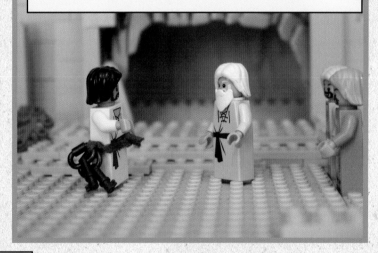

SOLOMON'S TEMPLE CONTAINED THE OLD ARK OF THE COVENANT, WHICH HELD THE TEN COMMANDMENTS (THE WORD OF GOD), THE ROD OF AARON (SYMBOLIZING THE HIGH PRIESTHOOD), AND THE MANNA (BREAD FROM HEAVEN).

CATHOLIC CHURCHES CONTAIN TABERNACLES, WHICH HOLD THE NEW COVENANT, JESUS. HE IS THE WORD BECOME FLESH, THE HIGH PRIEST, AND THE BREAD FROM HEAVEN.

1 KGS 2:17-18, JN 2:3, 2 CHR 3:1, MAT 16:18, 1 KGS 8:1-4, CCC 1183

MAT 1:1-16

"YET ON THAT DAY, SAYS THE LORD, I WILL SHEAR THAT PEG."

SO, AS PROPHESIED, JESUS, WHO IS A DESCENDANT IN THE LINE OF DAVID, TOOK THE KEYS OF AUTHORITY OF THE DAVIDIC KINGDOM WHEN HE "SHEARED THE PEG."

JESUS RENAMED SIMON PETER AND SAID TO HIM,

YOU ARE ROCK (PETER),

AND UPON THIS ROCK (PETER) I WILL BUILD MY CHURCH,

AND THE GATES OF HELL WILL NOT PREVAIL AGAINST IT!

I GIVE YOU THE KEYS TO THE KINGDOM OF HEAVEN.

WHATEVER YOU BIND ON EARTH IS BOUND IN HEAVEN;

AND WHATEVER YOU LOOSE ON EARTH IS LOOSED IN HEAVEN.

MAT 16:18-19

THE AUTHORITY OF THE DAVIDIC KINGDOM AND THE KEYS WERE "SHEARED WITH THE PEG." CHRIST GAVE THE KEYS AND THEIR AUTHORITY TO PETER, WHO WAS PLACED IN A SEAT OF HONOR AS THE FIRST POPE OF CHRIST'S CHURCH, THE NEW JERUSALEM.

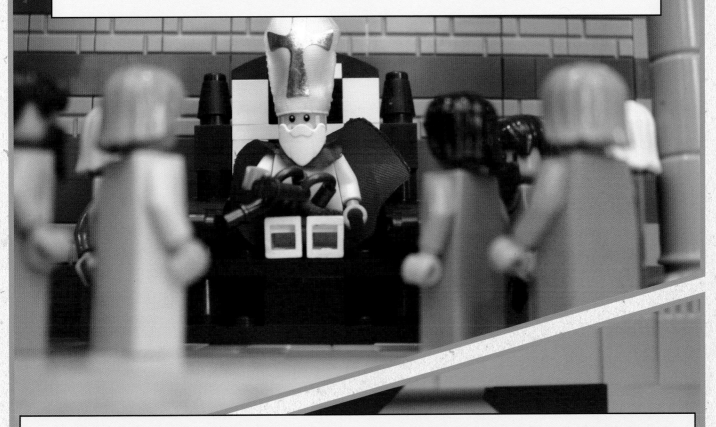

AND JUST AS AUTHORITY WAS PASSED DOWN IN THE DAVIDIC KINGDOM, PAPAL AUTHORITY HAS BEEN PASSED DOWN FROM GENERATION TO GENERATION WITHIN CHRIST'S CHURCH, WHICH WAS GIVEN THE KEYS AND BUILT ON THE ROCK JUST LIKE IN THE DAVIDIC KINGDOM.

POPE ST. JOHN PAUL II, PRAY FOR US!

THAT'S HOW JESUS STARTED THE CHURCH. THE FRAMEWORK FOR HIS CHURCH WAS APOSTOLIC.

WE NEED TO STAY WITHIN THAT FRAMEWORK BECAUSE

THE BIBLE TELLS US THAT THE CHURCH IS THE PILLAR AND FOUNDATION OF TRUTH!

JESUS TOLD HIS APOSTLES, WHO WERE THE FIRST BISHOPS, THAT HE WOULD SEND THEM THE HOLY SPIRIT. THE HOLY SPIRIT WOULD LEAD THEM INTO ALL TRUTHS.

236

JESUS SAID, "THE FATHER HAS GIVEN ME ALL AUTHORITY IN HEAVEN AND EARTH!"

WITH THE AUTHORITY GIVEN BY THE SON, THE MISSION FROM THE FATHER, AND THE GUIDANCE OF THE HOLY SPIRIT, THE APOSTLES (BISHOPS) CONTINUED TO GROW CHRIST'S CHURCH BY ANOINTING MORE APOSTLES.

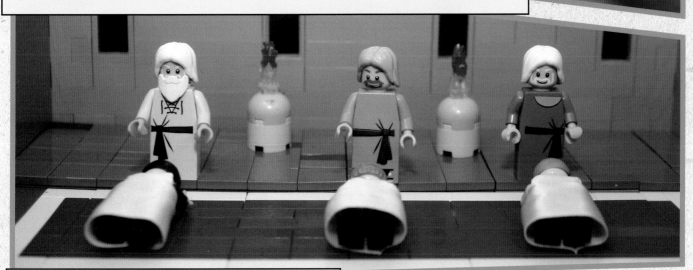

FOR EXAMPLE, AFTER JUDAS DENIED CHRIST THROUGH HIS BETRAYAL AND DEATH, PETER USED THIS AUTHORITY TO FILL THE CHAIR OF JUDAS WITH A NEW APOSTLE, MATTHIAS.

THE APOSTLES ALSO USED THIS AUTHORITY TO DRIVE OUT DEMONS IN CHRIST'S NAME.

MAT 28:18, CCC 77, ACTS 1:12-26, ACTS 16:18

JESUS ALSO TOLD HIS APOSTLES,

AS THE FATHER HAS SENT ME, SO NOW I SEND YOU!

THINK ABOUT THAT! THE FATHER SENT HIS SON (JESUS) TO DESTROY AND FORGIVE SIN!

THEN THE SON SENT THE APOSTLES ON THE SAME MISSION: TO DESTROY SIN THROUGH HIS CHURCH AND THE SACRAMENTS!

JN 20:21-23, CCC 858

SO THE APOSTLES BAPTIZED, WHICH RESTORES SANCTIFYING GRACE AND DESTROYS SIN.

THEY HEARD CONFESSIONS, WHICH RESTORES SANCTIFYING GRACE AND DESTROYS SIN.

THEY CONFIRMED, WHICH COMPLETES THE SANCTIFYING GRACE RECEIVED AT BAPTISM AND SEALS THE SOUL WITH THE GIFTS OF THE HOLY SPIRIT.

THEY CONSECRATED THE EUCHARIST, WHICH GIVES ACTUAL GRACE AND DESTROYS SIN.

THEY WITNESSED MARRIAGES, WHICH GIVES ACTUAL GRACE.

THEY ANOINTED THE SICK, WHICH GIVES ACTUAL GRACE AND DESTROYS SIN.

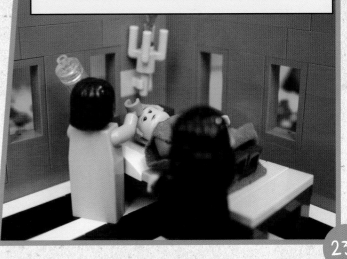

ACTS 8:36-38, ACTS 19:18, HEB 6:2, 1 COR 10:16, 1 COR 7:8-9, JAS 5:14

THE APOSTLES ALSO ANOINTED MORE PRIESTS TO HOLY ORDERS, WHICH GAVE THEM ACTUAL GRACE AND THE AUTHORITY TO DESTROY SIN!

THOSE PRIESTS WERE SENT ON THE SAME MISSION: TO DISTRIBUTE GRACE THROUGH CHRIST'S CHURCH AND HIS SACRAMENTS!

DID YOU KNOW THAT, AFTER JESUS ASCENDED INTO HEAVEN, A MAN NAMED SAUL WAS BRUTALLY KILLING CHRISTIANS?

ST. STEPHEN, FIRST CHRISTIAN MARTYR, PRAY FOR US!

ONE DAY AS SAUL WAS ON HIS WAY TO THE TOWN OF DAMASCUS, A GREAT LIGHT FROM HEAVEN SHONE UPON HIM. HE WAS SUDDENLY BLINDED AND FELL TO THE GROUND.

HE HEARD A VOICE SAYING, "SAUL, SAUL, WHY DO YOU PERSECUTE ME?"

THEN HE FELT SORRY FOR WHAT HE HAD DONE. SO HE CAME TO THE CHURCH.

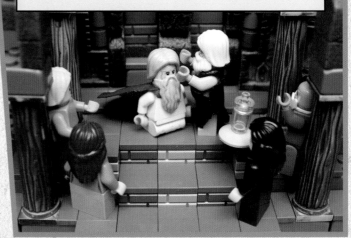

1 TM 4:14, ACTS 9:1-12

BISHOPS (EPISCOPATE)

PRIESTS (PRESBYTERATE)

DEACONS (DIACONATE)

CCC 1554

BISHOPS HAVE AUTHORITY OVER THEIR ENTIRE DIOCESE (AREA) AND ALL OF THE PRIESTS AND DEACONS IN THAT DIOCESE.

BISHOPS HAVE THE FULLNESS OF THE PRIESTHOOD,

Baptism

Anointing

Reconciliation

Holy Orders

Eucharist

Confirmation

Marriage

WHICH MEANS THEY ALONE HAVE THE AUTHORITY TO OFFER ALL SEVEN OF THE SACRAMENTS ON CHRIST'S BEHALF.

ST. IGNATIUS OF ANTIOCH SAID,

WHERE THE BISHOP IS, SO TOO IS THE CATHOLIC CHURCH.

ST. IGNATIUS OF ANTIOCH, PRAY FOR US!

THIS IS BECAUSE THE CHURCH HAS THE RESPONSIBILITY TO DISTRIBUTE GOD'S GRACES THROUGH THE SACRAMENTS.

AND, ORDINARILY, IT IS A BISHOP WHO BESTOWS THE SACRAMENT OF CONFIRMATION,

C.C.C. 1560, C.C.C. 1594, C.C.C. 1536, C.C.C. 1536

ONLY BISHOPS CAN BESTOW HOLY ORDERS.

ALTHOUGH PRIESTS CAN CONFIRM WHEN SOMEONE IS IN DANGER OF DEATH OR WHEN THEY BAPTIZE OR RECEIVE AN ADULT INTO THE CHURCH.

CCC 1560-1562

248

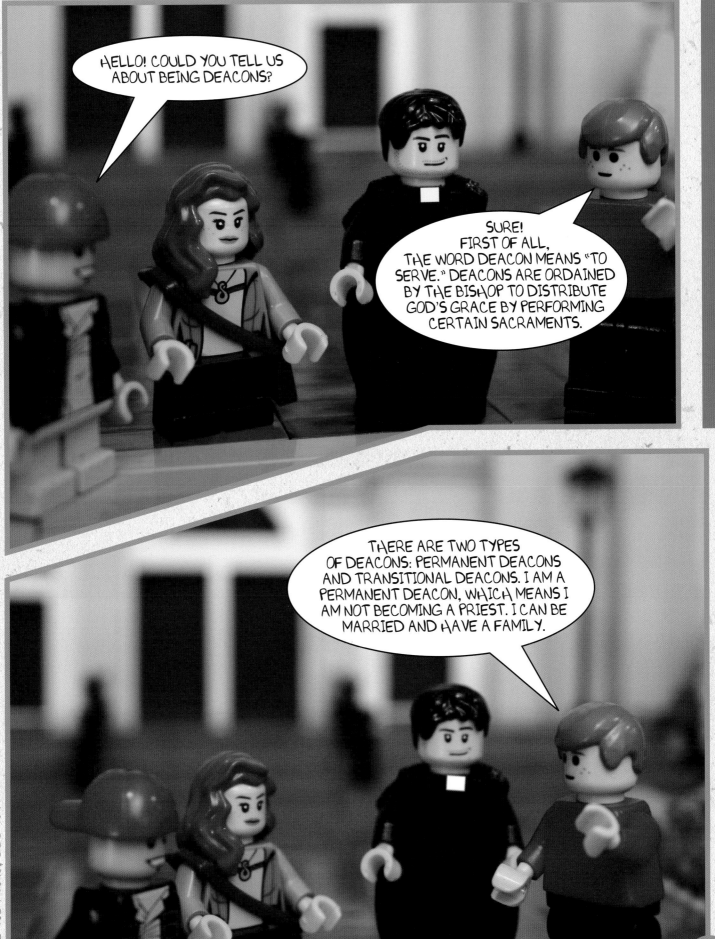

WE CAN ALSO SERVE THE CHURCH IN OTHER WAYS. DURING HOLY MASS, WE CAN READ THE GOSPEL, GIVE THE HOMILY, SERVE AT THE ALTAR, AND DISTRIBUTE THE HOLY EUCHARIST.

WE CAN ALSO IMPART CERTAIN BLESSINGS ON PEOPLE, EXPOSE THE BLESSED SACRAMENT FOR ADORATION, AND BLESS PEOPLE WITH THE MONSTRANCE.

THANK YOU FOR HELPING US UNDERSTAND YOUR VOCATION!

WELL, WE BETTER BE ON OUR WAY. IT'S TIME FOR ADORATION.

THANK YOU!

REMEMBER, YOU ARE NEVER TOO YOUNG TO BEGIN DISCERNING YOUR VOCATIONS! GOD BLESS YOU!

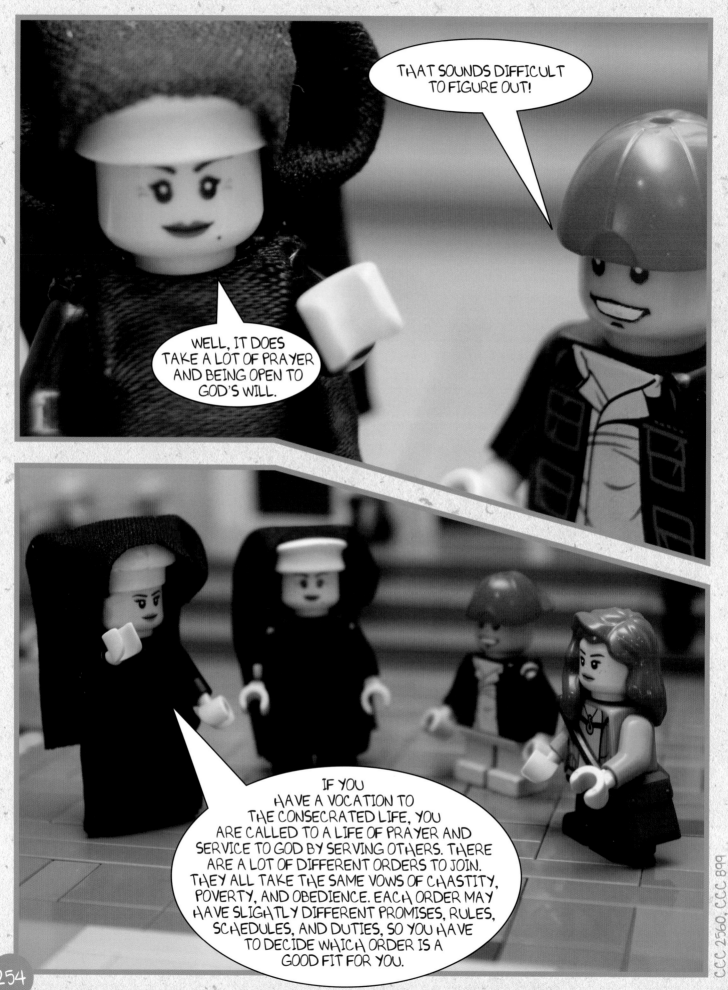

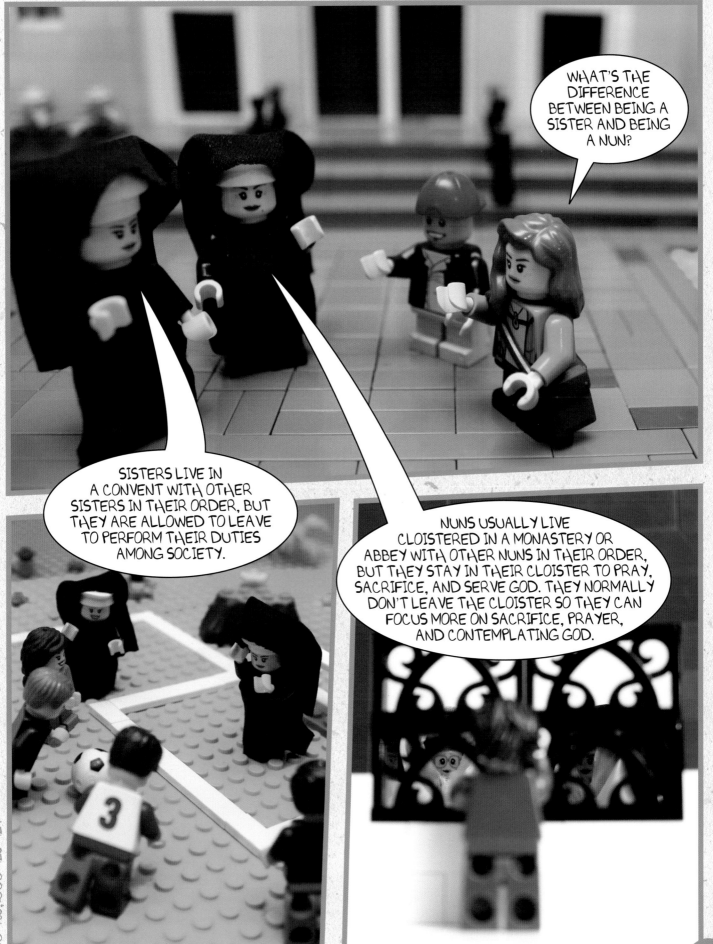

CCC 930, CCC 920-921

BROTHERS ARE SIMILAR TO SISTERS IN THAT THEY TAKE VOWS AND LEAD LIVES OF PRAYER, SACRIFICE, AND SERVICE AMONG SOCIETY. BROTHERS ARE NOT ORDAINED WITH HOLY ORDERS.

MONKS ARE SIMILAR TO NUNS IN THAT THEY ALSO TAKE VOWS AND LEAD LIVES OF SACRIFICE, SERVICE, AND PRAYER. THEY ARE TYPICALLY CLOISTERED IN A MONASTERY AND USUALLY DON'T GO OUT AMONG SOCIETY. SOME MONKS, HOWEVER, CAN ALSO BE ORDAINED WITH HOLY ORDERS AND BE A PRIEST OR DEACON.

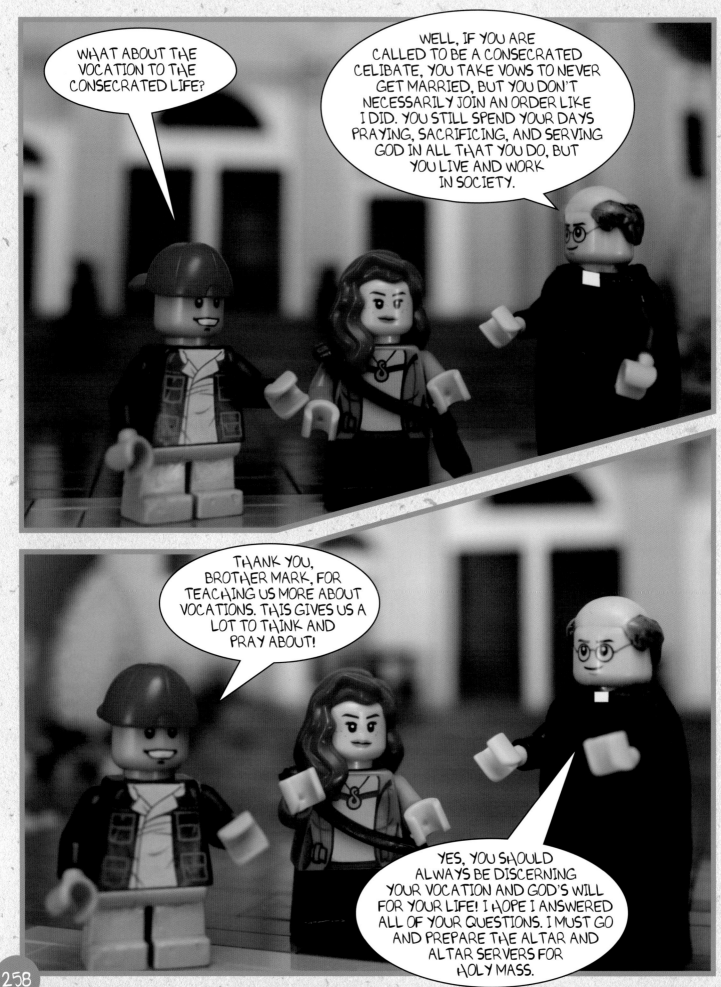

CCC 935, CCC 1536

ANOINTING OF THE SICK

JN 3:16-22, CCC 1, CCC 27, CCC 1020

CCC 1514, CCC 1517

EXTREME UNCTION (ANOINTING WITH HOLY OIL),

AND VIATICUM (THE EUCHARIST).

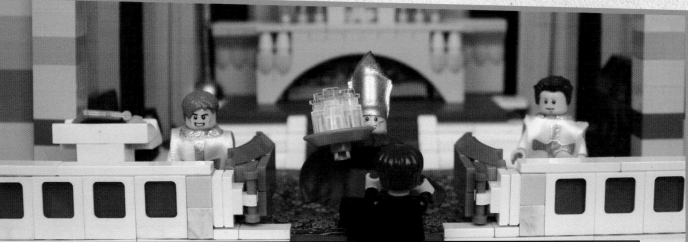

CCC 1517, CCC 1524-1525, CCC 1512, CCC 1297

THE OLEUM INFIRMORUM (OIL OF THE SICK) MARKS US FOR GOD AGAIN, JUST AS THE OILS USED FOR BAPTISM AND CONFIRMATION PLACED AN INDELIBLE MARK ON OUR SOUL. ALL THREE OF THESE OILS ARE BLESSED BY THE BISHOP ON HOLY THURSDAY.

ST. JOSEPH WAS CHOSEN BY GOD TO CARE AND INTERCEDE FOR JESUS AND MARY,

AND AT THE END OF HIS LIFE, HE DIED IN THE ARMS OF JESUS AND MARY.

IF WE HAVE A DEVOTION TO HIM, HE CAN ADVOCATE FOR US, AS WELL.

HE IS KNOWN AS THE TERROR OF DEMONS!

MAT 1:20

WELL, IN THE BOOK OF JAMES, IT SAYS THAT IF SOMEONE AMONG YOU IS SICK, SEND FOR THE PRIEST.

REMEMBER, ANOINTING OF THE SICK HAS THREE PARTS: PENANCE, EXTREME UNCTION, AND VIATICUM.

FIRST, THE PRIEST OFFERS **PENANCE** (RECONCILIATION), WHICH IS WHEN THE PRIEST HEARS CONFESSION AND GIVES ABSOLUTION.

NEXT, THE PRIEST ADMINISTERS **EXTREME UNCTION**, WHICH IS WHEN HE PRAYS OVER THE SICK PERSON AND ANOINTS HIM OR HER WITH OLEUM INFIRMORUM (OIL OF THE SICK).

FINALLY, THE PRIEST ADMINISTERS **VIATICUM** (THE EUCHARIST), WHICH IS BREAD FOR THE JOURNEY.

IT'S CERTAINLY POSSIBLE THAT THIS SACRAMENT CAN BRING PHYSICAL HEALING. BUT LIKE ALL OF THE SACRAMENTS, THE MOST IMPORTANT HEALING IS SPIRITUAL.

DOES THAT HEAL THE PERSON'S SICKNESS?

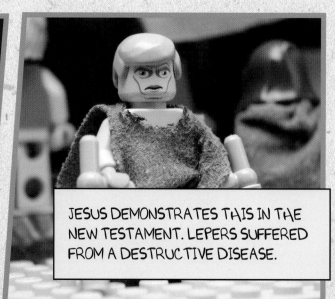

JESUS DEMONSTRATES THIS IN THE NEW TESTAMENT. LEPERS SUFFERED FROM A DESTRUCTIVE DISEASE.

IN FACT, IT WAS SO DANGEROUS, THEY HAD TO BE REMOVED FROM THE COMMUNITY.

REMEMBER, THAT'S EXACTLY WHAT SIN DOES TO US: IT REMOVES US FROM GOD'S COMMUNITY.

WHEN JESUS HEALED THE LEPERS, HE SHOWED US A PHYSICAL TRUTH AND AN EVEN GREATER SPIRITUAL TRUTH!

CCC 1503, MAT 8:1-4, NUM 5:2, GEN 3:23, LK 17:11-19

LK 17:11-19, LK 5:23, CCC 1524-1525

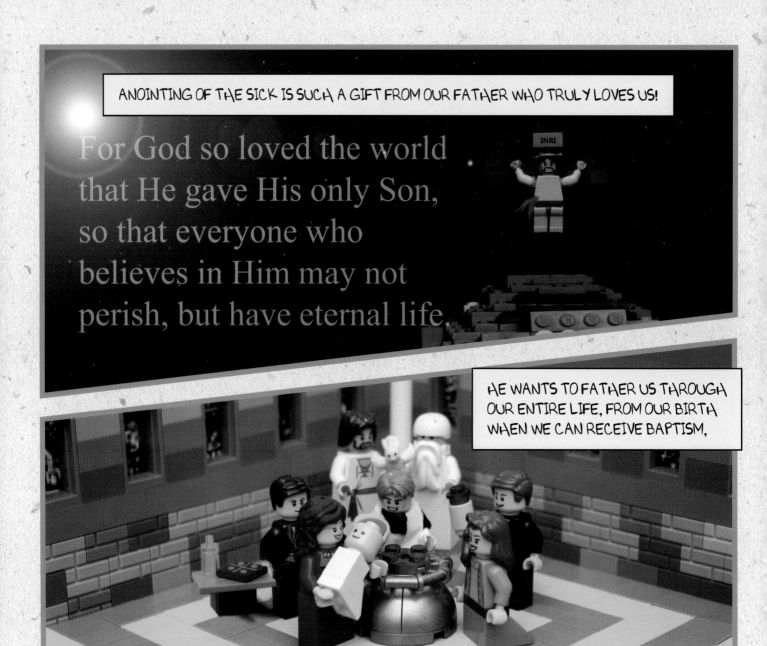

ANOINTING OF THE SICK IS SUCH A GIFT FROM OUR FATHER WHO TRULY LOVES US!

For God so loved the world that He gave His only Son, so that everyone who believes in Him may not perish, but have eternal life.

HE WANTS TO FATHER US THROUGH OUR ENTIRE LIFE, FROM OUR BIRTH WHEN WE CAN RECEIVE BAPTISM,

ALL THE WAY THROUGH TO OUR DEATH WHEN WE CAN RECEIVE ANOINTING OF THE SICK. HE GAVE US THE SACRAMENTS SO WE CAN DRAW NEAR TO HIM AND ULTIMATELY BE ETERNALLY UNITED WITH HIM!

JN 3:16, CCC 1525

274

ANOINTING OF THE SICK OFFERS REMISSION OF THE ETERNAL PUNISHMENT (HELL) INCURRED BY MORTAL SIN.

IT CAN ALSO REMOVE TEMPORAL PUNISHMENT (PURGATORY) FOR SIN AND GIVE US STRENGTH TO ENDURE THE FINAL BATTLE FOR OUR ETERNAL SOUL.

OR, IF IT'S GOD'S WILL, IT CAN RESTORE THE BODY TO HEALTH!

"JUST AS A CHIMNEY GETS DIRTY FROM THE SOOT LEFT BEHIND,"

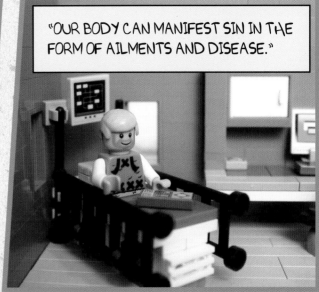

"OUR BODY CAN MANIFEST SIN IN THE FORM OF AILMENTS AND DISEASE."

"AND THE ANOINTING OF THE SICK CAN REMOVE SIN AND CLEANSE OUR BODY TO RESTORE HEALTH. BUT MOST IMPORTANLY,"

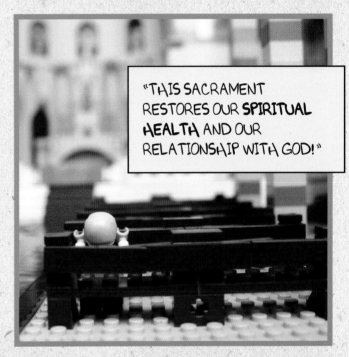

"THIS SACRAMENT RESTORES OUR **SPIRITUAL HEALTH** AND OUR RELATIONSHIP WITH GOD!"

OUR SALVATION WAS PURCHASED BY CHRIST'S SUFFERING AND DEATH ON THE CROSS.

INRI

TO RECEIVE SALVATION, WE HAVE TO CONFORM OUR LIFE AND OUR WILL TO GOD'S PERFECT WILL AND TRUST IN HIS DIVINE MERCY! THERE IS NO BETTER WAY TO ACCOMPLISH THIS THAN TO LIVE A SACRAMENTAL RELATIONSHIP WITH JESUS CHRIST, JUST AS HE INSTRUCTED! ONCE WE RECEIVE THE SACRAMENTS OF INITIATION - **BAPTISM, CONFIRMATION,** AND THE **HOLY EUCHARIST** - WE CONTINUE TO GROW IN GRACE FOR OUR STATE IN LIFE THROUGH THE SACRAMENTS OF SERVICE - **MARRIAGE** AND **HOLY ORDERS.** AND WE CAN RECEIVE CONTINUOUS HEALING AND GRACE THROUGH THE SACRAMENTS OF HEALING - **RECONCILIATION** AND **ANOINTING OF THE SICK.**

ST. FAUSTINA KOWALSKA, PRAY FOR US!

CCC 1113, CCC 1134

REV 21:27, CCC 830

ABRAM/ABRAHAM – Born in the twentieth or nineteenth century B.C., in Ur of the Chaldeans on the Euphrates River. His father, Terah, named him Abram. The family migrated to Haran, where Terah died (Genesis 11:26-31). At God's behest, Abram, his wife, Sarah, his nephew, Lot, and all their followers moved on to Canaan (Genesis 12:4). When Abram was ninety-nine years old, God made a covenant with him, changing his name to Abraham and promising to make him the "father of a multitude of nations . . . . [Genesis 17:1-5] I will make you into nations and your issue shall be kings . . . I will give to you and your descendants the land you are living in, the whole land of Canaan, to own in perpetuity, and I will be your God" (Genesis 17:5-8). Hence he has been called the founder of the Hebrew people. Abraham's dedication to the will of God was tested when he was told to take his son, Isaac, to the land of Moriah (which later became the site of the Jerusalem temple) and sacrifice his son as a burnt offering. He obeyed without hesitation, but Isaac was spared at the last moment (Genesis 22). In his final days Abraham arranged to have his son marry Rebekah, one of his kinfolk (Genesis 24), and left Isaac all his possessions before he died at the age of one hundred seventy-five (Genesis 25).

ABSOLUTION – In the sacrament of penance, the act by which a qualified priest, having the necessary jurisdiction, remits the guilt and penalty due to sin. The new formula of absolution, since the Second Vatican Council, is: "God, the Father of mercies, through the death and resurrection of His Son, has reconciled the world to Himself and sent the Holy Spirit among us for the forgiveness of sins; through the ministry of the Church may God give you pardon and peace, and I absolve you from your sins in the name of the Father, and of the Son, and of the Holy Spirit." To which the penitent answers, "Amen." In this formula essential words are: "I absolve you." For centuries, the Church used the deprecatory form of absolution, e.g., "May God absolve you from your sins." This was really declarative in meaning, as is clear from the fact that in the whole of tradition the priest who absolved was looked upon as a judge who actually absolved, even though he used the subjunctive mood to express his affirmative judgment. (Etym. Latin *absolvere*, to free from; to absolve, acquit.)

ACTUAL SIN – Any thought, word, deed, or omission contrary to God's eternal law. All actual sins are classified on the basis of this division, where sinful thoughts are essentially desires, the words may either be spoken or otherwise articulated, the deeds involve some external manifestation, and omissions are failures to do what should have been done by a person in a given set of circumstances.

Sin is a human act that presumes three elements: objective malice in the action performed, or at least the person considers it wrong; actual advertence of mind by which the sinner is at least confusedly aware of the malice of his conduct; and consent of the will, which formally constitutes actual sin and without which the sin is said to be only material.

Every sin is a genuine offense against God. There is consequently no such thing as merely philosophical sin, which offends against right reason but is not at the same time a deliberate transgression of the divine law. Sin is theological by its very nature.

ADORATION – Acknowledgement that, because the whole Christ is really present in the Blessed Sacrament, he is to be adored in the Eucharist as the incarnate God. The manner of showing this homage differs among countries and has varied through the ages. The postcounciliar legislation for the Latin Rite requires that the Blessed Sacrament, whether in the tabernacle or exposed on the altar, is to be venerated by genuflecting on one knee.

ANOINTING OF THE SICK – Sacrament of the New Law, instituted by Christ to give the sick spiritual aid and strength and to perfect spiritual health, including, if need be, the remission of sins. Conditionally it also restores bodily health to Christians who are seriously ill. It consists essentially in the anointing by a priest of the forehead and the hands, while pronouncing the words "Through this holy anointing and His most loving mercy, may the Lord assist you by the grace of the Holy Spirit, so that, freed from your sins, He may save you and in His goodness raise you up." In case of necessity, a single anointing of the forehead or of another suitable part of the body suffices. Olive oil, blessed by a bishop, is normally used for the anointing, but any vegetable oil may be substituted in case of emergency.

The institution of anointing by Christ is an article of the Catholic faith, defined by the Council of Trent (Denzinger 1716). The Church further teaches that this sacrament is implied in Gospel reference to Christ sending out the disciples, who "anointed many sick people with oil and cured them" (Mark 6:13); moreover that the sacrament was promulgated by the Apostle James when he wrote, "Is anyone among you sick? Let him bring in the presbyters of the Church and let them pray over him, anointing him with oil in the name of the Lord. And the prayer of faith will save the sick man and the Lord will raise him up and if he be in sins, they shall be forgiven him" (James 5:14-15).

ASCENSION – Christ's going up to heaven forty days after his resurrection from the dead. All the creeds affirm the fact, and the Church teaches that he ascended into heaven in body and soul (Denzinger 801). He ascended into heaven by his own power, as God in divine power and as man in the power of his transfigured soul, which moves his transfigured body, as it will. In regard to the human nature of Christ, one can also say, with the Scriptures, that it was taken up or elevated into heaven by God (Mark 16:19; Luke 24:51; Acts 1:9, 11).

Rationalism has denied the doctrine since the earliest times, e.g., Celsus in the second century. It tries to explain the Ascension as a borrowing from the Old Testament or from pagan mythology, but in doing so omits the basic differences.

Doctrinally the Ascension means the final elevation of Christ's human nature into the condition of divine glory. It is the concluding work of redemption. According to the Church's common teaching, the souls of the just from the pre-Christian era went with the Savior into the glory of heaven. Christ's Ascension is the archetype and pledge of our own ascension into heaven. (Etym. Latin *ascensio*, an ascending, ascent.)

ASSUMPTION – The doctrine of Mary's entrance into heaven, body and soul. As defined by Pope Pius XII in 1950, the dogma declares that "Mary, the immaculate perpetually Virgin Mother of God, after the completion of her earthly life, was assumed body and soul into the glory of heaven."

While there is no direct evidence of the Assumption in the Bible, implicitly the Church argues from Mary's fullness of grace (Luke 1:28). Since she was full of grace, she remained preserved from the consequence of sin, namely corruption of the body after death and postponement of bodily happiness in heaven until the last day.

The Church does not rely on the Scriptures for belief in Mary's Assumption. The doctrine is rather part of the oral tradition, handed down over the centuries. It was therefore certainly revealed because, in reply to the questions, the Catholic bishops of the world all but unanimously expressed the belief that this was part of the divine revelations. In explaining the grounds for the Church's belief, Pius XII singled out the fact that Mary was the Mother of God; as the body of Christ originated from the body of Mary (*caro Jesu est caro Mariae*); that her body was preserved unimpaired in virginal integrity, and therefore it was fitting that it should not be subject to destruction after death; and that since Mary so closely shared in Christ's redemptive mission on earth, she deserved to join him also in bodily glorification.

BAPTISM – The sacrament in which, by water and the word of God, a person is cleansed of all sin and reborn and sanctified in Christ to everlasting life. (Etym. Latin *baptisma*; from Greek *baptisma*, a dipping.)

BRIDE OF CHRIST – See SPOUSE OF CHRIST

CHRISM – A consecrated mixture of olive oil and balsam. Blessed by a bishop, it is used in the public administration of baptism, confirmation, and holy orders; in the blessing of tower bells, baptismal water, and in the consecration of churches, altars, chalices, and patens. (Etym. Middle English *chrisom*, short for chrism cloth.)

CLOISTER – A covered walk enclosing a quadrangle around which monasteries are built. Also an enclosure for religious retirement. In canon law, restrictions to the free entry of outsiders within the limits of certain areas of the residences of men or women religious. (Etym. Latin *claustrum*, enclosure.)

COMMUNION OF SAINTS – The unity and cooperation of the members of the Church on earth with those in heaven and in purgatory. They are united as being one Mystical Body of Christ. The faithful on earth are in communion with each other by professing the same faith, obeying the same authority, and assisting each other with their prayers and good works. They are in communion with the saints in heaven by honoring them as glorified members of the Church, invoking their prayers and aid, and striving to imitate their virtues. They are in communion with the souls in purgatory by helping them with their prayers and good works.

CONFESSION, SACRAMENT OF – See PENANCE

CONFIRMATION – The sacrament in which, through the laying on of hands, anointing with chrism, and prayer, those already baptized are strengthened by the Holy Spirit in order that they may steadfastly profess the faith and faithfully live up to their profession. Confirmation is not strictly necessary for salvation, but it is eminently important in contributing to Christian perfection and there is a grave obligation to receive it in due time. (Etym. Latin *con-*, thoroughly + *firmare*, to make firm: confirmatio, fortification, strengthening.)

CORPORAL WORKS OF MERCY – The seven practices of charity, based on Christ's prediction of the Last Judgment (Matthew 5:3-10) that will determine each person's final destiny. They are: 1. to feed the hungry; 2. to give drink to the thirsty; 3. to clothe the naked; 4. to shelter the homeless; 5. to visit the sick; 6. to visit those in prison; and 7. to bury the dead.

COVENANT – In the Old Testament an agreement between God and Israel in which God promised protection to the Chosen People in return for exclusive loyalty. "If you obey my voice and hold fast to my covenant, you of all nations will be my very own" (Exodus 19:5). Moses presented Yahweh's offer to his people, who promptly "answered as one, 'All that Yahweh has said we will do.'" The compact was sealed (Exodus 19:8). Many years later Jeremiah prophesied that a new covenant would be offered. "Deep within them," Yahweh promised, "I will plant my law, writing it on their hearts" (Jeremiah 31:31-34). Ezekiel foresaw that God would "make a covenant of peace with them, an eternal covenant" (Ezekiel 37:26). Its universal character was foreshadowed by Isaiah, to whom it was revealed by Yahweh, "so that my salvation may reach to the ends of the earth" (Isaiah 49:6). In the New Testament, when Paul was explaining to the Corinthians the institution of the Eucharist at the Last Supper, he repeated Christ's words: "This cup is the new covenant in my blood, Whenever you drink it, do this as a memorial of me" (I Corinthians 11:25). This master idea of the New Testament is reinforced in the Letter to the Hebrews: "It follows that it is a greater covenant for which Jesus has become our guarantee" (Hebrews 7:22). Christ himself is the new covenant between God and his people. (Etym. Latin *convenire*, to agree, to come together.)

DISCIPLES – One who is learning or has learned. In the New Testament the word describes any follower of Jesus' teaching (Matthew 10:1). During his public ministry it referred as well to his twelve chosen aides, but in the Acts of the Apostles they are always referred to as Apostles (Acts 1:26). (Etym. Latin *discipulus*, pupil, follower.)

EASTER – The day commemorating Christ's Resurrection from the dead. It is the greatest of all Christian festivals, having the central place in the liturgical year. It is the Christian feast linked with the Jewish Pasch. The exultant Alleluia is constantly repeated in the Mass and Divine Office, the Vidi Aquam replaces the Asperges, and the Regina Coeli the Angelus. The Easter season continues from Easter Sunday to Trinity Sunday inclusive. (Etym. Anglo-Saxon *Eastre*, Teutonic goddess of dawn and spring.)

EDEN – The beautiful garden in which God put Adam and Eve. After they disobeyed him, they were expelled (Genesis 2, 3). It is a word used in Scripture to suggest an ideal place to live (Isaiah 51:3; Ezekiel 31:9).

EMMAUS – A village about seven miles from Jerusalem. It was on the road to Emmaus that two disciples met the risen Jesus and accompanied him to the village (Luke 24:13-35). Not until he broke bread at supper did they recognize him. Then he disappeared and they hastened back to Jerusalem to tell the Apostles of the encounter.

EUCHARIST – The true Body and Blood of Jesus Christ, who is really and substantially present under the appearances of bread and wine, in order to offer himself in the sacrifice of the Mass and to be received as spiritual food in Holy Communion. It is called Eucharist, or "thanksgiving," because at its institution at the Last Supper Christ "gave thanks," and by this fact it is the supreme object and act of Christian gratitude to God.

Although the same name is used, the Eucharist is any one or all three aspects of one mystery, namely the Real Presence, the Sacrifice, and Communion. As Real Presence, the Eucharist is Christ in his abiding existence on earth today; as Sacrifice, it is Christ in his abiding action of High Priest, continuing now to communicate the graces he merited on Calvary; and as Communion, it is Christ coming to enlighten and strengthen the believer by nourishing his soul for eternal life. (Etym. Latin *eucharistia*, the virtue of thanksgiving or thankfulness; from Greek *eucharistia*, gratitude; from *eu-*, good + *charizesthai*, to show favor.)

EXAMINATION OF CONSCIENCE – Reflection in God's presence on one's state of soul, e.g., in preparation for the sacrament of penance.

EXTREME UNCTION – See ANOINTING OF THE SICK

FRUITS OF THE HOLY SPIRIT – Supernatural works that, according to St. Paul, manifest the presence of the Holy Spirit. The one who performs them recognizes God's presence by the happiness he experiences, and others the divine presence by witnessing these good works (Galatians 5:22-23). They are, in other words, identifiable effects of the Holy Spirit. In the Vulgate text they are: charity, joy, peace, patience, benignity, goodness, longanimity, mildness, faith, modesty, continency, and chastity.

GENUFLECT – Bending of the knee as an act of reverence. Customary when passing before the Blessed Sacrament in the tabernacle, entering the pew for divine worship, and during certain ceremonies to the Cross. A double genuflection of both knees simultaneously was commonly made before the Blessed Sacrament exposed in a monstrance. The new directive since the Second Vatican Council specifies: "One knee is bent before the Blessed Sacrament, whether reserved in the tabernacle or exposed for public adoration" (*Eucharistiae Sacramentum*, 1973, number 84). Genuflections are also made to the Pope, to a cardinal, and to a bishop in his own diocese.

GETHSEMANE – The garden lying outside Jerusalem on the Mount of Olives where Jesus spent the agonizing hours praying prior to his arrest (Mark 14:32-52, John 18:1-12). (Etym. Aramaic *gat semane*, oil press; Greek *gethsēmanei*.)

GIFTS OF THE HOLY SPIRIT – The seven forms of supernatural initiative conferred with the reception of sanctifying grace. They are in the nature of supernatural reflexes, or reactive instincts, that spontaneously answer to the divine impulses of grace almost without reflection but always with full consent. The gifts are wisdom (*sapientia*), understanding (*intellectus*), knowledge (*scientia*), fortitude or courage (*fortitudo*), counsel (*consilium*), piety or love (*pietas*), and fear of the Lord (*timor Domini*).

GODPARENT – Sponsors who make profession of faith for the person being baptized. Solemn baptism requires godparents. The godparent assumes an obligation to instruct the child in the event of the death or neglect of the parents, in order to fulfill the baptismal promises. Being a godparent creates a spiritual relationship that is recognized in ecclesiastical law.

GRAVE SIN – The transgression of a divine law in a grievous matter with full knowledge and consent.

The matter may be serious either in itself (as blasphemy) or because of the circumstances (as striking one's father or mother) or on account of its purpose (as telling a lie in order to destroy a person's character). Sufficient knowledge of the serious nature of a sinful action is present if one is clearly conscious that the act is mortally sinful, say because the Scriptures or the Church identify certain acts as seriously offensive to God. It is enough that one knows that what one intends to do may be a mortal sin, but does it anyhow. Indifference to the laws of God is equivalent to disobeying them.

Full consent is present when one freely wills to commit an action although one clearly knows it is gravely sinful. No sin is committed if one does not will the deed, no matter how clear one's knowledge may be. After all, the essence of sin is in the free will. Thus, too, a person does not sin who, with the best of will, cannot dispel obscene or blasphemous thoughts and desires, even though he or she well knows they are gravely sinful. The resolution to perform an action is not the same as the pleasure or satisfaction experienced in the emotions, nor the same as a compulsive idea, "I like the sin." One sign of partial knowledge or not full consent would be the fact that a person does not complete an action when this can easily be done, or is so minded that the person would rather die than commit a grave sin.

HELL – The place and state of eternal punishment for the fallen angels and human beings who die deliberately estranged from the love of God. There is a twofold punishment in hell: the pain of loss, which consists in the deprivation of the vision of God, and the pain of sense, which consists in the suffering caused by outside material things. The punishment of hell is eternal, as declared by Christ in his prediction of the last day (Matthew 25:46), and as defined by the Fourth Lateran Council, stating that the wicked will "receive a perpetual punishment with the devil" (Denzinger 801). The existence of hell is consistent with divine justice, since God respects human freedom and those who are lost actually condemn themselves by their resistance to the grace of God.

HOLY DAYS OF OBLIGATION – Feast days to be observed by attendance at Mass and rest, as far as possible, from unnecessary servile work. The number and dates of these vary among countries. In the United States there are six holy days: Solemnity of Mary on January 1; Ascension of Our Lord, forty days after Easter; Assumption of the Blessed Virgin, August 15; All Saints' Day, November 1; Mary's Immaculate Conception, December 8; and Christmas, or the birth of Christ, December 25. On holy days the pastor of every parish is required to offer or have offered a special Mass for his parishioners.

HOLY ORDERS – See ORDERS, SACRAMENT OF

HYSSOP – A plant of unknown identity, mentioned in the Scriptures. Found in Egypt, Sinai, and Canaan, it was used to sprinkle the blood of the paschal lamb or victims of sacrifice. It is referred to in the Psalm Miserere and in the Church's prayers.

JERUSALEM – Ancient city in Palestine, the religious and political center of the Jewish people, situated on the crest of a chain of mountains that cross Palestine from north to south. Originally called Salem, it was the capital of King Melchizedek about 2100 B.C. (Genesis 14). First mentioned in the Book of Joshua (10, 15), the inhabitants were known as Jebusites. When the Promised Land was parceled out, Jerusalem was assigned to the tribe of Benjamin. Its most famous rulers were King David, who brought the Ark of the Covenant into the city, and his son Solomon, who built the

first Temple. A second Temple was built in the sixth century B.C., and the third (and last) was the work of Herod the Great, who ruled as a vassal of Rome from 37 to 4 B.C. The Christian history of Jerusalem begins with the short ministry of the Savior, culminating in his death, resurrection, and ascension. The Apostles lived and taught there for some time after Pentecost, and met in Jerusalem for their first council about A.D. 49. The Apostle St. James the Less was the first Bishop of Jerusalem, where he was condemned by the Sanhedrin and martyred in A.D. 62.

JEWS – Those who adhere to Judaism both as a religion and a people. Originally the name was restricted to the subjects of the kingdom of Judah. But after the Babylonian exile it became the common name for the race descended from Jacob and for the followers of the Mosaic religion.

LAST RITES – See ANOINTING OF THE SICK

LAST SUPPER – The last meal taken by Christ with his apostles, the night before his Passion. On this occasion he instituted the Holy Eucharist and the priesthood, and gave the apostles the long discourse on the Trinity and Christian charity, as recorded by St. John. He then proceeded to Gethsemane and the Agony in the Garden.

MANNA – The name given in Scripture for the miraculous food sent to the Israelites in the desert (Exodus 16:4-36). There are natural exudates from trees and shrubs in Arabia that yield, during two months in the fall, a minute quantity of edible substance. But their limited supply, with characteristic taste, makes them totally unlike what the Bible describes as the manna of the Exodus.

MARRIAGE – See MATRIMONY

MATRIMONY – Marriage, but a more appropriate term for legal and religious use. It is the proper term for the sacrament of marriage, and refers more to the relationship between husband and wife than to the ceremony or the state of marriage.

MELCHIZEDEK – A king of Salem and a priest. When Abraham returned from battle after rescuing Lot, Melchizedek greeted him and gave him a blessing in honor of his victory (Genesis 14:18-20). In return Abraham offered him tithes because of his priesthood. In a Psalm devoted to the dual role of priest and king, David exclaimed, "Yahweh has sworn an oath which he never will retract, You are a priest of the order of Melchizedek and forever" (Psalm 110:4). There are only two references to this priest-king in the Old Testament. In the New Testament the Epistle to the Hebrews associates Christ's priesthood with Melchizedek's by quoting in three successive chapters the invocation from Psalm 110: "You are a priest of the order of Melchizedek and forever." This is also the biblical basis for the Catholic doctrine that, once a man is ordained a priest, his priesthood, like Christ's "in the line of Melchizedek," is forever (Hebrews 5, 6, 7).

MERCY – The disposition to be kind and forgiving. Founded on compassion, mercy differs from compassion or the feeling of sympathy in putting this feeling into practice with a readiness to assist. It is therefore the ready willingness to help anyone in need, especially in need of pardon or reconciliation.

MESSIAH – The Hebrew word for "Anointed One." The equivalent word in Greek is Christos. In the Old Testament it was sometimes applied in a general sense to prophets or priests (Exodus 30:30), but more specifically it referred to the coming of one who would usher in a period of righteousness and conquer sin and evil (Daniel 9:26). In the New Testament the Evangelists made it clear that they knew Jesus was the long-anticipated Messiah (Acts 2:36; Matthew 16:17; Galatians 3:24-29). Those who refused to accept Jesus interpreted the promised kingdom to be a worldly domain and looked forward to a messiah who would be a military leader to help Israel triumph over her enemies.

MONSTRANCE – A symbol of the Blessed Sacrament since the monstrance is the sacred vessel which contains the consecrated Host when exposed or carried in procession. It is a well-known emblem of St. Clare, who is reported to have repulsed unbelievers who assaulted her convent of nuns by presenting to their gaze Christ in the monstrance. St. Peter Julian Eymard, founder of the Blessed Sacrament Fathers, is symbolized carrying the monstrance and blessing the people with it. St. Thomas Aquinas has the monstrance among his many emblems as the author of the famous hymns "Lauda Sion and Pange Lingua," written to honor the Eucharistic Lord. St. John Neumann, who first established the forty hours' devotion in America, and St. Paschal Baylon, patron of Eucharistic Congresses, are both represented in art with the monstrance. (Etym. Latin *monstrans*, from *monstrare*, to show, point out, indicate.)

MORTAL SIN – An actual sin that destroys sanctifying grace and causes the supernatural death of the soul. Mortal sin is a turning away from God because of seriously inordinate adherence to creatures that causes grave injury to a person's rational nature and to the social order, and deprives the sinner of a right to heaven.

The terms mortal, deadly, grave, and serious applied to sin are synonyms, each with a slightly different implication. Mortal and deadly focus on the effects in the sinner, namely deprivation of the state of friendship with God; grave and serious refer to the importance of the matter in which a person offends God. But the Church never distinguishes among these terms as though they represented different kinds of sins. There is only one recognized correlative to mortal sin, and that is venial sin, which offends against God but does not cause the loss of one's state of grace. (Etym. Latin *mors*, death.)

MOSES – The greatest figure in the Old Testament, the founder of Israel, lawgiver, leader, and proponent of monotheism. Of the tribe of Levi, he was born in Egypt during a persecution when all the Hebrew male children were to be killed. Exposed on the Nile, he was rescued by Pharaoh's daughter and educated at court. God appeared to him in a burning bush and told him to deliver his people with the help of Aaron. The plagues did not make Pharaoh relent, until the death of every firstborn forced him to yield. Moses then led the Israelites through the years' long exodus, but he is excluded from the Promised Land because of his lack of confidence at the "Waters of Contradiction." The prophet died on Mount Nebo after pronouncing the three memorable discourses preserved in Deuteronomy. He was buried in the valley of Moab, but no one knows where.

NEW JERUSALEM – In biblical language the Heavenly City of the angels and saints after the Last Day. As described by St. John in the prophetic vision: "I saw the holy city, and the New Jerusalem coming down from God out of heaven, as beautiful as a bride all dressed for her husband" (Apocalypse 21:2).

NICENE CREED – There are two creeds that have the same name. The original Nicene Creed was issued in A.D. 325 by the Council of Nicaea. It was composed by the Fathers of the Council in their conflict with Arianism and contains the term *homoousios* (consubstantial). It is comparatively short, ends with the phrase, "and in the Holy Spirit," and has attached to it four anathemas against Arianism. The more common Nicene Creed is more accurately the Nicene-Constantinople Creed. It came after the first ecumenical Council of Constantinople (381), is the creed now used in the liturgy, including the added phrases "and the Son," and "died," and differs from the preceding in that it: 1. has more about the person of Christ; 2. omits the phrase "from the substance of the Father" after homoousios; 3. says more about the Holy Spirit; 4. adds the articles on the Church, baptism, the resurrection, and eternal life; and 5. contains no anathemas. The full text reads: "I believe in one God, the Father almighty, maker of heaven and earth, of all things visible and invisible. I believe in one Lord, Jesus Christ, the Only-Begotten Son of God, born of the Father before all ages. God from God, Light from Light, true God from true God, begotten, not made, consubstantial with the Father; through him all things were made. For us men and for our salvation he came down from heaven, and by the Holy Spirit was incarnate of the Virgin Mary, and became man. For our sake he was crucified under Pontius Pilate, he suffered death and was buried, and rose again on the third day in accordance with the Scriptures. He ascended into heaven and is seated at the right hand of the Father. He will come again in glory to judge the living and the dead and his kingdom will have no end. I believe in the Holy Spirit, the Lord, the giver of life, who proceeds from the Father and the Son, who with the Father and the Son is adored and glorified, who has spoken through the prophets. I believe in one, holy, catholic and apostolic Church. I confess one Baptism for the forgiveness of sins and I look forward to the resurrection of the dead and the life of the world to come. Amen."

NOAH – Son of Lamech and father of Shem, Ham, and Japheth. Yahweh was so embittered by the corruption and faithlessness of the world that he decided he would wipe out the human race in a flood. The one exception he made was Noah and his family. He gave Noah detailed instructions about the construction of an ark strong enough to remain intact (Genesis 6). Then he instructed him to take aboard his family and two specimens of every kind of animal and bird, male and female, so that after the flood the world could be repopulated. Noah obeyed Yahweh. Every living being outside the ark was destroyed when the flood submerged the earth (Genesis 7). After several months Noah had proof that the waters receded enough for all to leave the ark, which was now resting on Mount Ararat (Genesis 8). God promised, "Never again will I strike down every living being . . ." (Genesis 8:21). "There shall be no flood to destroy the earth again" (Genesis 9:11). Noah's sons became the eponymous ancestors of the great races in the repopulation of the world.

OIL OF THE SICK – The olive oil blessed by the bishop of a diocese for use in the sacrament of anointing of the sick. Commonly abbreviated O.I. (*oleum infirmorum*, oil of the sick) on oil stocks used by priests. Until 1874, when Pope Paul VI published the new Order of Anointing the Sick, olive oil was prescribed for the valid administration of the sacrament. This is no longer necessary. Any oil from plants is permissible in case of necessity; and the blessing by a bishop, though ordinarily required, may now be supplied by a duly authorized priest and, in emergency, by any priest.

OLD TESTAMENT – A term denoting the time from the origin of the human race to Christ; also the primitive, patriarchal, and prophetic revelation; and the Old Covenant of Yahweh with the Israelites. But most commonly, the Old Testament means the collection of books that the Catholic Church believes are divinely inspired, and that are not the New Testament. In biblical order they are: Genesis, Exodus, Leviticus, Numbers, Deuteronomy, Joshua, Judges, Ruth, I and II Samuel, I and II Kings, I and II Chronicles, Ezra, Nehemiah, Tobit, Judith, Esther, I and II Maccabees, Job, Psalms, Proverbs, Ecclesiastes, Isaiah, Jeremiah, Lamentations, Baruch, Ezekiel, Daniel, Hosea, Joel, Amos, Obadiah, Jonah, Micah, Nahum, Habakkuk, Zephaniah, Haggai, Zechariah, and Malachi.

ORDERS, SACRAMENT OF - The sacrament that, by the imposition of a bishop's hands, confers on a man the grace and spiritual power to sanctify others. There are three forms of this sacrament, also called sacramental orders, namely diaconate, priesthood and episcopate. They are not, however, three sacraments, but only one sacrament that is separately administered with three successively higher sacramental effects. It is certain that every baptized male can be validly ordained, although it would be highly illicit to ordain him before the age of reason. It is likewise certain that every baptized male can be validly ordained a priest without previously being ordained a deacon. However, the more probable teaching is that a baptized male cannot be validly consecrated a bishop unless he has previously been ordained a priest.

ORIGINAL SIN – Either the sin committed by Adam as the head of the human race, or the sin he passed onto his posterity with which every human being, with the certain exception of Christ and his Mother, is conceived and born. The sin of Adam is called originating original sin (*originale originans*); that of his descendants is originated original sin (*originale originatum*). Adam's sin was personal and grave, and it affected human nature. It was personal because he freely committed it; it was grave because God imposed a serious obligation; and it affected the whole human race by depriving his progeny of the supernatural life and preternatural gifts they would have possessed on entering the world had Adam not sinned. Original sin in his descendants is personal only in the sense that the children of Adam are each personally affected, but not personal as though they had voluntarily chosen to commit the sin; it is grave in the sense that it debars a person from the beatific vision, but not grave in condemning one to hell; and it is natural only in that all human nature, except for divine intervention, has it and can have it removed only by supernatural means.

PASCHAL MYSTERY – The title of a document, Paschalis Mysterii, issued by Pope Paul VI on May 9, 1969. In this document he approved a reorganization of the liturgical year and calendar for the Roman Rite. Its purpose was "to permit the faithful to communicate in a more intense way, through faith, hope and love, in the whole mystery of Christ, which . . . unfolds within the cycle of a year." Paschal Mystery is a general term to describe the redemptive work of Christ, especially the events of the Last Supper and the Passion, reaching their climax on Easter Sunday. (Etym. Latin *paschalis*, from *pascha*, Passover, Easter; from Greek *pasha*; from Hebrew *Pesah*, *Pesach*.)

PASSOVER – The Jewish Pasch celebrated annually as commanded by God to commemorate the deliverance of the Israelites from the bondage of Egypt. Its main feature was the sacrificial meal, ending with eating the paschal lamb, followed by the seven-day Feast of the Unleavened Bread. At the time of Christ the Passover meal united the Jewish family from sunset to midnight on the fifteenth of Nisan. Its last celebration by the Savior was the occasion for instituting the Eucharist and the priesthood of the New Law.

PENANCE – The virtue or disposition of heart by which one repents of one's own sins and is converted to God. Also the punishment by which one atones for sins committed, either by oneself or by others. And finally the sacrament of penance, where confessed sins committed after baptism are absolved by a priest in the name of God. (Etym. Latin *paenitentia*, repentance, contrition.)

PENTECOST – Feast commemorating the descent of the Holy Spirit on the Apostles. It takes its name from the fact that it comes about fifty days after Easter. The name was originally given to the Jewish Feast of Weeks, which fell in the fiftieth day after Passover, when the first fruits of the corn harvest were offered to the Lord (Deuteronomy 16:9), and, later on, the giving of the law to Moses was celebrated. In the early Church, Pentecost meant the whole period from Easter to Pentecost Sunday, during which no fasting was allowed, prayer was only made standing, and Alleluia was sung more often. (Etym. Greek *pentēkostē*, the fiftieth day.)

PROMISED LAND – The land of Canaan, generally thought to be the whole of western Palestine. It was promised to the Israelites by God after their sojourn in the desert (Exodus 12:25).

PROPHET – The biblical term "nabi" means one who spoke, acted, or wrote under the extraordinary influence of God to make known the divine counsels and will. Yet commonly associated with this primary function to proclaim the word of God, a prophet also prophesied by foretelling future events. His role, then, was to both proclaim and to make the proclamation credible.

RECONCILIATION, SACRAMENT OF – See PENANCE

RESURRECTION, BODILY – The universal return to life of all human beings, to occur soon before the last judgment by God's almighty power. Each individual soul will be reunited with the selfsame body with which it was united on earth. While all the dead will rise, only the just will have their bodies glorified.

RITE – In general, the manner and form of a religious function. Hence the words and actions to be carried out in the performance of a given act, e.g., the rite of baptism, or the rite of consecration, the Roman Rite. The term in its widest ecclesiastical sense refers to the principal historic rituals in the Catholic Church, whose essentials are the same as derived from Jesus Christ. The four parent rites in Catholicism are the Antiochene, Alexandrine, Roman, and Gallican. Some religious orders have their own rites. In all cases, however, the ritual must be approved by the Holy See. (Etym. Latin *ritus*, religious custom, usage, ceremony.)

SABBATH – The Jewish day of rest, with elaborate prescriptions for its observance. Failure to observe the Sabbath was one of the principal accusations of the Pharisees against Jesus. It began on Friday night at sundown and ended on Saturday at sundown. No manual labor was done on the Sabbath. This meant complete withdrawal from business and trade interests, and giving oneself to family, friends, and religion. On the preceptive side, the Sabbath was to intensify home life, deepen one's knowledge of religious history and religion, and above all concentrate on prayer and things of the spirit. Already in apostolic times (Acts 20:7) Christians transferred the Sabbath from the seventh to the first day of the week. Moreover, the Catholic understanding of Sunday as a Sabbath (rest) has never been as rigid as that of some Protestant groups, e.g., the Puritans.

SACRAMENT – A sensible sign, instituted by Jesus Christ, by which invisible grace and inward sanctification are communicated to the soul. The essential elements of a sacrament of the New Law are institution by Christ the God-man during his visible stay on earth, and a sensibly perceptible rite that actually confers the supernatural grace it symbolizes. In a broad sense every external sign of internal divine blessing is a sacrament. And in this sense there were already sacraments in the Old Law, such as the practice of circumcision. But, as the Council of Trent defined, these ancient rites differed essentially from the sacraments of the New Law, they did not really contain the grace they signified, nor was the fullness of grace yet available through visible channels merited and established by the Savior. (Etym. Latin *sacramentum*, oath, solemn obligation; from *sacrare*, to set apart as sacred, consecrate.)

SACRED CHRISM/SACRUM CHRISMA – See CHRISM

SANCTIFYING GRACE – The supernatural state of being infused by God, which permanently inheres in the soul. It is a vital principle of the supernatural life, as the rational soul is the vital principle of a human being's natural life. It is not a substance but a real quality that becomes part of the soul substance. Although commonly associated with the possession of the virtue of charity, sanctifying grace is yet distinct from this virtue. Charity, rather, belongs to the will, whereas sanctifying grace belongs to the whole soul, mind, will, and affections. It is called sanctifying grace because it makes holy those who possess the gift by giving them a participation in the divine life. It is *zoē* (life), which Christ taught that he has in common with the Father and which those who are in the state of grace share.

SANCTUARY LAMP – A wax candle, generally in a red glass container, kept burning day and night wherever the Blessed Sacrament is reserved in Catholic churches or chapels. It is an emblem of Christ's abiding love and a reminder to the faithful to respond with loving adoration in return.

SCAPULAR – An outer garment consisting of two strips of cloth joined across the shoulders, worn by members of certain religious orders. Originating as the working frock of Benedictines, it was adopted by other religious communities and is now considered a distinctive part of the monastic habit. It symbolizes the yoke of Christ. A scapular is worn under one's secular clothes, in abbreviated form by tertiaries associated with the religious orders. Tertiary scapulars vary in size and shape; their color corresponds to that of the monastic family. As a further development, the Church has approved some eighteen blessed scapulars as two small pieces of cloth joined by strings and worn around the neck and under the clothes. Best known are the five scapulars of: Our Lady of Mount Carmel (brown), the Passion (red), Seven Dolors (black), Immaculate Conception (blue), and the Holy Trinity (white). (Etym. Latin *scapulare*, *scapularium*, "shoulder cloak," from Latin *scapula*, shoulder.)

SEAL OF CONFESSION – The grave duty of keeping absolutely secret all sins that are told in sacramental confession and anything else that is told by the penitent and is related to the confession. It is an obligation binding in the natural law, the divine law of Christ, and in the positive law of the Church. It binds the confessor and any other person who in any way discovers what was confessed. Under no circumstances may any of this information be revealed unless the penitent freely gives permission.

SEAL OF CONFIRMATION – To establish or determine irrevocably, in the sacrament of confirmation, when a bishop anoints a person with chrism and says, "[Name], be sealed with the Gift of the Holy Spirit." Thus, by confirmation a baptized Christian becomes permanently marked as a witness of Christ and is enabled to preserve, profess, and communicate the faith even (if need be) with the price of his blood.

SIN – "A word, deed or desire in opposition to the eternal law" (St. Augustine). Sin is a deliberate transgression of a law of God, which identifies the four essentials of every sin. A law is involved, implying that there are physical laws that operate with necessity, and moral laws that can be disregarded by human beings. God is offended, so that the divine dimension is never absent from any sin. Sin is a transgression, since Catholicism holds that grace is resistible and the divine will can be disobeyed. And the transgression is deliberate, which means that a sin is committed whenever a person knows that something is contrary to the law of God and then freely does the action anyway. (Etym. Old English *synn*, *syn*, sin; Old High German *sunta*, *suntea*, perhaps to Latin *sons*, guilty.)

SPIRITUAL WORKS OF MERCY – The traditional seven forms of Christian charity in favor of the soul or spirit of one's neighbor, in contrast with the corporal works of mercy that minister to people's bodily needs. They are: converting the sinner, instructing the ignorant, counseling the doubtful, comforting the sorrowful, bearing wrongs patiently, forgiving injuries, and praying for the living and the dead. Their bases are the teaching of Christ and the practice of the Church since apostolic times.

SPOUSE (BRIDE) OF CHRIST – Primarily the Church, founded by Christ, which St. Paul elaborately describes as espoused to Christ. Also a woman who vows her chastity to God in order to be more like Christ and more intimately united with him. Among certain mystics, such as Sts. Teresa of Avila and Catherine of Siena, an extraordinary union in prayer with the Savior.

TABERNACLE – A cupboard or boxlike receptacle for the exclusive reservation of the Blessed Sacrament. In early Christian times the sacred species was reserved in the home because of possible persecution. Later dove-shaped tabernacles were suspended by chains before the altar. Nowadays tabernacles may be round or rectangular and made of wood, stone, or metal. They are covered with a veil and lined with precious metal or silk, with a corporal beneath the ciboria or other sacred vessels. According to the directive of the Holy See, since the Second Vatican Council, tabernacles are always solid and inviolable and located in the middle of the main altar or on a side altar, but always in a truly prominent place (*Eucharisticum Mysterium*, May 25, 1967, II, C). (Etym. Latin *tabernaculum*, tent, diminutive of *taberna*, hut, perhaps from Etruscan.)

TEN COMMANDMENTS – Also called the Decalogue, they are the divinely revealed precepts received by Moses on Mount Sinai. Engraved on two tablets of stone, they occur in two versions in the Bible. The earlier form (Exodus 20:1-17) differs from the later (Deuteronomy 5:6-18) in two ways. It gives a religious motive, instead of a humanitarian one, for observing the sabbath; and in prohibiting avarice, it classes a man's wife along with the rest of his possessions, instead of separately.

With the exception of forbidding graven images and statues and the precept about the Sabbath, the Ten Commandments are an expression of the natural law. More or less extensive sections of the Decalogue are found in the law of other ancient people However, the Ten Commandments excel the moral codes of other religious systems in their explicit monotheism, their doctrine of God's awesome majesty and boundless goodness, and their extension of moral obligation down to the most intimate and hidden desires of the human heart. The following is a standard Catholic expression of the Ten Commandments: 1. I, the Lord, am your God. You shall not have other gods besides me. 2. You shall not take the name of the Lord, your God, in vain. 3. Remember to keep holy the Sabbath day. 4. Honor your father and your mother. 5. You shall not kill. 6. You shall not commit adultery. 7. You shall not steal. 8. You shall not bear false witness against your neighbor. 9. You shall not covet your neighbor's wife. 10. You shall not covet anything that belongs to your neighbor.

TREE OF LIFE – A tree that stood next to the Tree of Knowledge in the middle of the Garden of Eden (Genesis 2:9). It conferred on anyone eating its fruit the gift of immortality (Genesis 3:22).

THEOPHILUS – Possibly a government official or a person of high rank to whom Luke dedicated his Gospel. Most likely a potential convert, as may be inferred from Luke's final words in the introduction: ". . . how well founded the teaching is that you have received" (Luke 1:4). Luke also directed Theophilus' attention to the Acts of the Apostles, addressing him by name in the opening sentence (Acts 1:1). (Etym. Greek *theophilos*, beloved of God.)

TRANSUBSTANTIATION – The complete change of the substance of bread and wine into the substance of Christ's body and blood by a validly ordained priest during the consecration at Mass, so that only the accidents of bread and wine remain. While the faith behind the term itself was already believed in apostolic times, the term itself was a later development. With the Eastern Fathers before the sixth century, the favored expression was meta-ousiosis, "change of being"; the Latin tradition coined the word transubstantiatio, "change of substance," which was incorporated into the creed of the Fourth Lateran Council in 1215. The Council of Trent, in defining the "wonderful and